PATRIOT LOST

A Memoir

JONATHAN SCHERCK

ISBN: 0615369278
ISBN-13: 9780615369273

For my princesses, Chloe and Sidney.

"Well, Doctor, what have we got—
a Republic or a Monarchy?"

"A Republic, if you can keep it."

Taken from the notes of Dr. James McHenry, a Maryland delegate to the
Constitutional Convention of 1787. The response is attributed to Benjamin
Franklin—at the close of the convention, when asked as he left Philadelphia's
Independence Hall on the final day of deliberation.

INTRODUCTION

As the tumultuous two term administration of George W. Bush and Richard B. Cheney drew to a close in January of 2009, many Americans who voted for these men were ambivalent about what they had done with the power they wielded as President and Vice President of the United States—powers spelled out in the U.S. Constitution and, more directly, powers bestowed by the American people by a razor thin margin in 2000 and (more decisively a second time) in 2004.

On the one hand Bush and his vice president had seen to it that not a single more terrorist act was committed on American soil following the terrible events of September 11, 2001. Much of America also approved of the strict constructionist judges President Bush nominated for confirmation as new Supreme Court justices. The nominees—now sitting as Chief Justice John Roberts and Justice Samuel Alito—each had extensive judicial records suggesting that they would not "legislate from the bench." Rather, they would adhere to the judiciary powers enumerated in the United States Constitution. They would serve the Constitution (and thereby the American people) by *interpreting* the relevant laws of the cases that came before them on the high court; laws *made* by Congress and *enforced* by the Executive. I was among those Americans who preferred to look back on the Bush-Cheney years from this more sanguine, conservative point of view.

But at the same time, I believed something had gone horribly wrong under President Bush and Vice President Cheney's watch. As successful as these men were in waging the Global War on Terrorism, there had been a grave unspoken misstep in America's foreign policy. The error I'm referring to was similar to the Iraq WMD intelligence debacle and ensuing war, as it too was ultimately a product of America's senseless addiction to foreign oil. But in the end, this other error was altogether different. This subsequent disaster was a result of the Bush administration's need to retain a key partner (as some saw it) in America's battle with Al Qaeda; it was rooted in a rigid unwillingness to differentiate between short-term advantage and the long term good.

This egregious mistake had to do with the Executive branch of our nation's government deciding unilaterally to renege on its obligations under the Nuclear Non-Proliferation Treaty, the world's nuclear arms control agreement ratified by the U.S. Senate on March 13, 1969. It was, "L'etats, c'est moi" ("I am the state"), as the "Sun King" Louis XIV was saying in seventeenth century France, less than one hundred years before the sixteenth Louis got his head chopped off by a disapproving French mob.

It was a similarly arrogant approach to decision making that I witnessed from my perspective as a Collection Management Officer (CMO) at the Central Intelligence Agency—from mid-January 2005 to April 3, 2007—that compelled me to write this book.

To the extent, as some readers might question, that I chose to include much of my personal story in this account, I have two reasons for having done so. The first is that I wrote this for myself and my family. I wanted this account to be coherent not just for the American public, but for my family and me— particularly my two daughters, both of whom were born while I was working as a CMO in CIA's Counter-Proliferation Division (CPD).

The second is that I think it is important for people to understand who is making such a serious claim about the Cheney vice presidency. I feel that had I decided to just go to the press with this—as I very easily could have—that it may have amounted to little more than a fleeting entry on some savvy Washingtonian's national security blog, just one more rumor added to the many that have come before it on the topic. Telling my story alongside *the* story adds credibility to my account of the peculiar and tragic interplay between Dick Cheney's Office of the Vice President and CPD's Near East Branch.

As I will lay out in much greater detail, I believe the People's Republic of China delivered a turn-key nuclear ballistic missile system to the Kingdom of Saudi Arabia over the course of several years beginning no later than December 2003. This illicit transfer, a flagrant violation of the Non-Proliferation Treaty, occurred while Dick Cheney was managing both the intelligence and foreign policy portfolios of the George W. Bush administration. Cheney wielded unprecedented influence over foreign policy matters as vice president, a level of authority that had been a pre-requisite for Cheney to accept the position as Bush's number two back in 2000.

Dick Cheney would prove to be a new kind of vice president—one that actually made decisions, one that made policy. The traditional vice presidential chore of attending state funerals around the globe (as established by Cheney's forty-five predecessors) would not be on this vice president's agenda. Mary Matalin, who served as one of Cheney's advisors, summed it up well; Dick Cheney took it upon himself to manage all of the "steely issues" of the Bush administration. When it came to matters of national security and energy, President Bush may have retained final say, but the policy outcome was almost invariably and unmistakably Cheney.

I believe that these two men were not only cognizant of the strategic oil-for-nukes deal between Saudi Arabia's King Abdullah and China's President Hu Jintao, but that they also chose to look the other way. It was a wicked deal, most likely discussed (if not closed) in January 2006 when King Abdullah travelled for his first time as king to Beijing, notably becoming the first ever Saudi monarch to visit China. Of note is that President Hu would visit Abdullah in Riyadh only a few months later in April, immediately following a stop in Washington for meetings with President Bush. Vice President Cheney was almost certainly in the room, as he always was when the important decisions were made. This whole affair was handled thusly, almost entirely by word of mouth, directly from president to king and king to president—and between president and vice president.

From Dick Cheney's standpoint, there would have to be very little in writing that anyone could point to in official U.S. government channels that might someday see the light of day. Preferably nothing. Discussion of the matter with his advisors was kept to an absolute minimum. Obviously, there would be no steady demand for intelligence on this matter as there had been years earlier for even a small hint that Saddam Hussein was arming himself with such weapons. And so it would be that just as there was no "smoking gun" intelligence reporting to justify President Bush's decision to topple the Iraqi leader under the pretense of weapons of mass destruction, I too have no concrete proof that Saudi Arabia is today a nuclear power.

The vantage point I had working in CIA's Counter-Proliferation Division—the basis for this claim—was hardly ideal. I was a contractor supporting America's intelligence community. As a contractor working at CIA (and there were not a few of us back then, only a few years following 9/11), I served as a middleman between HUMINT collectors in the field overseas and policymakers downtown at the White House and National Security Council. But in this role, I was one of only a few individuals in Washington with access to what was being said overseas at the time about Saudi Arabia's procurement of a new ballistic missile system from China. I read things, I heard things, I saw things. Admittedly, I did not see all—but I saw enough.

Along with my own view of how this short-sighted policy was adopted by the White House, I offer my own thoughts on how we might find our way out of not only this national security conundrum, but also perhaps some of the malaise that struck the American psyche forcefully back in the fall of 2008, just as Barack Obama and the campaign for "hope and change" was emerging as successor to the Bush years. I urge the reader to take my thoughts for what they're worth, either with a grain of salt or to heart.

* * *

While I did take the course Elements of Political Theory as an undergraduate at Georgetown University, I don't pretend to have an expert grasp of the field of political science. I just wasn't a very good student. However, I do believe that the wisdom of history's great political thinkers—philosophers such as Aristotle and John Locke, for example—that their contributions belong every bit as much to Main Street America as to those in academia who contemplate the science on a daily basis.

When I think back to what I learned from Father Schall there on Georgetown's hilltop (that Aristotle's *Ethics* is more a prescription for the political realm, while his *Politics* is in many ways concerned with the family as it *ought* to be), I see implications for what I saw unfold in Washington from my unique perspective at CIA.

Speaking of great thinkers, as Socrates once said, "All I know is that I know nothing." Likewise, I don't know precisely what President Bush and Vice President Cheney knew about the ultra-secret energy-for-security partnership that took shape between Riyadh and Beijing during Bush's two terms in office. Unfortunately, I don't have the insight of the fly on the wall when Hu made that stop in Washington on his way from Beijing to Riyadh in the spring of 2006. Nor was I ever present when Presidents Bush (father and son) had their many intimate conversations with a man who would become almost family-like to them, Saudi Arabia's Prince Bandar bin Sultan—or "Bandar Bush" as George W. would come to refer to him.

But what I do have is confidence in my understanding of what I saw going on, to "connect the dots" as they say. In this sense, I know what I believe.

1 / AIR FORCE BRAT

When I was ten years old, I remember being out on the Tidal Basin near the Jefferson Memorial in Washington, DC. I was in one of those paddle boats with my mother's sister, my Auntie Lorri. She was visiting from Boston.

I looked over and said, "I just don't know what my parents want me to do with my life." I was still six years away from getting my drivers license.

My aunt looked at me and said, "I think it's more what do *you* want to do with *your* life?"

Over twenty years later, with two abbreviated careers working for the federal government behind me, I finally understand what Auntie Lorri was getting at.

My family and I were living at the time an hour south of Washington in the suburban community of Montclair. We had a nice four bedroom home that overlooked a great man-made lake, one that I spent a lot of time on as a kid. I would take the John boat out; my friends and I would fish off the dock. It was a great house for my brothers and me to grow up in.

One day in the summer of 1986, just before I was to start at Graham Park Middle school in Dumfries, Virginia, my dad pulled me aside to tell me that he was planning to take a year off from his time working at the Pentagon. The Air Force had selected him to serve as a research associate for the coming academic year at Tufts University's Fletcher School of Law and Diplomacy in Massachusetts. He would be splitting his time between teaching a course and writing a thesis. It was a great opportunity for him, he explained.

The down side was that he would be gone away from home for weeks at a time during the school year. Was I ok with this? My dad wanted to make sure.

Yeah, it would be ok. A few weeks later, as my dad prepared for the academic year away from home up in the Boston area, I started the sixth grade.

Virginia's Prince William County Public Schools were ahead of the curve even back in the mid 1980s. We middle schoolers learned how to build a birdhouse *and* how to cook and sew—boy or a girl, it didn't matter. Today in 2010, many years later, the whole boy/girl thing *really* doesn't matter anymore when it comes to—well, just about everything. We've gone from a little home economics classroom instruction for Jill *and* Jack (a good thing I think) to quite unchartered territory. Not only is it much more common for the dad to stay at home with the kids while mom goes off to work—something I'm doing myself these days as I write this—you also now have entirely new definitions of family itself. Children are growing up in households with "two dads" or "two moms." To be honest, I'm concerned about how far we're stretching the concept of family in America. But I digress.

I don't know what possessed me, but for my sixth grade home economics (ahem) *knitting* project I decided I would make my dad a pillow for the desk chair of his new faculty office at Tufts. It was simple enough, nothing more than a square of burgundy and white yarn was all. But, surprised as I was that my teacher had asked the entire class to knit something of yarn, I must say I was rather impressed with the end result.

Mid-way through that first semester, my dad brought me up to Boston for a weekend visit. I packed the pillow with me as a surprise gift. It didn't exactly look like a dove holding an olive branch—the Fletcher School's logo—but my dad knew instantly what it was.

* * *

As I followed my dad around campus that weekend (he was still getting to know where things were himself) I kept seeing this funny phrase everywhere. On school letterhead, on sweatshirts at the bookstore, etc. I knew it was Latin, but I had just started my first semester of French at Graham Park, so I needed some help. *Illegitimus Non Carborundum* it read.

"Don't let the bastards grind you down," my father told me. Unlike me, he had taken Latin when he was a boy.

The Fletcher School is the oldest graduate school in the United States dedicated to the study of international relations. It was established in 1933 as a partnership between Tufts and nearby Harvard University. As my father explained, there were no law classes taught there, per se. But there was plenty on the topic of international relations and defense, the reason the Air Force had given my dad a year to study and teach there as a research fellow.

By June 1987, he had completed his thesis, "Implementing a Department of Defense Acquisition Information System: Potential Organizational Problems and Possible Solutions." My dad used to joke about the Pentagon buying $500 hammers and $1,000 toilet seats. Knowing my dad—and knowing how well DoD spends money—I'll bet this thesis is still relevant today. He returned from Fletcher for a second tour in the DC area, this time at the Defense Communications Agency in northern Virginia.

* * *

Whether it was more my own predisposition to keep up with current events and, for example, meditate on Reagan's decision to bomb Libya—as the U.S. military did in 1986 when it was discovered that the Libyan government had played a role in the April 5, 1986 bombing of a German discothèque—or rather the ongoing dialogue I had on these same events with my father, I can't say for sure. I just know that when the teacher across the hall back in fifth grade was, for whatever reason, trying to come up with the name of the Israeli prime minister at the time, I was able to answer without hesitation. "Shimon Peres," I said.

I remember several occasions that my brother Mike and I would go into work at the Pentagon with my dad—on a *Saturday* morning. My younger brother Jeff would be home with mom, as he was still too young for such outings. My dad would park in the nearly empty parking lot and drag us along for a quick stop at his office.

"I have to check on something," he would say. "It won't take but a minute." Finally (thirty minutes later) we would be off to the Pentagon Officers Athletic Club—the "Po-Ak," as my dad would pronounce the acronym.

Almost every visit, as we walked by the POAC racquetball and squash courts, my dad would tell us about some high ranking foreign dignitary he had seen playing with the SecDef (Secretary of Defense) earlier in week. One time it was Hosni Mubarak and one of the Pentagon's top chiefs. Mubarak was (and still is, even decades later) Egypt's president at the time.

In hindsight, the effect that these brief anecdotes from my father had on me at a very early age was essentially an underlying awareness that these guys—these Secretaries of Defense and Ambassadors from this or that country—were also just ordinary men. They *also* put their pants on one leg at a time, just like my dad—no matter what titles preceded their names. They went to the POAC. They played racquetball and squash. They even sweated, just like everybody else.

Previous notable POAC racquetball pairings (I would learn from my father) included Saudi Arabia's Prince Bandar Bin Sultan and former Secretary of State Colin Powell—only this was back in the 1970s when Powell was just a young Army officer. I'm sure there were not a few times that my dad was getting a workout in at the POAC with the Saudi ambassador facing off with some deputy secretary of defense in a nearby racquetball court.

But what I remember most about the time I spent with my dad those weekends as a young boy growing up near Washington were all the movies we would go to. I mean tons of them. Week after week, there was always something my dad or I wanted to see. And we loved most every one of them. Classics like *Top Gun*, *The Untouchables*, *Rain Man*, *Coming to America* and *Wall Street*. My dad played the stock market throughout his adult life—rather successfully truth be told—so he really enjoyed this last one, director Oliver Stone's depiction of 1980s greed in New York. "Greed is good."—as Michael Douglas' character Gordon Gecko famously declared.

Family summer vacations during those years were a four and a half hour drive south to the beaches of North Carolina's Outer Banks. My parents would rent a beach house in Nags Head for the week where my brothers and I would go from the rough surf of the Atlantic during the day fighting the "Imperial Japanese Navy" (as my dad used to playfully pretend), to relatively quiet evenings on the Albemarle Sound. As the sun set, we would wade around mid-calf in the salty water of the grand estuary, crabbing baskets in hand. I remember one time getting a little too close to one of the critters and, boy, did he let me know it. My big toe throbbed for the rest of the night.

* * *

My dad's mother "Kitty," my grandmother, made it down from Massachusetts one summer with her older sister Stasia who had flown in from northern California. As my dad told the story once, Kitty had won a speed typing competition in New England during the early years of the FDR administration— back in the 1930s. Somehow this prompted a job offer in Washington, DC. She would begin work as a secretary at the U.S. Department of Agriculture, one of thousands of new bureaucratic positions that were being added quickly to federal payrolls at the time.

Kitty and her sister Stasia Polucha, both not yet married at the time, packed up together and left Blackstone, Massachusetts for the nation's capital. This was some time prior to my grandmother and grandfather meeting and having my father. Soon after arriving in DC, not only was Kitty working as a new federal employee, but Stasia had herself also found a new government position. Federal jobs were almost literally growing on trees back then. Such was the era of FDR's "New Deal."

* * *

Somehow I had always known that my dad's relationship with his mother was a strained one. He much preferred talking with his Aunt "Sta" that week on the Outer Banks, as I recall. Whatever it was between he and his mother— and I wouldn't find out myself until later in life—the bitterness between my dad and grandmother really came out one afternoon while passing time on the Albemarle Sound.

I remember my grandmother very casually commenting on a seagull that had flown by. "Look at the seagull!" she exclaimed, a little too enthusiastically. My dad looked over at her with an unmistakable look of disgust on his face.

"Look at the seagulls…look at the seagulls," he mocked her under his breath with a trace of venom in his voice. My dad was ridiculing his mother right in front of his own sons.

By the end of our vacation to the Outer Banks that year, "look at the seagulls" had become code for "our dad doesn't care much for his mom."

* * *

My dad's next assignment, this time away from the DC area, was McClellan Air Force Base in Sacramento, California. My father and older brother headed out on the cross-country trek by car in the summer of 1989. My mom, younger brother and I would follow months later almost half-way into my freshman year of high school after the house in Virginia had finally sold. In what would be the first of several cross- country road trips for me, we headed west in the family Dodge Caravan.

My brothers and I were already headed our separate ways by this point. Older brother Mike would take his time settling in to the undergraduate criminal justice program at California State University Sacramento. He wisely took a semester off from school and spent some time working as a chair lift operator on the ski slopes of Squaw Valley in Tahoe. My younger brother Jeff, meanwhile, wasn't even in middle school yet there in the fall of 1989. As I was adjusting to my third (and thankfully *final*) set of freshmen year teachers at Roseville's Oakmont High School, Jeff still had several years of elementary school yet to go.

I had some friends in high school but was admittedly a bit of a *nerd* throughout. I played on the tennis team, but gravitated more to academic pursuits— not that it came naturally to me. I did something called Academic Decathlon (kind of a well organized annual *Trivial Pursuit* competition) and also participated in a handful of speech contests as a student at Oakmont.

I enjoyed these activities, but too often in the back of my mind I was thinking about how something would look on my college applications. By my junior year, it was clear that my grades and extracurricular activities were going to have to offset a rather lackluster SAT score. I think I took that damn test no less than four times between my sophomore and senior year. I maxed out at a cumulative score of 1220. Top score back then was 1600.

One of the out of the ordinary things I did was to pursue an internship in Governor Pete Wilson's office in Sacramento. My dad would drop me off at the commuter train on the outskirts of downtown on his way to work at McClellan AFB, and then he'd pick me up on his way home. I worked in Wilson's legislative affairs branch a few days a week the summer between my junior and senior year.

Like most internships I was there mostly to just watch and listen, but I do recall feeling more a part of the action when I would be asked to hand carry freshly signed bills over to the California Secretary of State's office. Literally, the governor would sign an Assembly or Senate bill into law—they were actually just small 5 x 8 inch newsprint-looking booklets—and someone would have to walk the signed copy a few blocks from the capital building to be recorded. It was a good ten minute walk through Sacramento's scorching summer heat, but I always volunteered. It was a rather menial chore in the grand scheme of things, but I enjoyed it.

That August, my parents footed the bill for a plane ticket to Houston where I served as a "youth delegate" to the 1992 Republican National Convention. This was the year that George H. W. Bush went down in defeat to the young charismatic governor from Arkansas while saying "read my lips... no new taxes" one too many times—a promise the elder Bush of course broke during his first and only term as president.

I remember meeting three people that week in Houston. John McLaughlin, a Washington political pundit and host of "The McLaughlin Group." I always liked the way he broke down the issues he discussed on his weekly talk show, always with great insight but also with just enough sarcasm to remind you that—obvious as the solution may seem—it just wasn't going to get done. This was Washington after all. I also got my picture taken with 1992's Ms. Texas, something I rather enjoyed.

And then there was my run-in with a CBS reporter by the name of Ed Bradley. Bradley, who has since passed away, was on one side of me in an aisle not far from the main stage podium. Coming down the aisle on my other side was Vice President Dan Quayle, whom Bradley very much wanted to ask a question of. As Quayle drew closer, Bradley began shouting his urgent question over my head. As I recall it had something to do with comments Quayle had made earlier that summer at a speech in San Francisco about the actress Candice Bergen's character Murphy Brown—specifically, the fact that she was a single mom—on the popular television show of the same name.

Whether Ed Bradley's politics as a popular reporter from CBS' *60 Minutes* news show had anything to do with it that night, it was clear that Quayle's handlers wanted as much space as possible between the vice president and Mr. Bradley. And, lucky me, I was right there in between the two of them. As Quayle was escorted past, I somehow (*wink, wink*) became part of the fracas keeping Bradley from getting his question through. Quayle's handlers were of course quite happy with me as I played the role of the flakey junior delegate from California. (I have to admit, I was having some fun with this.) Bradley, not surprisingly, had taken issue.

"If you do that again, we'll sue!" Bradley puffed in my face moments after Quayle had been safely whisked away from any pesky reporters' questions.

Whatever wise-ass response I had for Bradley must have been a good one because the crowd around me started to cheer me on. Fun as it was, though, I much preferred having my picture taken with Ms. Texas.

2 / POTOMAC FEVER

I took the overachiever route out of high school by somehow squeaking through the undergraduate admissions process of Georgetown University's School of Foreign Service—Bill Clinton's alma mater. I went from a solid 4.0 at the end of my junior year at Oakmont High School to something not quite so perfect by getting a "D" in my first semester of calculus senior year—as in *Didn't* much care to learn about how to calculate the area of a *Donut*. (Rather than employing several tricky equations to determine their surface area—one of the supposed virtues of this higher level of mathematics—I much prefer to eat them.) It turned out that this slip-up wouldn't matter in the end. I had a brief chat with the school's Dean Steigman during my first week on campus and all was forgiven.

The other reason I say I "squeaked" into Georgetown was that there had been more applications to the School of Foreign Service for fall 1993 entry than any other year in the school's history. I don't have the exact number, but it was a lot—very likely due to Bill Clinton's (class of '68) election to the presidency in the fall of 1992.

But the real luck from Our Lady of the Admissions Office came on my way to a second place finish in the state of California in the American Legion's annual oratorical contest. In 1993, the state semi-finals were held in the small town of Yreka in the northern-most part of California near the Oregon border. Who do I meet as I'm finding my mom a seat in the audience there in the town of Yreka but a good Catholic priest by the name of Ray Devlin. Father Devlin happened to have a close Jesuit friend who taught at the nation's oldest Catholic university in Washington, DC. Devlin must have enjoyed my speech on Article V of the U.S. Constitution because not long afterwards, on my behalf, he picked up the phone and called Father James V. Schall, SJ, Professor of Government at Georgetown. I would wind up taking Father Schall's Elements of Political Theory my freshman year.

Incidentally, I went on to the state finals held in the Pacific Palisades neighborhood of southern California, but lost to a real charmer from Fresno. Nevertheless, I chalked the whole experience up as a win. And I would be remiss if I didn't mention that my success in that competition was due in no small part to a man by the name of Ben Davidian. Davidian, an attorney in Sacramento at the time, had served as a judge in the first round held in Roseville. He handed me his card after I won saying that I still had a lot of work to do on the extemporaneous portion of the competition, but that he thought I could do very well in the following rounds if I put some work into it.

As a high school student in northern California himself years before, Ben had won not only first place at the state level but then went on to win the whole enchilada at the national level finals in 1969. Aspiring to do the same I gave him a call and, true to his word, he took some time out from his busy schedule to coach me alongside my high school speech teacher Kathleen Sirovy. Ben now serves as a Superior Court judge in Sacramento County. Mrs. Sirovy is today the principal of Oakmont High School.

* * *

As much as the "D" in Calculus could have forever damned my chances of getting into a good school, I believe the serendipitous encounter with the Good Father of Yreka made certain that I would be on my way. And on my way I was. My dad wrote me a letter to mark my departure back to Washington from the airport in Sacramento. He handed it to me as I was boarding the plane. As I read it again years later—now in my mid-thirties—I'm struck by how prescient it was about the "twists and turns" life can take.

I was miserable at Georgetown by the end of my freshman year and wound up having to take six classes during the spring semester of my senior year just to graduate on time. It was the old "careful what you ask for."

I just never got comfortable as a college student there on the banks of the Potomac. Socially I was a loner, just not able to relate to my mostly northeast boarding school peers. They had been groomed for success at schools with names like Philips Exeter, Deerfield and Choate. This former Air Force brat probably would have been much more content just going to U.C. Davis back in California.

Academically, with few exceptions, I always felt like I was operating on a different wave length than my professors. Being a solid student in a California public high school does not mean you're going to be a superstar in the classrooms of one of America's top universities. That said, while my grades didn't reflect it, I learned plenty about how the world works during those four years on the Hilltop. But when my dad asked me where I stood in my graduating class, I had to put the best face on it that I could.

"I'm at the top of the bottom seventh," I told him with a straight face. He was none too pleased. To make matters worse, there was a real look of surprise on his face. I felt I had let him down.

Worse still, I really didn't know what to do with this prestigious Foreign Service degree. Over time, I did eventually do the logical thing and apply to the State Department's Foreign Service Officer program. But they proceeded to reject me. Twice.

That rejection would come years later, however. As graduation from Georgetown grew closer—and with little clue as to what else I was going to do out of the gate—I decided I would join the Navy. (My dad had been career Air Force and so I had to be at least a little different.) So off I went in the summer following graduation to Officer Candidate School—to U.S. Naval Air Station, Pensacola, Florida.

After being "on the bubble" my final weeks at OCS (that is to say one step away from washing out to the next class—if not getting kicked out entirely), I managed to earn a commission as an officer in the world's (still) most powerful and technically advanced navy—although the Chinese are doing all they can of late to catch up.

"Be fair, firm and professional," Gunnery Sergeant Seals, U.S.M.C. told his class of freshly minted Naval officers at graduation.

* * *

Several months after leaving Pensacola in November 1997, I would meet my dad in Boston for the weekend. I was temporarily assigned to SWOS (Surface Warfare Officer School) in Newport, Rhode Island—less than a two hour drive from Beantown. He was well retired from the Air Force by then, himself working as a contractor at McClellan Air Force Base. He had flown in from California for some business meetings at his company's headquarters in Andover, Massachusetts.

As we headed out of town, we didn't go to Andover or back to Newport. And we certainly didn't drive west to the town of Blackstone where my dad had grown up as a kid. He hated that town and the memories from it in a way that even today, years after his death, I can't fully comprehend.

Instead, we drove north to spend a night in the quiet and pleasant tourist town of Kennebunkport, located on Maine's southern Atlantic coast. We put meaning into the words "ate like kings" those 24 hours together. For dinner that night we each had a plate of jumbo baked stuffed lobster. That meal could have lasted us well into the next day, but of course we woke up the next morning only to gorge on tall buttered stacks of the best blueberry pancakes I will ever have. This weekend trip to Maine is one of my fondest memories with my father.

After consuming enough pancakes to feed an entire family, my dad and I took a much needed walk to the outskirts of town. He wanted to show me Walker's Point—also known as "the Bush compound"—the summer home of George H. W. Bush, the 41st President of the United States. I was eager to see it myself.

I doubt there's a more perfect combination of architecture and geography anywhere else along America's eastern seaboard. If there is, I'd sure like to see it. The "Summer White House" as it was called is, as you would expect, an impressive vacation mansion with fantastic panoramic views of the Atlantic. My dad and I were only able to see the place from a distance of course, but you could still imagine the sublime ambience experienced by folks lounging in its sitting rooms.

Built in 1903, the original owner was a St. Louis banker by the name of George H. Walker. His daughter Dorothy Walker Bush and her husband

Prescott Bush (also a banker and later a prominent U.S. senator from Connecticut) inherited the mansion. It has remained in the Bush family ever since.

Standing there admiring Walker's Point in 1998, still half drunk on blueberry pancakes, my own father and I didn't have the foggiest clue what Prescott Bush's grandson and some guy named Karl Rove were cooking up right around the same time in the governor's office in Austin, Texas. The nationwide political campaign that would lead to the tumultuous two term presidency of George W. Bush was still in its embryonic stages.

But I did know a few general things about the Bush family beyond whatever plans W. had for the Oval Office back then. The Bushes had done quite well for themselves between their collective success in the banking sector and, later in the twentieth century, as big Texas oil men. And along with much of America, I knew of the high-flying ambassador from Saudi Arabia, too—this flamboyant Prince Bandar who I had seen not a few times as a kid in the 1980s on NBC's Sunday talk show *Meet the Press*. "Bandar Bush," as our country's 43rd president would come to affectionately call him, had himself spent plenty of downtime with the Bushes there on Walker's Point.

All of this together—banking, oil, a considerable political legacy and, of course, exclusive ties with the ruling family of oil-rich Saudi Arabia—all added up to, well, a magnificent summer home on the Atlantic. That, and a hell of a lot more, as I would begin to see firsthand years later while working a particular issue at the George H. W. Bush Center for Intelligence, the CIA.

* * *

I think I did a fair job during my tour as the Damage Control Assistant aboard USS Princeton (CG 59), home ported in San Diego, California. My responsibilities included management of the ship's Repair Division (R-Division, for short), the division of shipboard firefighters and plumbers—or "hull technicians" as they're known in Navy-speak.

"So you make sure all the *shit pumps* work properly," my dad would tease me over the phone from home in Sacramento. This was exactly the case. I remember one guy in my division, HT2 Korinta, bragging to me about how he had once cleared a really bad clog in one of the ship's toilets using only his hand. He used a glove of course. I hope.

As my tour aboard USS Princeton came to a close in the summer of 2000, I was treated to the U.S. Navy's traditional "Hail and Farewell" send-off. A dinner was held for me and several other officers who were also moving on to their next assignments. The event took place in the backroom of a restaurant in town near the U.S. Naval Weapons Station at Seal Beach in California, as the ship was being loaded with a new arsenal of cruise missiles for her upcoming deployment out to the Pacific.

I remember carrying on a bit too long that evening when it came time for me to say something about what had been a very full junior officer tour. The two years had included a six month deployment to the Persian Gulf and a lengthy ten-month overhaul in the shipyards of San Diego just north of the 32nd Street Naval Base. I hope he doesn't mind me saying, but I had some rather blunt advice for my successor in the Damage Control Assistant position, Ensign Francis Tam. With the rest of the wardroom sitting there in this otherwise festive room to hear everything I needed to say to him, I spoke directly and probably a bit too candidly to my replacement.

"Use common sense," I told Francis, none-too-subtly. "*A lot* of common sense…And make them do it," I said, referring to his new role as officer-in-charge of Princeton's R-Division. I just had my doubts about whether he was up to the job—whether his heart was in it—and wanted to let him know it. Not that he wasn't a sharp guy, but he just didn't seem to have an interest in running a division of twenty or so men aboard a warship.

I myself certainly had my share of down days on Princeton, but whether the men in my division were performing maintenance on a firefighting station or taking care of a malfunctioning toilet in one of the ship's heads, I was always of the mind—particularly in front of my men—that their work was vital to overall operations.

In retrospect, my comments to my replacement that night should have been made in private. But I'll blame this oversight on the beer I had just prior to waxing eloquent—not a bad thing, mind you, if you're a more introverted type trying to talk from the gut to a group of fellow military officers.

* * *

My last morning onboard USS Princeton, I remember knocking on the door of the Executive Officer's stateroom. Commander Bryan McGrath was the ship's number two in command. He wanted to see me before I departed.

A large black pirate flag with skull and crossbones was draped on the bulkhead behind him as it had been shortly after his arrival months earlier. Some sort of classical music was playing, spilling out into the empty hallway of "Officer Country," as it's referred to in the Navy. The rest of the wardroom was already out on the ship's quarterdeck waiting to see me off.

Upon hearing me knock, McGrath kicked his feet from his desk, put down the book he was reading and turned his chamber music down low. He quickly wished me luck in Norfolk, Virginia (my next assignment) and then, leaning forward at me, he grabbed hold of my knee.

"And try not to be so *negative*," he said, staring me straight in the eyes and shaking my leg for added effect.

This to the young lieutenant whose father would too often recite out loud to his son the line from Shakespeare's *Macbeth*—that life is "a tale told by an idiot, full of sound and fury, signifying nothing."

Minutes later on the quarterdeck, I saluted McGrath and Princeton's commanding officer before going ashore. My time on Princeton had been gratifying in many ways, but it had also been a very long two years.

I wasn't a negative person, I told myself as I walked down the pier. I was a realist. And I was happy to be moving on.

* * *

In Norfolk, I was less an officer, but still a gentleman. I was living near downtown in the quaint neighborhood of Ghent when a young female sailor moved into my apartment building.

Whereas I was assigned to a surface fleet destroyer squadron in nearby Portsmouth, Christa, my new neighbor, was a rescue swimmer and computer specialist assigned to a command miles away at Fort Story in Virginia Beach.

So, in the grand scheme of things, we were at separate commands and were serving in entirely different "communities" of the Navy. Still, the whole fraternization thing was in the back of my mind as I was first getting to know Christa. I was, after all, an officer. She had enlisted.

It's safe to say, however, that my difference of opinion in the way Uncle Sam conducts certain aspects of military affairs in modern times started right there in Norfolk. The idea that I was fraternizing soon became the last thing on my mind as Christa and I began dating.

"Is this a *date?*" Christa asked, mid-way through what I certainly considered to be one of our first dates.

"Well, yeah," I said. "Is that ok?"

While her smile seemed to suggest that it probably was, I had decided for myself that it definitely was. My loner bachelor existence as an already jaded young naval officer suddenly had a bright side. Christa and I started spending all kinds of time with each other; dinner dates, jogs together along Norfolk's waterfront and, of course, not a few trips to the movies.

Over those first few months, I realized that we had more in common than the Navy and our choice in a Ghent neighborhood apartment. Christa had also gone to high school in California, only she was living in southern California near San Diego while I was up north just outside Sacramento. And, underneath the social butterfly that she was in Norfolk, I was happy to find that Christa and I shared a mostly conservative political point of view.

Just as importantly—our differing status in the Navy notwithstanding—our paths in life had crossed. And we were very much enjoying our time together.

* * *

As it turned out, Christa and I both separated from the Navy late in the summer of 2001. I asked her to follow me back to California where I was going to start a graduate program in public policy at U.C. Berkeley, and she accepted.

Graduate school seemed the logical thing at the time—because that's just what junior officers coming out of the military do if they don't choose to make a career of it, as my father had. They get out of the service and go back to school for another degree.

I still had a strong interest in government and politics at the time, despite having once been admonished by a more senior naval officer to steer clear of such work as it would only "stunt my moral growth." But I wasn't yet so skeptical as Christa and I drove cross-country in our rented U-Haul truck.

The plan (to the extent that I had one) was to study government some more, get this public policy degree under my belt and then find myself a "normal" job—whatever that might be. But that was just it, I never knew clearly for myself what *it* was. There was no crystallized *goal* in my mind, an essential element to success as I've come to learn in life. A Georgetown education, four years in the Navy, and now a graduate degree in public policy. It was all supposedly leading somewhere, I told myself. But *where?*

The destination was always just sort of out there in the future, lacking any clear definition. Was I going to be a chief of staff for some state senator in Sacramento? Or was I perhaps going to wind up as a Capitol Hill staffer back in Washington someday? I didn't know the answer.

Within weeks of arriving in Berkeley, this career in government and politics that I had vaguely imagined for myself since I was a young kid was beginning to look more and more like a mirage. I approached a member of the school faculty to discuss the second thoughts I was already having about the program. I was finding much of the material and class discussion to be dry and mostly intuitive. And the more liberal atmosphere of Berkeley obviously wasn't a natural fit for me—something that, in hindsight, I should have given much more thought to before enrolling.

"Oh, give it a few more weeks," I was told. I hadn't yet adjusted back to student life. I just hadn't given the program a chance.

But then 9/11 happened. Almost instantly, I felt like an even bigger fish out of water. The first campus-sponsored symposium to talk about the heinous events was called (strangely sympathetic in my view) "Sources of Anger." What the hell kind of a title was that?

Over three thousand Americans had just been brutally slain in the World Trade Center Towers, at the Pentagon and aboard United Flight 93—as its heroic passengers foiled at least part of the terrorists' plot, by selflessly crashing their plane to earth in the Pennsylvania countryside. Yet there some of us were on the campus of U.C. Berkeley only a few days later, discussing the "anger" of the Islamic fascists who had orchestrated these horrific events.

Oh, those nineteen hijackers were *angry*, alright. Angry that the rest of the world wasn't letting them have their way in rebuilding a society rooted in centuries old religious hatreds and cruelty towards women. These men who knocked down the Twin Towers in New York were indeed angry that the "Great Satan" of America didn't agree with their nihilistic justifications for suicide-bombing their way to political power.

On September 11th, 2001, this "anger" had boiled over like never before in history to make a most fateful declaration to the civilized world—on American soil: Either agree with our worldview, or we will continue to indiscriminately kill you and your children.

When our self-appointed class president (I, for one, don't recall there ever being a vote on the matter) announced just before class a week later that one of his top five priorities for the remainder of the semester would be to eliminate the use of *paper* cups at the school house water cooler—I knew it was time to move on.

3 / BREAKING THE MOLD

Christa and I were living in a small one bedroom on Oxford Street in Berkeley, just north of campus, when I asked her to marry me.

It had only been a little over a year since we first met and, to say the least, my parents weren't exactly thrilled with the idea of me and Christa together—let alone *marriage*. Indeed, I hadn't even broached the subject with Christa's own father.

So, we eloped to Lake Tahoe where we were married at "Love's Chapel" on November 23, 2001. We had a great dinner at the Dory's Oar restaurant on the south shore before staying the night at Caesars.

As newlyweds, the first stop out of Berkeley for Christa and I was the state capital, Sacramento. I had gone to high school in nearby Roseville, closer to the foothills of the Sierra mountains.

Before leaving Berkeley, I turned up a contact of a contact from my internship days years earlier in Governor Pete Wilson's office. This led to a job offer from a man by the name of Joe Rodota, a former senior advisor to the governor. Now, while Rodota was once described to me as a "cold prickly," I myself had just dropped out of graduate school and was now married. I took the job.

Rodota was a known *"pol,"* with experience in government that went back to the days of the Reagan administration. He hired me to coordinate a project for a major electronic documents firm in Silicon Valley that had designs on the emerging state government markets in Sacramento and Austin, Texas.

I did what I could, but in the end it was a shit product. I knew it, and Rodota knew it too. He proceeded to fire me the week after Christmas. I have no idea what he wound up doing with his embryonic government consulting firm, but I do know that he went on to advise Arnold Schwarzenegger in what would be a successful bid to unseat California's democratic governor at the time, Gray Davis.

I really can't say anything bad about that brief detour through Sacramento. I didn't know a thing about electronic documents or how state government could benefit from them beyond what common sense dictates: reduces costly use of paper products and saves trees. Kind of like what the "president" of my class at Berkeley had in mind, I suppose.

But, to be honest, I don't think Rodota had much more insight on the topic himself. That said, he did give me a full month's pay as severance which Christa and I were able to use while we got our bearings straight again at her parents' home near San Diego.

Eight months later, I went to work for one of the major U.S. federal contracting firms, Booz Allen Hamilton. I was—in the view of Booz executives, at least—a "financial analyst." In reality, though, I was a novice Microsoft Excel spreadsheet jockey, doing what I could to track about $30 million that the Department of Defense appropriated on an annual basis to upgrade and maintain the shore component of the U.S. Navy's Global Command and Control System, known by its acronym GCCS-M. (The 'M' stands for maritime.)

Once again, I didn't have a lick of experience for the job I had been hired to perform, but this time it didn't matter. Because this time, the customer wasn't some high-speed company in Silicon Valley that would fire your ass after the first project if they didn't like the product. No, this time the ultimate customer was the United States Government, the biggest, most bloated company in the history of the world—a two hundred year old company defined by an acute lack of accountability in its management chain and a strong aversion to strategic thinking. But more on this in a bit.

By Thanksgiving 2002, Christa and I had been living in San Diego for over a year. I was working a steady job and Christa was taking a few classes at the nearby city college. Life was good except for the fact that my mom and dad still didn't like the fact that I had a) married behind their backs and b) dropped out of graduate school. My parents were expecting me to take my Georgetown degree and shoot for the moon out of the Navy. But there I was, treading water in San Diego (not a bad place to do so, by the way) as a low-level government contractor.

I knew that my parents—my father especially—had rejected Christa and me together due to the circumstances under which we met in Norfolk. The fraternization factor and related matters made ours a doomed relationship from the very start in my parents' eyes. But now that Christa and I had moved on from the Navy, now that I was (still) on my own supporting myself—why did I continue to be in the doghouse with my parents? In the end, wasn't I allowed to marry who I wanted to marry? Wasn't I allowed to drop out of school if I decided I didn't want it anymore? The answer from my parents seemed to be, quite simply, *no*.

As much of a (*realistic*) pessimist as I had become growing up as my father's son, Christa is—in important and good ways—my polar opposite. She has a way of living life that embraces the day. Rather than fixating on how things could be going better, she invariably sees the glass as half full. OK, I'll admit it—the "negativity" isn't in her. Christa connects with the moment. She *lives*.

Unfortunately, my father would just never recognize this about us.

* * *

Full stop. Sometime in the late summer of 2002, my father was bouncing on a trampoline in rural Missouri (*this*, I would have enjoyed seeing, as you can perhaps imagine) attending the wedding of one of my cousins on my mom's side. He would later tell me that he came down hard—and painfully—from his final jump, and at that moment knew that something wasn't quite right inside.

A few months later—and completely out of the blue—Christa and I were invited to my parents' in Roseville for Thanksgiving dinner, which happened to coincide with Christa's and my first wedding anniversary. My mom's mom—my *Babcia* (Polish for "grandmother")—even flew out from Blackstone, Massachusetts. It was Happy Thanksgiving *and* Happy Anniversary…my parents had gone from not talking to me for the better part of a year to (relatively speaking) rolling out the red carpet for Christa and I.

Not that I was complaining, but something was not in order.

After dinner that night, my dad took me for a very short walk down the street with Dudley, the family dog. Dudley and I used to hunt pheasant together at Beale Air Force Base in northern California back when I was in high school. That night, Dudley was along for a final walk with us as my father explained to his son that he was dying.

Something was very wrong, my father told me. The doctors weren't sure of the exact cause, but they would know within a few weeks, maybe sometime before Christmas.

It was a short walk because that's all my dad could handle. For years, he and I would take much longer walks with the dog, talking about the last movie we had seen or the latest issue of the day in national and international politics. Not this time.

It's not that this Thanksgiving visit didn't go a long way to repair—in my father's view—the damage done by his *officer* son who had gone off and married an *enlisted* woman. It did. For the first time, I think my dad finally started to see that Christa is good for me, despite a less than traditional start.

The problem was that this occasion there in the fall of 2002 had been precipitated by death itself. My father knew he only had a short time to live and so he wanted to make amends while he still had time. The result was rather forced and strained. But, "better late than never" truly is better.

I made the trip from San Diego to Roseville again only a few short weeks later. It was just after Christmas 2002. I'll never forget the sight of my father arriving home with my two brothers from yet another hopeless round of chemotherapy.

I say "hopeless" because this wasn't just any cancer. This was pancreatic cancer. He was a different man entirely as he got out of the car in the garage that afternoon. The volume of his face had been sucked away. He was bottom heavy from the edema. Not so much his backside and hips, but his legs and feet. He was a swollen mass of man, literally being weighted down to earth. My dad died less than a week later on January 2, 2003.

He had been everything to me as a boy. He had been why I wanted so very much to attend Georgetown University. He had been why I decided to join the military. And, even after his death, he would be the reason that I would explore a career in government service throughout the rest of my young adulthood. My choice in a wife had formed a bitter wedge between us, but we remained father and son in the end.

* * *

My last moments with my dad are still vivid in my mind. I wanted to get on the road early that morning for the long drive south along California's Interstate 5 highway. It was likely that I would be returning to Roseville very soon, but in the meantime life went on in San Diego with work.

I carefully walked my father down the stairs from his bedroom to the kitchen table where he would have yet one more read of the morning newspaper.

To be clear, my father didn't just read the newspaper. He *loved* reading newspapers. The man was a voracious reader in general, mostly history and biographies from the non-fiction genre. But he was also not one to discriminate on the fiction side of the house; mysteries, spy thrillers and, invariably, one or two odd-balls from the current best selling lists. He'd have his current menu of books stacked five and six deep right next to his chair in the family room. When he picked from it at random from one day to the next, it may have seemed arbitrary, but of course it was all dependent on whatever mood he was in at the time.

And so it wasn't just the local *Sacramento Bee* newspaper on the table that morning, but *The New York Times* as well. Years earlier, when he was still in the Air Force, he would even bring home a copy of the day's *Wall Street Journal*.

Even though he knew I was about to get on the road that morning, he tossed me the front section of *The New York Times* as if I were going to sit with him for a final read—just as I had since I was a kid. I'll take the local, you take the national paper, he was saying to me.

To this day, I know I wouldn't have been able to read one word of that paper without breaking down in tears. I kissed him on the head one last time and walked away.

4 / LAX

Less than a week after my father's passing, I had an interview at the Dou-bletree Hotel near LAX International Airport. I could see the commercial jets taking off and landing as I made my way in from the parking lot. It had been a long drive north from the apartment in downtown San Diego, but I was anxious to get on with it. I had made the first cut during a phone interview only a few weeks before.

The guy on the other end of the phone line, a retired CIA case officer, wanted to know the top three national security intelligence priorities as I saw them. I told him Vladimir Putin: "I'd want to be a fly on the wall at the Krem-lin," I said. "I'm not sure the guy can be trusted." I spoke as if my opinion mattered, something I think they look for in new recruits.

Number two was Al Qaeda, a safe answer. Less than two years after 9/11, that was a no-brainer.

"And I think this Hugo Chávez down in Venezuela is a national security problem," I said flatly. I think he liked that answer, too.

The subsequent interview in a room of the Doubletree went on for well over an hour. I was more relaxed in that interview than I've ever been in any interview in my life. I had such a nothing-to-lose attitude. I felt loose and confident. I didn't care if my answers were right or wrong.

I honestly don't remember any of the questions posed to me specifically, al-though I do remember telling the interviewer very matter-of-factly about half-way through that I had buried my father only a week before. I remember him watching me for a sign of emotion—which there was, but probably too briefly. I cleared my throat and it was on to the next question. A few weeks later, I was asked to continue the hiring process with a trip to northern Virginia.

I gave my company and the Navy's GCCS-M program manager some bogus story about having to spend some extra time in Roseville with my mom to help square things away following my father's death. I felt a little guilty using this as an excuse; I had already taken a lot of time off over the preceding months. But I knew my dad would have approved, so I didn't give it too much thought.

I can't remember how many multiple choice questions I answered during the start of that second phase of CIA's hiring process. Hundreds and hundreds—if not over a thousand.

The next day, I was interviewed by a psychologist who wanted to know—among other things—whether I had ever performed any sort of deviant sexual act. I told him I once engaged in anal sex. Once. His eyebrows and lower lip contorted a little. Was that it? he wanted to know. Yeah, that was it.

There was a second, more traditional interview on the final day very similar to the one I had at LAX. I answered more questions about why I wanted to work in intelligence. Was this *really* a career I wanted to pursue? I, of course, wasn't *entirely* certain. But—for the purposes of the interview—yes, I was certain. And then I flew back to California.

A few weeks later, I got a letter in the mail saying I had been selected to be a student in the upcoming class of new hires starting in January 2004. I would be attending the Agency's famous "Farm" to learn the tradecraft fundamentals of international espionage—American style.

I knew my mom was proud of me joining the CIA. And I know my father would have been, too. I would be starting my very brief and *highly atypical* intelligence career there at Headquarters in Langley, Virginia almost a year to the day after his death.

5 / CAPITOL HILL

The schedule for the first weeks of indoctrination at CIA was flexible enough that Christa and I were able to do some quality house hunting, both on the weekends and during the week.

We were fortunate to have some old friends let us stay with them at their home on Military Road in Northwest Washington for that first month in town, a favor Donna and Tom would graciously repeat a few years later—and under very different circumstances—as my time in the nation's capital was drawing to a close.

After some dead-end searches elsewhere in the District, we settled on a small 1,100 square foot row house on 14th Place in Northeast Washington. Technically, it was a block east of "historic" Capitol Hill, but to Christa and me we were living on the Hill. All we needed now, as a new Washingtonian couple, was a dog.

We had actually already made arrangements for the arrival of our first puppy months earlier—even before making an offer on our first home together—while still living in California. Stephanie Crowley was a well known breeder of Afghan Hounds, living in Frederick, Maryland, not too far from where we were staying in Northwest, DC. Christa and I ventured out on a very cold January day to the farm where Stephanie's kennel was located to see her latest litter of Afghan puppies.

"Prada," as my wife would almost instantly name her, was the third of the litter that Stephanie showed us that morning. Christa knew Prada was the one immediately. I also liked her just fine, although I was rather partial to the first one Stephanie had shown us. Prada was the smallest of the litter, Stephanie noted without a hint of judgment. Did we really want the runt? I remember thinking to myself.

"Would you take a little less for her then?" I asked hesitantly. I was still bowled over by the sticker price of the breed. Not your average priced puppy, for sure.

"No," Stephanie replied curtly, her voice still thick with an English accent even after years of living in the States. "I don't sell my dogs by the pound."

There would be no arguing with that. And, as is often the case, there was no arguing with Christa either. She had already made up her mind. Prada was the one.

But, I kid you not, a few weeks later—after Christa and I had finally moved in on Capitol Hill—Prada puked her guts out on the ride home from Stephanie's. It was so bad that we actually had to pull over at the Turkey Run exit of the George Washington Parkway just to get all of the puppy vomit cleaned up off the middle armrest of our Volkswagen.

I didn't know it at the time, but Prada's nausea was an ominous sign of things to come for me in my abbreviated career in the U.S. intelligence community.

The very next exit following Turkey Run on the parkway? CIA Headquarters.

6 / DOWN ON THE FARM

There have been books written by both lifetime veterans of the CIA, as well as those who have gone through the Agency's "Farm" training only to then complete a single overseas tour before deciding it wasn't for them. Count me as one of the latter. But it didn't take even a single assignment overseas for me to realize that I wasn't a CIA *lifer*.

At the time I was in-processing at CIA, management was instructing new hires to decide for themselves on one of three separate career tracks: the "tip of the spear" Operations Officer (OO), the "middle man" Collection Management Officer (CMO), or the almost strictly home-based Staff Operations Officer (SOO). I remember having the conversation early on with Christa in our apartment in San Diego, soon after getting the offer letter. My gut told me that I was best suited for collection *management*, but my ego was pushing me to opt for OO. That's what James Bond is, after all. I mean, who had ever heard of a Collection Management Officer?

Also during this initial in-processing, my fellow Class 14 classmates and I were assigned our Agency pseudonyms. These were fake names, rumored to be taken at random from some old edition of the London phonebook, which would follow us through our careers as American intelligence officers. Mine would be (I loved it)—Winston P. Smoakes.

Throughout the account that follows of my working on the Saudi WMD issue, I will refer to the people I worked with by their real-life first names *only*—to protect their identity—or, in other cases, by either the first or last name of their pseudonym. It would be commonplace during my time at CIA, both in training and, ultimately, as a contractor (as I'll explain), that people were known by their pseudonyms only—their real life names rarely, if ever used.

For reasons still beyond me, all new hires in the CIA's Directorate of Operations, regardless of their track, were required to submit to the pressure cooker training of the Farm—the Agency's notoriously taxing field operations training course. Before leaving our families behind in the metro Washington area, my class and I had heard all sorts of rumors about how much of a mind game it was down there. (I say "down there" because it's located south of Washington, but technically the location is classified, so I'll leave it at that.)

Sure enough, not unlike the early misgivings I had soon after arriving on the campus of U.C. Berkeley, I knew within weeks after arriving at the Farm that I wasn't in the right place. This was far more than just an aversion to the inhospitable training environment. I had been through worse at Officer Candidate School in Pensacola. No, my problem with the Farm was that I simply couldn't get onboard with what they were training me to do there.

* * *

My first real epiphany that I was once again in the wrong place actually occurred during a brief pre-Farm send-off by then-deputy director for Operations (DDO) Steve Kappes. (His is a high profile and public position, thus my use of his real first and last name.) This particular address to Class 14, held at Headquarters, was during his first time as head of the Directorate of Operations, Kappes having just succeeded James Pavitt in the position. Together, these two men had been numbers one and two (Pavitt and Kappes, respectively) overseeing the CIA's Directorate of Operations during the controversial lead-up to the Iraq war in 2002 and early 2003.

Kappes would later return to Headquarters in May 2006, again as DDO, this time under newly appointed CIA Director Michael V. Hayden. This came after a brief hiatus in London for Kappes, while Congressman Porter Goss (himself a former case officer) was at the helm of the Agency.

To his credit, Steve Kappes did not see eye to eye with Director Goss on personnel issues—among many other things, for sure. Porter Goss' brief tenure as the head of CIA mid-way through the Bush administration is notable for a nasty scandal involving a California congressman and Goss' own choice for DDO, Kyle "Dusty" Foggo, a former CIA case officer who was ultimately sentenced to 37 months in federal prison after being convicted on bribery and money laundering charges.

Kappes was of course "legendary" within the Agency, having served as station chief in Moscow, New Delhi and Frankfurt. But as he introduced himself to me and my fellow classmates that morning, what really struck me about the man was his unbridled arrogance. At the end of his "pep" talk to Class 14, Kappes stood there on the stage with his hands on his hips, eyeballing as many of us as he could. To the most promising young talent the country had to offer at the time in the midst of a still-unfolding Global War on Terror, he said, with a none-too-subtle accusatory tone, "And if I ever catch any of you trying to advance your personal careers at the expense of one of your classmates—I will personally hunt you down and *punish you.*"

As he left the stage, it occurred to me that Kappes had very likely just revealed to me and the rest of the class the means by which he himself had attained such a lofty position within his beloved Agency. He was exhibiting a little guilt, it seemed. Surely, neither I nor any of my classmates had done anything during our brief time at Headquarters up to that point to warrant such stern admonishment.

What a jackass, I thought to myself. I was seated in the aisle seat of my row as the man exited the auditorium, chin high in the air as he hit his stride. I so wanted to stick my leg out and trip his pompous ass to the floor.

* * *

There were other indications over and above my response to the deputy director's motivational words that clued me in to the fact that I wasn't exactly on the right track. There was the memorable mentoring session I had with one of the Agency's renowned Cold War warriors who, prior to the fall of the Soviet Union in the Eastern Bloc, had performed his fair share of official business on behalf of the U.S. government.

In the midst of some frank talk about the ins and outs of his former tradecraft, he broke to a short anecdote about his time back in the day working the tricky terrain of communist Bulgaria. Real or embellished (who could tell?), he recalled a particular pedestrian bridge crossing that involved the mortal fear of a rumored poison-tipped umbrella in the hands of adversaries. Making your way through an approaching wave of people, he explained to me, it would take just a poke from an inconspicuous parasol and you'd suddenly be at the mercy of some trace amount of a highly lethal substance.

"You think that's funny?" my seventy-year-old instructor asked with equal parts curiosity and edge. His underlying tone wasn't far from that of actor Robert De Niro's character Travis Bickle in the 1976 movie *Taxi Driver,* when Bickle is talking to himself in the mirror: "You talkin' to me?...Who the fuck do you think you're talking to?" I'm not kidding. He even had some of the same look as De Niro.

My instructor's question was prompted by a seemingly irreverent smirk that had spread wide across my face, a problem I've had my whole life to be honest. I too often wear my heart on my sleeve.

"No, it's not funny," I countered, trying in vain to suppress the grin.

The problem was that I actually did find some humor in the old codger's war story. The thought of a bunch of dedicated Cold War intelligence officers running around Sofia trying to poke each other with toxin-tipped umbrellas was—well, it kicked up an only half-muffled guffaw.

But the lingering smirk was not out of a lack of respect, as it was obviously perceived. It was rather a direct response to the insanity of it all.

* * *

Whether my all-too-brief immersion in Berkeley culture had any part in it, I would turn spouses' weekend that fall at the Farm into spouses' *and family pets'* weekend.

You see, as much as I wanted Christa to be part of the festivities—a real morale booster for us spies in training, as you can imagine—there was a problem. Prada was still only a pup and there was no way in hell that Christa was going to leave that dog all by her lonesome in some kennel in Washington over the weekend. Was there any way Prada could *come with?* Christa wanted to know.

"You mean, down *here*?" I hesitated.

"Yeah, why not?" Christa replied, in typical Christa fashion. I can't count the number of times over the years that she's made similar pushing-the-envelope type suggestions to me, only for me to answer with an "oh, I don't know about that…" Spouses' weekend was a prime example of this.

I had to ask my OTB (officer training branch) chief, Don, whether this would be alright, for my wife to bring our dog down from Washington. He was a little surprised by the question, but not overly so. The instructor staff there at the Farm encouraged full participation in the event. Happy marriages make for happy CIA officers. As a young kid growing up in an Air Force family, I had experienced much the same thing at various summer picnics we would attend with the families of my dad's Pentagon co-workers.

"Sure, I don't see why not," was Don's surprising response. "But I'll have to check to make sure it's OK. What kind of dog is it?"

"Prada. My wife named her," I was quick to point out. "She's an Afghan Hound."

Now this part actually did take Don a little by surprise. "Really?! An *Afghan*, huh?"

Yep. With two hot wars going on at the time in Iraq and Afghanistan, there I was trying to sneak Christa's Afghan hound into the CIA's clandestine operations training facility. Don, the nice guy that he was, would see what he could do.

I can only imagine the grief he probably got in the instructor's lounge from the more hard core Agency pros for pushing that one through with management. Don, the Farm instructor, who turned Class 14's "Spouses' Weekend" into "Bring the Family Pet to Work Day." *Geesh*.

But things would turn out just fine. It was sort of fun actually. Prada played nice in my apartment room that day while Christa accompanied me around "campus" (although somehow it just wasn't like our time in Berkeley together). That same night, while all the other couples were looking for something to do, Christa and I took Prada for a walk on the Farm.

* * *

I'm even more convinced in hindsight that the CMO tracked folks just didn't need full blown Farm treatment, and not just because certain CMO's are prone to bringing their Afghan hounds along for a day of training.

The OO is the guy out in front—the "pitch" man, the one meeting with assets overseas who (hopefully) know things that policymakers in the U.S. government need to know. The CMO, on the other hand, acts as a sort of middle man in the way he guides the intelligence collection effort. It's quite common, for example, for the questions that get asked of assets overseas by the OO to be entirely generated by the CMO, who may or may not take part in the actual meeting.

In my case, having chosen the CMO path, it was no doubt useful for me to learn about the methods and techniques used by the Operations Officer in his interactions with intelligence assets. But for me to be required to undergo *all* of the very same training—and do it well—was, in my humble opinion, overkill. After having almost quit a first time (early on in the Farm training), I finally did just that down towards the end with only about a month to go.

I clearly remember the final role playing scenario in which I was pretending to be some sort of international businessman meeting with a prospective asset who offered access to sensitive information concerning a notional chemical production facility. The instructor, as they all tended to do with me, was giving me a hard time with my cover story—i.e. my fake business persona and all that went with it.

The problem, of course, wasn't so much my cover story itself, but rather *how* I was delivering it. It just wasn't me to be acting like someone I wasn't. And so, naturally, I was doing a pretty shitty job of it. Thank goodness our country has people who are able to do this—and they do it very well—but, if it's not you, it's *not you*. And it wasn't me.

Somewhere about halfway into my pitch I lost my patience when the instructor dug in his heals on the question of why my company would be interested in hiring someone like him. He just wasn't buying it—or, to be more exact, he wasn't buying *me*. I repeated my answer one last time. No dice.

Finally, I just looked at him and said very matter-of-factly, "I think we've got the wrong guy."

I said "we" as in me and my pretend company, but the instructor knew exactly what I was getting at. I thanked him for his time, walked him to the door and, still playing the role for the hell of it, said to him, "We'll be in touch if we have anything else for you." I shook his hand and closed the door. By that afternoon, I had convinced Don (this time more forcefully than months before) that I really did need to check out.

The next day, I had to say it all over again to the director of the Helms Center. (The training center is named after former CIA director Richard Helms.) The deputy head of the school was also with us during the exit interview and said something to me that I still appreciate today.

"Know thyself," he said, nodding his head slightly in agreement with my rationale for self-selecting out of the training.

In other words, he understood. This isn't your cup of tea. Good luck to you.

7 / THROUGH REVOLVING DOORS

Upon my return to Headquarters back in the Washington area, I was still adamant about wanting to work for the Agency as a CMO. I wrote it into the letter they had me write for the record to document my decision to self-select out of the Farm.

CIA's Human Resources division was only half cooperative on this. A board was held to decide that, yes, I could remain in the Directorate of Operations, but that the only positions available to me would be either SOO, or the still-nascent "targeting" track.

As the name implies, targeteers are the ones who decide which people are worth pursuing for foreign intelligence; who in the world is worthy of development for possible recruitment by the CIA? I had little interest in targeting, and even less in the SOO track. I had quit my job in "74 degrees and sunny" San Diego to join the CIA as a *CMO*, and if that was no longer a possibility, it was time for me to move on.

I also sent an email directly to Michael V. Kostiw, one of the higher-ups on CIA's "seventh floor"—the term is synonymous with the Agency's policy-making crowd, as it's where the director's and various deputies' offices are located. I was intent on voicing my frustration with the Agency's inflexible training policy. On November 16, 2004 Winston P. Smoakes—I still had my cool *nom de plume* at that point—wrote:

> "Just as the CMO needs the OO to provide the raw material that serves as the basis for CMO work, the OO needs a CMO perspective to optimize operational efforts. Despite what the average OO might claim, the typical

CMO really does bring something extra to the table in terms of how he thinks about a case."

Not surprisingly, I never got a reply from Mr. Kostiw. Beyond the several layers of CIA management between him and this Farm drop-out, the tone of my note was a bit snarky wasn't it? Had I been in his shoes—at the time Kostiw was serving as senior advisor to CIA Director Porter Goss—after reading the first paragraph of my email, I would have likely just hit the "delete" button myself.

Even so, my point was a good one. The CMO and OO are two entirely different animals. And, the director's right-hand man or not, I figured Kostiw would at least consider my thoughts on the matter. He had, after all, gone through the same training pipeline himself decades earlier before serving several years as an Agency officer. That much I knew as Winston waxed eloquent via email to the seventh floor.

What I did not know—prior to doing my homework for this book—was that Michael Vincent Kostiw (after serving in the CIA in the late 1970s, and before going to work on Capitol Hill for U.S. Representative Porter J. Goss) had, mid-way through his career in the federal government, climbed his way up America's big oil corporate ladder to the lucrative post of vice president for international government affairs of ChevronTexaco, as the company was known at the time.

Founded in 1879 as Standard Oil of California, it had been Mr. Kostiw's predecessors in the executive offices of Chevron Corporation who oversaw the company's rather worthwhile oil exploration ventures in the Middle East, in particular the sands of Saudi Arabia. In the early 1950s, the company would discover the world's largest oil field on the Arabian Peninsula, Saudi Arabia's *Ghawar.* Sometime thereafter, the Saudis in Riyadh would begin buying up shares of the Standard Oil subsidiary that was now enjoying unprecedented profits—at considerable expense to the royal family, of course.

By 1980, this same corporate off-shoot—then known as the Arabian American Oil Company (ARAMCO)—was wholly owned by the Saudi royal family. The name was ultimately changed to Saudi Arabian Oil Company (Saudi Aramco) in 1988. Over the next twenty years, it's clear that America's Chevron Corporation adjusted just fine to the change in control over oil drilling operations inside the kingdom. In 2008, Chevron reported a net income just shy of $24 billion.

Now, I have no idea how well Mr. Kostiw got to know Condoleezza Rice during his tenure as a Chevron government affairs executive, but it's certainly notable that Ms. Rice is herself a former member of Chevron's board of directors. Perhaps the two at least crossed paths when she chaired Chevron's public policy committee, a position that Rice would eventually resign from on January 15, 2001, to become President George W. Bush's National Security Advisor. Rice would hold the post throughout Bush's eventful first term in office before moving on to become the 66th U.S. Secretary of State.

Still wearing her National Security Advisor hat on January 10, 2003, however, it was of course Condoleezza Rice who made the now infamous statement to CNN anchorman Wolf Blitzer regarding the false specter of WMD in Iraq. Just months before the U.S. military invasion of Saudi Arabia's belligerent neighbor to the north, Rice noted ominously:

"The problem here is that there will always be some uncertainty about how quickly [Saddam Hussein] can acquire nuclear weapons. But we don't want the smoking gun to be a mushroom cloud."

It was hard to argue the former Stanford professor's point at the time, wasn't it? Indeed, no person in their right mind wants a mushroom cloud. But I'm getting ahead of myself.

* * *

So in January 2005, exactly a year after arriving in Washington to work for the CIA, I was unemployed and living with my wife…who happened to be due with our first child only one month later. For the first time in my adult life, I really had no idea what I was going to do for a job.

Fortunately, by virtue of the fact that I had just recently self-selected out of Agency training, I did have something that was highly sought after by the many start-up intelligence contracting companies that had sprung up in northern Virginia and suburban Maryland since 9/11—a TOP SECRET/HCS security clearance. The HCS stands for "HUMINT (Human Intelligence) Collection System."

During one of my interims in the Agency's Central Eurasian Division reports shop the previous summer, I met a fellow Georgetown alum by the name of Foxwell. He was a native Washingtonian and, while I had gone off into the Navy after graduation to figure out what I wanted to do with my life, he had chosen to remain in the DC area. He got his masters degree in Russian studies and was well into his career as a CMO by the time we met at Headquarters.

An experienced CMO, Foxwell showed me the ropes of collection management. His office handled incoming reporting from all the "Icky"-stans— as they were collectively known, tongue-in-cheek, of course; Uzbekistan, Tajikistan and, my focus during those six weeks as Foxwell's apprentice, Turkmenistan.

At the time, Turkmenistan was being ruled by a psychotic named Saparmurat Niyazov, the self-proclaimed "President for Life" of the Turkmen homeland. *Türkmenbasy*—"Father of All Turkmen," as he preferred to be called. While North Korea's Kim Jong Il had a penchant for porn, Donald Duck cartoons and fine cognac, the Bashi had his own peculiar approach to leading a country.

For example, the Bashi renamed the months of the year after himself and members of his family. He banned television news anchors and reporters from wearing any make-up. And he was no fan of false teeth either, gold ones in particular. Speaking on the merits of good oral hygiene, the Bashi once explained:

> "I watched young dogs when I was young. They were given bones to gnaw to strengthen their teeth. Those of you [in the audience] whose teeth have fallen out did not chew on bones. This is my advice."

The Bashi has sadly since passed, suffering massive cardiac arrest in December 2006. But in the summer of 2004, when I was learning how to be a CMO at CIA Headquarters, his antics constituted the bulk of the intelligence reporting that I helped process under Foxwell's mentorship.

* * *

Being immersed for the first time in the world of intelligence at CIA during the summer of 2004 had been eye opening indeed. Like most American kids, I had grown up on an image of the CIA that more closely resembled the travails of the most famous member of the British intelligence service—"Bond...James Bond." Somehow, the life and times of the Bashi, sensational as they were, just didn't live up to such expectations.

There were certainly times during these first months at Headquarters that I did see traces of CIA's Hollywood mystique. For example, the Agency's Division of Science and Technology (the bureaucratic equivalent of Bond's "M" at CIA) conducted an informational briefing for my class one day that demonstrated some real *whiz-bang* capabilities that left many of us impressed, myself included. There were a few other such moments of awe during that first year, but not many.

Life at Headquarters was really much like every other government entity I had experienced up to that point in my life—state, federal or otherwise. It was made up of people, after all. People who go home to their families at the end of the day. People who often—for better or worse—go to the trouble of jumping through this or that administrative hoop to get promoted to the next level of the management chain. And, in terms of the subject matter of the work, that too was often rather lackluster and mundane. This human side of the business of *human* intelligence was driven home by a tragic event that took place during my first summer at CIA.

I had studied abroad in Turkey for a semester during my sophomore year at Georgetown and so, naturally, I was curious to find out more about the nature and tempo of U.S. intelligence out of that country. Over the Agency's online instant messaging system, I reached out to the Headquarters CMO who handled the Turkey account.

When I finally met him in his office one Friday afternoon, I wasn't surprised to hear that reporting was fairly brisk out of Turkey, the "Old Man of Europe." Ankara is a NATO ally and Turkey borders both Iraq and Iran. Turkey's population is ethnically Turkish, not Arab (as PBS's news anchor Gwen Ifill once famously made the mistake of assuming), but its population is almost entirely Muslim. These factors had become even more important in U.S.-Turkish relations in the post-9/11 era.

Turkey's Headquarters CMO was obviously farther along in his career than me. After getting "certified" at the Farm, he had already done several tours overseas and was now serving in one of the better CMO slots at Headquarters. As we spoke, he seemed to genuinely appreciate my own interest in the Turkey account and promised to answer any questions I might have in the future as I made my way through training and on to my first assignment overseas as a CMO. After chatting for ten minutes or so, we shook hands and said goodbye. Minutes later, I was heading south down the GW Parkway on my way home for the weekend.

When I returned to Headquarters the following Monday, I was stunned—to say the least—to find out that this same man had committed suicide over the weekend. Within seconds of hearing the news, I realized that I had been one of the last people he spoke with at Headquarters that previous Friday afternoon. I learned what everyone in his office had been only partly aware of themselves—the fact that he and his wife were in the midst of a difficult divorce.

His wife had been a professional ballerina. *A ballerina*. They even had a child together. She had recently left him for another man. Burdened with this reality, he went home for the weekend that previous Friday and swallowed a bottle of prescription pills.

* * *

Without any real clue of what I wanted to do now that I had left the Agency, I got in touch with Foxwell. He agreed to have lunch with me in northern Virginia just after New Years in 2005.

Foxwell is a real upstanding guy. Not only is he an intelligence professional, he's also the father of two sharp kids, a devoted husband and one hell of a saxophone player. He records on the side, plays the occasional gig in the DC area, and is undoubtedly the highlight of Sunday service at the church he and his family attend.

Over lunch, Foxwell suggested I submit my resume to the small intelligence contracting company he had just joined, SpecTal, LLC. SpecTal had a corporate office in nearby Reston, Virginia. Having few other options, I contacted SpecTal's hiring boss, a former Agency employee herself by the name of Katherine, and was scheduled for an interview soon thereafter.

Naturally, during the course of the interview, Katherine was curious about why I had dropped out of the Farm. But not only did she like my response to the question, I was rather heartened to hear that her own work experience as an Agency employee not long before had included some of the very same frustrations.

At the end of the interview, she asked me how much I had in mind in terms of salary. Having done a little research on what intelligence contractors were making at the time, I told her $100K. I felt funny putting that number out, especially since it was almost double what I had been making in San Diego with Booz Allen just a year before, but there it was.

A few days later, a FedEx package arrived at the row house with an offer letter from SpecTal. Starting annual salary: $100K. I took the job.

But more than the pay and, more importantly, the fact that I would be able to work at CIA after all—*as a CMO, no less*—there was another factor involved that made me jump at the offer. Chloe, our first daughter, would be born on a beautiful snowy February morning only a few weeks later at Sibley Hospital in Washington. The women at SpecTal sent flowers, which Christa very much appreciated.

And, by that point, Christa and our baby girl were covered by my new company's health insurance plan—which *I* very much appreciated.

* * *

John, the mid-career GS-13 intelligence officer I went to work for as an (ahem) experienced intelligence contractor was himself seemingly already aware that he wasn't a CIA lifer. My SpecTal handler, Kathy, introduced me to him one morning in January 2005, during what I at least considered a serious hiring interview with the customer.

I distinctly remember two things about this initial meeting with John. One was that his office was completely empty except for his desk, two chairs, his computer and maybe one or two books on chemical and biological weapons. The only other things in his windowless basement office at Head-quarters were a healthy green potted plant—doing just fine even without the sunlight—and a rather scary looking circa WWII gas mask.

The other thing I recall sitting there in John's office, anxious to prove that I'd be worth my premium contractor's salary, was my mentioning the fact that I had once traveled to Turkey and Syria as a college student.

"It's been a while since I've been over there," I said earnestly, "but I learned a lot." This was, after all, CIA's Near East Counter-Proliferation reports shop; I had to have some sort of real life qualification for the job. I had been to the Persian Gulf, too, years before as an officer in the Navy, but for some reason I didn't think this counted for much in the CIA's Counter-Proliferation Division (CPD).

"Syria, huh?" John said. He just looked over at Kathy and smiled.

The next day, I began settling into my cubicle in CPD—as a *collection management* contractor. Never mind that—whereas I had dropped out of graduate school—most of the Agency's CMOs had earned advanced degrees at some of the world's top colleges and universities. Never mind, too, that after dropping out of U.C. Berkeley, I had then proceeded to drop out of Farm training. As I was still learning, once you're *there* in life, *how* you got there often just doesn't matter.

I had come east from California to be a Collection Management Officer at the Central Intelligence Agency and—what do you know?—there I was going to work in the Agency's Counter-Proliferation Division. This was the very branch of CIA that played an integral role in the controversial run-up to the second Gulf War just a few short years earlier. This was the same division of CIA made famous by a related scandal involving the now famous former CPD case officer, Valerie Plame and her husband, Ambassador Joe Wilson.

Word quickly got around to some of my former classmates about how I had left the Farm only to return as a Headquarters CMO. When that first paycheck from SpecTal arrived, I must admit I was a little self conscious of the fact that I was making such great pay while most of Class 14 had to settle for more modest civil service salaries. Not only that, I came to find out later that spring that some of them were going without proper health and dental cover-age because their pending assignments overseas presented various "cover issues" that prevented them from enrolling in regular employer-based plans. They were, understandably, not happy campers.

Can you imagine, you quit your $175K a year job working at an investment bank in New York to work for the CIA, and you don't even have health coverage in your first year on the job? Believe it. Good thing I had coverage through SpecTal when Chloe was born.

* * *

By early 2005, as I was just beginning in CPD's Near East branch (CP/NE)—literally in the basement of CIA, Valerie Plame's office had moved a few floors up. Her twenty-year career, however, was drawing to a premature close after she had been "outted" as a CIA employee back in 2003 by *Chicago Sun Times* columnist Bob Novak and—as she and her husband would later allege—high ranking Bush administration officials including the Vice President's chief of staff I. Lewis "Scooter" Libby and Richard Armitage at the State Department.

Considerable differences in time working for the Agency and the fact that I was working as a contractor aside, in the end, my time working in the basement of CPD would have significant commonalities with Valerie Plame's own experience—and that of her Joint Task Force Iraq colleagues—in those same spaces back in the pre-war 2002 timeframe.

Honest to God, the sign hanging over my desk there in the basement of New Headquarters Building (built adjacent to the CIA's better known Old Headquarters Building) read "IRAQ REPORTS," as in all the so-called "intelligence" about aluminum tubes and yellow cake Uranium that went into President George W. Bush's infamous 2002 State of the Union address to Congress. Remember that one? It was Bush's famous "Axis of Evil" speech in which he falsely (as the country would later learn) claimed that Iraq was hiding a nascent nuclear weapons program from U.N. weapons inspectors.

I could hardly believe my eyes standing there in my new cubicle. How was that sign *still* hanging in that office, several years after it had become clear to the world that the WMD part of the Bush administration's justification for the war in Iraq had been all hype?

I didn't even ask—not John or anyone else. I got up on my desk and pulled that damn sign down.

But there were other remnants of the Iraq intelligence debacle, of course. You see, soon after my arrival John had me (a contractor) do a little house cleaning. Books—and I mean fancy bound printings of "analysis" covering the many alleged programs in Iraq--all thrown in the burn-bag as trash. CDs with who knows what on them. Trash. Not just suspect nuclear weapons sites, but write-ups on Saddam's chemical and biological kitchens of doom. Trash. Pictures, raw notes from case officers of meetings with assets—probably even that infamous source *Curveball*. Trash.

I mention this not at all to suggest that I was an unwitting accomplice in some sort of ongoing cover-up. That's almost certainly not the case. *Right?* By early 2005, Congress had already done its due diligence with this corner of CIA and had subpoenaed all the relevant notes and transcripts that had been handled by this office in the run up to the war against Saddam. *Right?*

"Trash," John told me as I filled burn-bag after burn-bag with the stuff. Trash.

What I was actually doing, of course, in following John's house-keeping requests, was disposing of miscellaneous remains of the sum product of the Joint Iraq Task Force—a critical component of what had been Dick Cheney's plot to justify the use of military force against Saudi Arabia's neighbor to the north.

* * *

That first year working in CP/NE is largely a blur, mostly because Christa and I were busy on Capitol Hill as first time parents. Bound by contract to only an eight-hour day, I was almost always home by five in the evening.

Not much for long work hours, I certainly wasn't complaining. I'm the type that will happily put the time in at the office *when necessary*. But this nonsense of hanging around until six at night—every night—just to hang around, that's just not in my playbook.

Weather permitting, by early evening Christa and I would be walking Chloe in the stroller in nearby Lincoln Park, a great urban park in the District situated halfway between the Capitol building and Robert F. Kennedy

Memorial Stadium where the Redskins used to play—and really should play again someday. It makes little sense to me—along with not a few die hard Washington fans—that the Redskins play in the town of Landover, *Maryland*. Not that I had much time for watching football that year. With a new job and a baby to help take care of, my hands were full.

Another reason working as a new intelligence contractor that first year in CPD is a bit hazy is that it took me some time to get a handle on what I was doing there. The analogy that the business of intelligence is a lot like the childhood game of *telephone* is fairly accurate.

Remember as a kid in the classroom or on the playground, getting in a circle and someone whispered "banana" or "elephant" into the first kid's ear? And then, eight or twelve kids later, the teacher asked your second grade friend Jessica right next to you what word you just whispered into her ear—and she says "spaghetti sauce"…remember that? That's what working as a CMO is like. Sort of. Only instead of "banana" or "elephant" it's "tritium triggers" and "anthrax."

Fortunately, this first year that I was handling WMD related intelligence on behalf of the American taxpayer (and the rest of the world, really—when you stop and think about it), I didn't screw anything up too badly. A report would come in from the field. I would read it and maybe change a word or two here or there so that it read more smoothly. Sometimes, when the information didn't seem quite right, I would run it by analysts and subject matter experts for a sanity check. I would incorporate their comments and, just as importantly, make note of any other information they would like to see in subsequent reporting from the source. Finally, I would coordinate it through my civil service bosses (first John, then his higher-ups) and then, "click"—out it would go as "disseminated" intelligence. Analysts at CIA, DIA, the NSC, Department of Energy, etc.—they would then be able to factor the information contained in the new report into their own analytic products—hopefully not those of the Iraq variety that I helped dispose of during those first few weeks on the job.

I want to state very clearly that the work done by intelligence professionals is in no way trivial. It's some of the most important work done by federal government employees. Particularly in this post-9/11 era, we need people on "that wall" (to quote Jack Nicholson's character in *A Few Good Men*) talking to people overseas who know things that bad people don't want Americans to know. We need the professional men and women of the U.S. intelligence community to monitor all the emails, cell phone chatter, "Tweets," satellite imagery and air travel of those people in the world who—for reasons good, bad, and insane—want to kill you, me, our mothers and our newborn babies. These people are most certainly out there, folks. Make no mistake. Never mind that we're going on 10 years now after the 9/11 terrorist attacks. As the bumper stickers suggest, we really must *never forget*.

But at the same time, the work done by the nation's intelligence professionals can also be utterly boring and mundane. Weeks can go by without so much as a blip in one's area of concern. This, of course, hasn't typically been the case since 9/11 in the counter-terrorism realm, but even in that busy world there is inevitably some down time.

Such was the case for me while working the WMD accounts of several lower priority Middle Eastern countries my first year in CP/NE. Former Farm classmates would drop by and ask me how things were going and I would sometimes want to change the subject to my newborn daughter or ask them about their pending departure for their first overseas assignment. I just didn't want to be perceived as a bump on the log, either by former classmates or by my new co-workers in CP/NE.

I think some of this pride was a result of the fact that I had served in the Navy for several years before arriving at CIA. I was, after all, in the pilot house that night in December 1998, helping to steer USS Princeton just a few short miles off the Iraqi coast as she lobbed Tomahawk cruise missiles at Saddam Hussein, a "tyrant and a despot," as Margaret Thatcher once referred to the brutal dictator. So it wasn't that I was no longer a patriot—working as a contractor there in CP/NE—it was that during my time as an officer in the Navy and then as a newbie intelligence officer in training, I just hadn't found the right fit for myself. I simply wasn't cut out to do twenty years at sea in the Navy. Nor was I cut out for a career in the country's intelligence bureaucracy.

As I write this, I can feel the judgment of some Americans who did choose to devote their lives to the military, intelligence and, in many cases, both. Some of them have even made the ultimate sacrifice in recent years in Iraq, Afghanistan and elsewhere around the world in the war against Islamic fascism. They are a most honorable class of American patriots, following in the footsteps of the many who gave their lives for the cause of freedom in the last century in the jungles of Vietnam, in Korea and—in terribly large numbers—on the beaches of Normandy.

* * *

By late 2005, this funk I was in began to lift.

I was called into my boss's office one morning. John had departed by that point and, to be perfectly honest, I don't even remember his replacement's name. John's successor was in the position only briefly. But I absolutely remember the question he had for me.

As part of management's reshuffling of things, he explained, did I want to begin working the Libya WMD account or—to my surprise—*Saudi Arabia*. I had to choose one or the other.

Now, Libya's Muammar Qaddafi had just recently come clean with his nascent weapons program, perhaps motivated to do so as Saddam Hussein was by then headed for the gallows in Baghdad. The Libyan leader had agreed to allow for full inspections of Libya's facilities. The Libya account, therefore (I remember thinking over the span of a minute or two in John's old office), would be mostly a sanity check on whatever inspections the U.N. would be conducting—and whatever additional *unilateral* checks the U.S. (CIA's own Steve Kappes, actually) had negotiated directly with Mr. Qaddafi under the table.

Saudi Arabia, on the other hand…The world's largest oil producer, but at the same time the country of origin for 15 of the 19 September 11th hijackers. I was having trouble there on the spot conceptualizing what the account would entail; nuclear, chemical or biological? All three, perhaps—or just the most obvious?

As a quick (but not irrelevant) aside—I had never in my life set foot in Saudi Arabia. When I was an ensign in the Navy aboard USS Princeton, we had pulled into the nearby port of Jebel Ali in the United Arab Emirates for liberty call a few months after unloading our Tomahawks into Iraq. The timing of *Operation Desert Fox*, I have to say, was always a little suspect to me. President Clinton had been knee deep in the Monica Lewinsky scandal at that exact point in his second term—and all of a sudden he decides to turn the Navy loose on targets in Iraq and Afghanistan? The former were suspect WMD sites; the latter were terrorist camps in the badlands of Afghanistan, owned and operated by some Saudi ex-pat by the name of Osama Bin Laden.

That said—and as fate would have it sitting there in my boss' office—I decided to take the Saudi account.

I didn't know it at the time, but over the next eighteen months in CP/NE, I was to get involved in a matter of utmost national security importance—a reality that, even as this book goes to press, has yet to see the light of day.

I also didn't know it that morning, but at the end of those eighteen months, I would be prematurely removed from the Saudi account by CIA management. "Don't bring a knife to a gun fight," a sympathetic colleague would later say to me in regards to my sudden departure.

Knives and guns, it turns out, would be the least of my worries. By the end of my time in CP/NE, I had stumbled much too far into the chilling (and perilously political) world of nuclear weapons proliferation.

* * *

I realized soon after starting on the Saudi account that our old friends across the pond were also curious about Riyadh's potential interest in a WMD capability. Towards the end of 2005, I joined Phil (a CP/NE targeting officer) and Derrick (CP/NE's Operations Boss at the time) in a conference room in Old Headquarters Building for a meeting with our British counter- proliferation colleagues.

My recollection of that meeting is, admittedly, somewhat vague. There were a lot of facts about Saudi Arabia's Strategic Rocket Forces, or SRF (the personnel and infrastructure constituting the Saudi military's ballistic missile capability), and various new terms and acronyms that I was still trying to get my head around.

But I clearly recall that by the time the meeting was over, I was no longer thinking of the Saudi account in the catch-all WMD sense, i.e. chemical, biological and/or nuclear. From that point on, the Saudi account, for me (along with every American and Brit in the room) was a question of whether Riyadh was looking to acquire a *nuclear weapons* capability.

The arguments differed slightly as to why the King of Saudi Arabia might be seeking a nuclear deterrent in an increasingly volatile Middle East, but the underlying logic was the same on both sides of the table. Iraq was still boiling over with bloodshed during the years immediately following the Saddam era. This instability alone had ripple effects throughout the region that could potentially threaten the security of the kingdom. But, much more importantly from a strategic standpoint, it was becoming apparent from Riyadh's Sunni Muslim perspective that Mahmud Ahmadinejad was just getting warmed up—with the blessing of Iran's Shia mullahs, no less—with his not-so-subtle threats of nuclear confrontation with Israel and the West. And while Saudi Arabia was not considered to be *that* kind of enemy in Tehran, Riyadh was certainly no ally.

Little was known in western intelligence circles in late 2005/early 2006 about the status of Iran's nuclear enrichment program, but everyone agreed on the general psychological profile of Ahmadinejad. Like North Korea's Kim Jong Il, Ahmadinejad was a few cards short of a full deck, although in very different ways. Whereas Kim Jong Il enjoyed passing time watching certain Disney character cartoons (Donald Duck, especially, as I understand), Ahmadinejad took a much more sober—but no less troubling—approach to his role as leader of another of President Bush's "Axis of Evil" countries.

According to Ahmadinejad, the Nazi Holocaust had been a myth—a well coordinated Zionist conspiracy designed to shore up global support for the state of Israel. Also according to Ahmadinejad, there were really no homosexuals living in Iran, although that deviant lifestyle—in his view—was quite common in societies such as the United States and Western Europe.

In the face of this mad man in Tehran, and with the continuing instability that has forever been the norm in the Middle East, there was little question that the Saudis were seeking to achieve a level of security over and above what their conventional military offered—a poorly coordinated patchwork of capabilities which, to be frank, will never be among the world's more potent fighting forces.

And with the hotly contentious decision by Riyadh early on during the George W. Bush administration to deny the Pentagon continued basing rights inside the kingdom (as had been the case for many years leading up to the summer of 2003—to include the first Gulf War), the security umbrella of the waning U.S. hegemon that once extended over the oil-rich kingdom had now shrunken back markedly in the region, receding to more junior Gulf turf including Qatar and Bahrain. Public pronouncements to the contrary aside, Riyadh desperately needed a new security blanket in this fast and radically changing geopolitical landscape.

The unique power of a nuclear weapons capability would more than suffice. Chemical and biological weapons were of course an option, but there had been no intelligence reporting and certainly nothing in the press over the years to suggest a covert program of either sort inside the kingdom. On the contrary, statements out of Riyadh relating to Saddam's use of chemical weapons on his own people during the 1990s suggested that the Saudis regarded such weapons as crude and inhumane.

No, if the House of Saud was seeking to ensure Saudi national security— and who could argue otherwise?—there was only one viable option. Riyadh would use the black gold buried deep beneath Saudi sand to become the world's first Arab nuclear power.

8 / GRAVEYARD SHIFT

My first real glimpse into the CIA's role in America's Middle East foreign policy came while reading a book in the dead of night. It was former CIA case officer Robert Baer's autobiographical *See No Evil*, published in 2002. Along with Baer's follow-up, *Sleeping With the Devil*, the book would become the basis for the 2005 film *Syriana*.

I read *See No Evil* while working the graveyard shift as a security guard at a defense engineering firm off the I-15 in north San Diego County back in the summer of 2002. Christa and I were living in an apartment at the time just down the street from her parents in Escondido and it would still be another several months before I started my illustrious career as a federal contractor, first on the Navy's GCCS-M program in San Diego.

As you can imagine, working as a security guard was not what I envisioned for myself less than a year out of the Navy with a Georgetown University degree in International Politics under my belt. From ten at night to six in the morning, my job was to conduct regular patrols of the engineering facility, both inside and outside its labs and office spaces. And I was expected to record the fact that I was actually doing so with this little *do-hickey* portable time-check device that I had to carry with me from station to station. Think mouse and cheese type behavior; I was the mouse, and the cheese was some sort of date/time stamp made on a ticker-tape contained in the device I was carrying around with me.

Someone, I was told, supposedly reviewed this record on an ad-hoc basis to verify that patrolman Scherck had actually conducted his appointed rounds during the previous night's shift. Truth be told, I never did see that ticker-tape with my own eyes. But just the thought of it served to prevent me from sitting on my ass the entire eight hours or, worse, falling asleep. So whether anybody was checking it the next day or not, that little *do-hickey* was doing its job.

When I was just sitting on my ass in the guard shack, it was very often in the back of my mind that the surrounding fields were infested with rattlesnakes. Every time I made one of my rounds, I was reminded of this by fluorescent yellow diamond-shaped signs reading "caution" under the likeness of a coiled-up, fanged reptile. Fortunately, there was the safe haven of the guard shack where I could pass the time reading a book or the latest issue of *Vanity Fair*.

What I remember most about reading Baer's *See No Evil* was the sense of despair I felt every time I read another anecdote about the hypocrisy and self-serving nature of America's policies in the Middle East, particularly when it came to matters involving the region's oil reserves. I got so bummed a few times that the rattlesnakes were the last thing on my mind as I made my hourly tour. The country of Adams, Lincoln and Theodore Roosevelt had, not unlike some dirty old man trolling the Las Vegas Strip, sold out its principles for short-lived energy needs. As a result, Baer argues forcefully, the United States put itself in great jeopardy over the many years leading up to the events of 9/11. The magnitude of the events of that day, while horrifying in their execution, should have surprised no one.

* * *

Baer's book certainly cracked the door a bit more for me on the institution of the CIA, America's quiet sentry in that part of the world. But it was hardly my introduction to America's schizophrenic dealings with the Middle East. This had come years earlier during my sophomore year of college while studying abroad in Turkey.

Faruk Tabak, a brilliant Turkish world historian, would continually harp in his lectures on the inherent contradictions of U.S. policy in the Middle East: America's unwavering support of Israel—no matter how vicious their latest military incursion into Palestinian territory; U.S. meddling in the internal politics of Iran going back to the days of Mossadeq; and the unseemly on-again, off-again relationship with Iraq's Saddam Hussein. Whether he was talking about U.S. hypocrisy in the Middle East or the problems the dollar was having at the time against the Japanese yen, Tabak's consistent theme that spring semester in Alanya there on Turkey's Mediterranean coast was that, not unlike the Ottoman Empire centuries before, American hegemony was in decline.

While I didn't always agree with what Tabak had to say, he had a wonderful teaching style. When he offered his view that America was on a steep and slippery slope, he did so not as a Turk teaching a group of impressionable young American students, but as an objective observer simply calling it as he saw it. He spoke often in vague generalities, but when pressed he was always able to support his propositions with numbers and statistics. Human history in the end, he suggested more than once, all came down to the numbers: populations of people migrating across continents, the price of bread, the number of human beings killed by famine or plague.

Tabak referred occasionally to an imaginary bubble of money (again, some number) that made its way over time from one part of the world to the next. In 1995, during my time as a student of his, he spoke of that bubble almost as a weatherman does of an impending cold front. It had moved from Europe to North America, where it had loitered for much of the twentieth century. But by the close of the Cold War, it had begun making its way over the Pacific to China. One need only look at America's debt situation with China today in 2010 to see that Tabak's forecast (among others, I must say) has been realized.

But in the years since 9/11, there's been as much talk of a second bubble of capital that Tabak also had on his radar. This bloated bubble of money—generated by billions and billions of gas station stops by millions of Americans on their way to the country's many K-Marts, McDonalds and Walmarts—has been floating from the United States to Saudi Arabia over the last fifty years. It has been described by historians and economists as the greatest transfer of wealth in the history of the world.

If you're a member of "Generation X" as I am (or a preceding generation) you might recall a particular *Saturday Night Live* episode back in the 1980s, the one with comedian Dana Carvey playing a senile southern United States senator. Sitting on a Senate committee with several of his esteemed colleagues, Senator Carvey observes about the American economy of the day—in a spot on southern accent, no less—"There's too much consooomin' goin' on out therrre!"

Over twenty years later it's still a memorable act. It's just not quite as funny anymore.

* * *

If the "Made in China" stamp on almost every toy I had growing up as a kid was evidence of the first movement of the Tabak-*ian* bubble, proof of the second transfer of American wealth would come in the form of the unabashed extravagance and jet set living of Saudi Arabia's ruling elite—the king in Riyadh and his extended royal family.

The poster child for this incredible disbursement of American capital—and power—had been Prince Bandar bin Sultan bin Abdul Aziz Al Saud, the Saudi diplomat who had gone from playing racquetball at the Pentagon gym with Colin Powell in the 1970s to serving as Riyadh's ambassador to Washington, a position he would hold for over two decades beginning in 1983 during Ronald Reagan's first term in office.

Prince Bandar would eventually step down as ambassador and return to the kingdom in late 2005, just before the death of Saudi Arabia's King Fahd. In October of that same year, the new King Abdullah appointed Bandar as Secretary General of a newly constituted Saudi National Security Council. Following his father's death, King Abdullah had undertaken a significant reorganization of the kingdom's government, its national security apparatus in particular. Bandar proceeded to liquidate most of his American assets, which included a 56,000-square foot mansion in the mountains of Aspen, Colorado, complete with racquetball court, indoor and outdoor pools, and a "snowmelt" driveway. The property went on the market in 2006 for an astonishing $135 million, a record in the history of American real estate.

Bandar had started out as a fighter pilot in the Saudi Air Force in the 1960s only to then come to the U.S. for various finishing schools. He spent some time at Maxwell Air Force Base in Montgomery, Alabama—the same base where my own father had attended Air Command and Staff College in the late

1970s. Bandar went on to receive his masters degree in international public policy from Johns Hopkins University.

Whether all of this grooming was a result of Bandar's own personal ambition, or if this track had been laid out for him by someone back in Riyadh, (probably a combination of the two), the end result was that for over twenty years Prince Bandar bin Sultan of Saudi Arabia served as nothing short of the power-broker-in-chief between Washington and Riyadh. In this influential position, he developed close personal relationships with several U.S. presidents, George H. W. Bush and son George W. in particular. While serving the interests of his home country, Bandar facilitated substantial arms deals involving top U.S. and European defense firms, among others around the globe. At the height of his day, he was the man that both King and President alike would go to on the more pressing issues of the day, including fluctuating oil prices, Arab-Israeli tensions, and everything in between.

It turns out that Bandar was hardly an honest broker through it all. As just one example, he was at the center of a particularly controversial arms deal known as Al Yamamah between British Aerospace and the government of Saudi Arabia. This sale of over one hundred British warplanes during the mid 1980s allegedly resulted in cash payments in the amount of US$2 billion (yes, that's a *b*, as in *Bandar*) to one of Bandar's personal slush funds. In 2009 the Saudi prince retained the services of America's former FBI director Louis Freeh, as legal proceedings continued in Europe and the United States in connection with the Al Yamamah scandal.

The ebb and flow of billions and billions of dollars from the U.S. and Europe to Saudi Arabia is of course the focus of many provocative books on the subject. *Sleeping With The Devil* (another illuminating book by Robert Baer) asserts that at least some of Bandar's wealth inadvertently financed perhaps two of the September 11th hijackers when his wife, Princess Haifa, made a particular donation in the amount of $130,000. I would not be at all surprised if this was the case, and perhaps it's naïve of me to think that the Bandars were themselves completely oblivious to how that money might someday be used.

* * *

But as I began working the Saudi WMD account in the Counter-Proliferation Division at CIA, these real world realities just weren't at the forefront of my mind. Rather, my focus was solely on the question of whether Saudi Arabia was pursuing WMD—specifically nuclear weapons.

From a historical standpoint, it was remotely possible—though highly unlikely—that the Saudis had already obtained a nuclear capability back in the 1980s, courtesy of China, when Prince Bandar brokered a deal with Beijing for CSS-2 ballistic missiles (much to the Reagan administration's chagrin). The Chinese-made CSS-2 is in fact reportedly capable of carrying both conventional and nuclear warheads. And for Riyadh, the acquisition of a corresponding nuclear device in the late 1980s would have been—the risk of broad international censure of both sender and recipient aside—a relatively simple matter of just another maritime shipment into Saudi Arabia's Jeddah Islamic Seaport. Delivery by air would have been an option, too, although much more risky from a logistics standpoint and certainly not as discreet.

But this rumor just didn't hold up to any real scrutiny. Riyadh would consistently deny the allegation throughout the 1990s. Much more importantly, there had been no real evidence in the press or in western intelligence channels to suggest that such a deal had been made.

As devastating a blow as the destruction of the World Trade Center Towers had been—a dastardly act planned and executed primarily by Saudi-born nationals—Saudi Arabia was not yet a nuclear power on September 11, 2001.

9 / FILLING A GAP

I had no immediate predecessor as CMO on the Saudi WMD account. The position was "gapped," as they say. Consequently, there was no turnover to speak of, as I had experienced during my time in the Navy.

In hindsight, this was the first red flag. Several strategically less significant countries in the Middle East had at least some sort of collection management coverage prior to my starting on Saudi; states like Syria and Yemen, where the concern was the potential for collusion between state-run chemical and biological programs and various terrorist organizations. CPD's reports chief, the CMO "boss" for the division, had either decided herself that it had become necessary to stand up a CMO on Saudi or, much more likely in my mind, someone above her on CIA's seventh floor had directed her to make it more a priority there in late 2005.

There was only one person at the working level in CPD with a handle on what might be going on WMD-wise with Saudi Arabia. He was a targeting officer named Phil who had been working in CPD since the pre-Gulf War timeframe. I gathered from Phil that he had had a few direct interactions with the vice president's chief of staff Scooter Libby in relation to the troubled Iraq intelligence reporting—if not with Vice President Cheney himself.

Phil's primary responsibility (as I was beginning on Saudi) was Pakistan; the aftermath of the A.Q. Khan shakedown and the growing instability in that country under then-President Musharaff. When I think of good people who work in the U.S. intelligence community, I think of guys like Phil. A mind as sharp as a tack, this guy could recall details from years old intelligence reporting or from a chaotic meeting just last week like nobody's business. When the talking heads in the American media would discuss the need for the CIA and

FBI to work better together in "connecting the dots" in the aftermath of 9/11, they were talking about guys like Phil. But no one was talking about Phil's "dots" because, at least as far as I could tell, he did a damn good job of connecting them.

While I sort of felt that I was working directly for Phil those first few months on Saudi, technically I was part of CPD's CMO cadre. I worked for the division's Near East (CP/NE) reports group chief, a position that saw several government staff CMOs come and go during my time on Saudi. Above the group chief position were the division's two deputy reports chiefs, Julie and Lolita. And above them was CPD's reports chief, who I'll refer to as Olivia. I would come to interact with Julie on a fairly regular basis in relation to the Saudi issue, but directly with Olivia on only a few occasions during my time working in CPD.

In addition to the targeting and reports components of CP/NE there was of course the operations element. Several more senior CIA officers rotated through the corresponding operations management position, but I came to work closest on the Saudi issue with a young desk officer named Tom. He was a sharp kid who, despite being a little wet behind the ears, fully grasped the gravity of the issue he had been assigned.

Whether or not it was a function of a drastic thinning of the ranks at CIA in the country's HUMINT collection capability—a direct result of deep budget cuts levied by the Clinton administration in the 1990s—Tom had not a lick of experience working in intelligence. He had been transferred from CIA's business operations division where he managed various contracts with a multitude of intelligence community private sector vendors and contractors. Nevertheless, and much to his credit, Tom got up to speed quickly on the Saudi desk and did yeoman's work during his time on the account.

* * *

"SIG," the acronym of a newly created branch of CPD, had originally been named the Suppliers and Interdiction Group, but was eventually renamed the *Strategic* Interdiction Group. As I and a few others in CP/NE would joke upon hearing of the name change, this seemed to signal a change in policy from the more objective stance—i.e. WMD proliferation is bad, end of discussion—to a more subjective approach.

In hindsight years later (and as I'll explain much more) this truly was a sign—coincidental or not—that CIA management under the Bush administration had been told, even following the disaster that took place over Saddam Hussein's alleged nuclear program, that there would now be some choice in the matter as to whether the United States would bother to interdict a given shipment of WMD in the world.

But, returning to the topic of SIG, the letters in the group's acronym remained the same, so in the end the name change didn't matter. SIG was still SIG and, as far as the Saudi team in CP/NE was concerned, the group still accomplished little to nothing. For this very reason, Phil (who would later relinquish his Saudi collateral duty to a full time and equally astute CIA officer), Tom and I would interact as little as possible with our SIG counterparts. There was either something strange in the water in SIG's spaces, or they knew something earth-shattering that we didn't know in CP/NE. I can't possibly imagine it was the latter.

Either way, it always seemed that I was starting from square one whenever I tried to engage Stephanie (my CMO counterpart in SIG) on the Saudi issue. Too often it was, *OK, the Saudis might be shopping around for nuclear missiles, but—as you know Jonathan—SIG does have a few other pokers in the fire.*

I was never actually told what those other priorities were, of course, but Stephanie never failed to remind me that there *were other priorities.*

10 / GET SMART

Phil showed me the ropes those first few weeks as I began working the Saudi account towards the end of 2005. He explained to me that Vice President Dick Cheney had personally seen to it that a very sharp CIA analyst named Steve (Phil's predecessor on the Saudi WMD matter) was assigned to the issue back in circa late-2003, when satellite imagery confirmed that an alarming shipment from China had arrived at the Jeddah Islamic Seaport on the west coast of Saudi Arabia.

As I was told by Phil, and later by others familiar with events, the containers that were part of that shipment from China to Saudi Arabia in December 2003 were of such concern to the Bush White House that the administration insisted that Riyadh allow U.S. observers to verify the return of these same containers back to China. But the concession that CIA got through covert channels from the Saudis was laughable: You guys can watch the containers getting loaded back—but with a pair of binoculars from the top of that hill over there—*away* from the pier. Sadly enough, the U.S. apparently had no choice but to accept.

This account was my introduction to the world of problematic Chinese maritime shipments into the Kingdom of Saudi Arabia through the Jeddah Islamic Seaport.

More telling information adding to this disconcerting story that the CIA had been forced to settle for "distance observation" as a means of verifying the return of illicit containers to China (an absurd proposition, which everyone involved at the time and afterwards acknowledged, as you simply cannot see what's in a shipping container without opening it up) came from an imagery analyst by the name of Joe at the National Geospatial-Intelligence

Agency (NGA). As an imagery expert at NGA, Joe worked to analyze the imagery collected over Saudi Arabia by America's spy satellites—to include the shipping activity at the seaport in Jeddah.

Very soon following the arrival of this troubling shipment into the Jeddah Islamic Seaport, Joe explained to me in person one day, the decision was made by longtime CIA veteran Charlie Allen to classify into oblivion the series of satellite images that had captured the arrival of these same shipping containers from China. From an imagery (IMINT) standpoint, it would be as if the shipment never happened.

I didn't have a clue who Charlie Allen was when Joe told me this. And, as it turns out, by the time I was hearing about Mr. Allen's role in the 2003 shipment, he was no longer even working at CIA Headquarters anymore. Subsequent to his mothballing of the Jeddah port imagery, Allen had been tapped by the Bush administration to oversee the creation of an intelligence shop at the newly established post-9/11 bureaucracy, the Department of Homeland Security.

According to several articles written in the press about Charlie Allen in 2009 at the time of his retirement from an unbelievable fifty year career in the U.S. intelligence community, the man was, as they like to say at CIA, a "legend." As a junior analyst fresh out of the University of North Carolina-Chapel Hill in the early 1960s, Allen had been part of the planning cell responsible for laying the groundwork for a new democratic government that was supposed to take shape following the U.S. invasion of Fidel Castro's Cuba.

Years later during the first Gulf War, Allen was assigned to develop targeting packages for the U.S. Air Force in its air campaign over Iraq. He and his team would mistakenly add to their target list a suspicious building in Baghdad, referred to as Public Shelter No. 25. Hundreds of innocent Iraqi civilians lost their lives when U.S. laser-guided bombs found their target.

As *U.S. News and World Report* reporter Alex Kingsbury wrote in his April 23, 2009 article titled "Legendary Spy Charlie Allen Knows the CIA's Secrets," by 2003, the time of the illicit Chinese shipment into Jeddah:

"Allen was coordinating collection efforts for the entire intelligence community. First for the director of central intelligence and later for the new director of national intelligence [John Negroponte], his job was to determine how to deploy a network of spy satellites, eavesdropping sensors, and human spies to go after targets from terrorists to nuclear-armed dictators. [Allen] called it being 'the night watch for central intelligence'. The post came with limited authority, but the man dubbed 'Charging Charlie' by colleagues wielded his formidable reputation to get things done."

This was the very same man at the working level of the U.S. intelligence community—just under then-CIA Director George Tenet—responsible for swallowing up the valuable information that the 2003 Jeddah satellite imagery would have offered Saudi WMD watchers only a few short years later.

It's probably unfair of me here to highlight only those examples of Mr. Allen's failures as a U.S. intelligence professional. But when it comes to his involvement in suppressing valuable IMINT on an issue as important as nuclear weapons in the hands of quasi nation-states—my purpose herein—I'm not interested in being diplomatic. By all accounts, (and, bear in mind, I heard the story from several separate reliable sources), Charlie Allen was a witting accomplice to a cover up of historic proportions within the Bush administration.

All of Mr. Allen's many years of good government service notwithstanding, this was not good intelligence work he was party to. The black-out of satellite imagery over Saudi Arabia's Jeddah seaport constituted denial and deception from *within* the U.S. government's own ranks. Charlie Allen and, of course, George Tenet himself were doing the bidding of a terribly misguided Bush administration hell bent on protecting an outdated and grossly flawed energy policy centered on the oil fields of the Middle East. And, as much as America was led to believe that the invasion of Iraq was a "slam dunk" at the time (as Director Tenet once famously referred to the Iraq WMD intelligence *trash*), I'm equally disheartened years later now knowing that the toppling of the Saddam Hussein regime in Iraq—while worthwhile on some levels—was mostly a product of this very same nonsensical addiction to foreign oil.

In a way, the analysis of all that transpired as a result of Bush's (read *Cheney's*) foreign policy in the Middle East is made almost too easy given Dick Cheney's role—both personally, but more as the personification of American interest in foreign oil—in *both* Gulf Wars; first as Secretary of Defense under Bush 41, and then as George W. Bush's Vice President. It's interesting to consider how the United States could have possibly entered into either conflict had Saddam Hussein never invaded Kuwait and, likewise, had the rise of Al Qaeda not resulted in an attack as galvanizing as 9/11. Without these tripwires, how else would America's military occupation of the lands bordering Saudi Arabia's oil fields been justified—beyond the obvious? As it was, 9/11 was only so much of a factor in rallying the American people behind a second face-off with the Iraqi dictator. Hence, Cheney's forced specter of a nuclear capable Baghdad.

Meanwhile, arriving in the Jeddah Islamic Seaport... (The irony and hypocrisy is almost too much, no?)

But, to the issue at hand, of all the rumors and speculation surrounding Saudi Arabia's acquisition of nuclear weapons, this suppression of imagery by high ranking U.S. intelligence officials is the closest thing to a "smoking gun" that I can point to as proof that the Bush White House had decided—as national policy—back as early as 2003 to turn a blind eye to Saudi Arabia's acquisition of nuclear capable ballistic missiles from China. The Bush administration, at its highest levels, had decided they needed to be able to claim ignorance if and when the significance of the December 2003 shipment someday came to light. Actual pictures of the event would make that exceedingly difficult. And so they were simply made to go away, courtesy of the likes of one Charlie Allen.

This is assuming that Bush and Cheney weren't already aware of the true nature of the December 2003 shipment through direct, high level communications with Riyadh—via Bandar Bush, of course. In that case, it may not have been a late night for Charlie Allen and company after all. Director Tenet's "night watch" would have known well in advance to see to it that counterparts at NGA quickly boxed up the incriminating imagery immediately upon arrival. Just make it disappear, NGA.

Unfortunately, disappear it did. And while the intelligence community lost whatever information was contained in those images from 2003 (*officially*, at least), the fact that they were never added back into the body of analysis at the working level of the Saudi issue—even years later—speaks volumes as to what was going on between Washington and Riyadh—and between Riyadh and Beijing.

* * *

An incident involving former Clinton administration official Sandy Berger comes to mind. Berger, who served as President Bill Clinton's National Security Adviser from 1997 to 2001, pled guilty in April 2005 to charges that he illegally removed classified documents from the National Archives, proceeding to then destroy some of them. After being sentenced to two years probation, 100 hours of community service and a fine of $50,000, Berger stated the following on the steps of district court in Washington:

> "I deeply regret the actions that I took at the National Archives two years ago, and I accept the judgment of the court. I'm glad that the 9/11 commission has made clear that it received all the documents it sought, all the documents that it needed, and I'm pleased to finally have this matter resolved."

I don't know about you, but I would have had more respect for Mr. Berger had he just apologized and then walked away. This need to clear one's name in Washington—even while everyone and their brother knows you did wrong—it just doesn't do anyone any good.

My gut tells me that the 9/11 commission would have also been interested in the untold number of official documents that Berger hid in his socks and stuffed down his trouser pants (yes, *literally*) only to then see to it that no one would ever be able to read them again. And while his court ordeal was ultimately "resolved," we'll never know what those destroyed documents may have said about the Clinton White House's thinking on a rapidly growing terrorist threat that was setting its sights on the Twin Towers in New York and several targets in Washington, DC—precisely during Mr. Berger's tenure as the country's National Security Adviser under Bill Clinton.

The point is that what goes on at the highest levels of the country's national security apparatus does have an impact—both positively and negatively—on the working level of the U.S. intelligence community. In a perfect world, this would go without saying. But in that same perfect world, we wouldn't have former top national security officials stealing documents out of the National Archives.

* * *

How could this possibly have been? How was it that, in the midst of the George W. Bush administration, the CIA and other parts of the U.S. intelligence community were being forced to put blinders on with respect to Saudi Arabia's acquisition of a new ballistic missile capability from China; missiles that (at least initially) the Bush-Cheney White House insisted that Riyadh return to their point of origin—under observation of the CIA, of course...from a hilltop near Jeddah port...using a pair of binoculars?

Missiles that, as subsequent imagery would indicate, were—almost without question—made to carry *nuclear warheads*?

Surely, the king in Riyadh wasn't going to get a pass just because of the close relationship the U.S. has enjoyed with Saudi Arabia's oil fields over all these years—especially after having just denied the Pentagon the option of using the kingdom as a staging base for the 2003 invasion of Iraq. *Was he?*

Surely, the Non-Proliferation Treaty that the United States, China and Saudi Arabia had entered into years before still meant something. *Didn't it?*

And, that decades old treaty that no one seemed to pay attention to anymore anyways aside, Washington wasn't going to stand idly by while China perpetrated such a flagrant violation of international norms. That just couldn't be. *Could it?*

* * *

As I got more deeply involved as CP/NE's Saudi CMO those first few months of 2006, I became the DO's working level point of contact for intelligence community counterparts working the Saudi question at various other federal agencies. If Saudi WMD was on the agenda at DIA, NGA or the newly created National Counter-Proliferation Center, I was usually the one management sent to represent DO equities.

I remember one particular brainstorming session in which several representatives of other agencies had a real ax to grind with CIA for the lack of HUMINT reporting being generated on Saudi. Being the dedicated contractor that I was, I offered a defense of collection efforts in the field, even though I knew full well that Headquarters management (and, consequently, CIA officers in the field) wasn't making it a priority. The Global War on Terror and war in Iraq together probably took up about 96% of station's time there in Riyadh, and let's just say that the issue of counter-proliferation didn't get much of the remaining 4%.

At one point, Derrick (one of the operations managers in CP/NE) got so frustrated with the lack of any HUMINT reporting that he decided to explore the possibility of a MASINT operation inside the kingdom. A surge in SIGINT collection (Signals Intelligence, e.g. the interception of cell phone communications, radio, etc.) coinciding with the arrival of one of the shipments from China had already been requested, but yielded no new information—at least that we knew of in CP/NE. As slim as the chances were, there were some of us who thought that a MASINT operation was at least worth a shot.

MASINT stands for measurement and signature intelligence. The idea was that if operators in country could get a sensor placed along one of the convoy routes used to transport incoming shipments away from the port in Jeddah to the nearby town of Ta'if, that it might be possible to infer the general size and weight of the newly delivered equipment.

Such sensors can measure the vibration of the earth as a truck and trailer rumble along—whether at a testing site in rural Nevada or in the sands of Saudi Arabia. Resulting measurements could then be compared to results of control tests conducted by the national labs here in the States, thus narrowing the list of potential equipment types—in this case ballistic missiles from China. As imprecise as the results would likely be, the MASINT option was seen as a possible means of obtaining at least a shred of data on the shipments arriving from China. At best, MASINT could help corroborate what the considerable amount of satellite imagery was telling us at the time.

Not surprisingly, chief of station (COS) Riyadh was quite skeptical that such an operation would be worth the risk. If station personnel were ever caught planting sensors along the roads near Jeddah, he argued convincingly in a meeting held in CP/NE's conference room, there was the potential for severe repercussions. Officers involved in such activity would be PNG'ed (declared *persona non grata* by the Saudi government) and would be forced to return home. That would be the least of Washington's worries.

Despite ever worsening relations between Riyadh and Washington in the wake of 9/11 and the invasion of Iraq in 2003, Saudi Arabia was still viewed by the Bush administration as a key ally in the War on Terror. And this is to say nothing of the tricky tightrope the U.S. has walked in its oil-based relationship with the kingdom ever since American-built oil rigs began pumping Saudi crude in the 1930s. A spy scandal involving U.S. intelligence officers attempting to monitor shipments of Chinese ballistic missiles into Saudi Arabia would open a nasty can of worms that the Bush administration would much prefer to just leave on the shelf. Such was the push-back CP/NE's MASINT proposal faced from the top U.S. intelligence official on the ground in Riyadh.

As much as I understood the root of the COS's reservations on the matter, I could hardly agree with him in principle. To me, such rationalizing was the top of a slippery slope that led straight to indifference at the working level of U.S. intelligence and, worse, complicity in these illicit transfers between China and Saudi Arabia. It was either a priority of the U.S. intelligence community to stay on top of this question, or it was not.

Hearing the COS, seated right next to me, talk in terms of unacceptable "blow-back" and other possible adverse repercussions for U.S.-Saudi relations only confirmed for me—quite emphatically—that it was not to be a priority.

* * *

But when all was said and done or, rather, *not* done at CIA, Saudi watchers throughout the intelligence community could always count on the latest imagery analysis from our colleagues at NGA.

More often than not, it was the "Le He," a shipping vessel that would make her way south from the east coast of China, down through the Straits of Malacca, across the Indian Ocean and finally up past the Horn of Africa into the Red Sea, before mooring at her customary berth at the Jeddah Islamic Seaport. The Le He was reportedly specially configured for the kind of sensitive missile shipments that NGA chronicled over the span of several years. The Office of Naval Intelligence typically provided tipper info on the impending arrivals, but sometimes this information came via other channels.

It became a mostly predictable (and depressing) slow motion fire drill: Here comes the Le He again. Will it, or won't it divert to Port Sudan across the Red Sea? Nope, straight into Jeddah again. SIG was interested sometimes, but could usually care less. As I explained, they had more pressing matters to tend to.

This inability of SIG to help track China's shipments to Saudi was really driven home when Phil plucked a highly valuable HUMINT target from a batch of candidates whom SIG personnel had (supposedly) vetted thoroughly for potential recruitment. I was still working on the Saudi account when the asset known by his cryptonym GCREDHOT finally started providing some promising feedback on the Chinese missile shipments. Unfortunately, I was to be ejected from CPD prior to seeing any substantive intelligence from this asset, as I'll explain.

* * *

Internal CIA meetings at Headquarters with counterparts from the Near East and East Asia geographic area divisions also often fell to me.

I would attend because I had to, but I usually hated every minute of it. By this I mean I had a visceral aversion to having to sit in a room with Agency staff and retired contractor types, many of whom never failed to roll their eyes at the idea that the Saudis in Riyadh were likely fairly far along in the process of acquiring a nuclear weapons capability.

Interesting. But how do we *really know this?*

Well, for starters, the endless parade of Chinese missile shipments arriving in Jeddah, based on imagery. There's also the volatile geo-political situation vis-à-vis Iran. China's unprecedented increase in oil imports from the kingdom, too, begs explanation. All of the above.

But by then the meeting had drifted to comments from some guest analyst out of the DI who had just spent several weeks analyzing the Saudi National Guard's role in foiling yet another attempt to blow up some critical segment of Saudi Arabia's oil pipeline network. These young academics in the DI were always eager to share their fresh insights with the DO side of the house.

11 / BEATING A DEAD HORSE

And so, it was with enthusiasm one Saturday afternoon in the spring of 2006 that I dropped everything and hopped into the car to head to Langley. I had gotten a call from the DO's watch office with a message that "Robbie in the DI" was requesting my presence at Headquarters.

Christa was still pregnant with Sidney and I had already begun grilling on the barbecue in the small backyard of our row house on Capitol Hill. *No problem*, as I started fixing a plate to go. A little aluminum foil over the top seconds later from Christa and off I went.

When I arrived, it turned out that—*surprise!*—another suspect shipment from China was arriving at the port in Jeddah. Our colleagues over at NGA were trying to clue us in yet once more. Robbie wanted me to draft an immediate ops cable to see if the DO's guys in country—case officers working on the ground in Saudi—could get eyes on the shipment, either as it was being unloaded at the port or as it was being trucked inland from Jeddah.

You might think it strange, as I did that afternoon, that a mid-level analyst in the Directorate of Intelligence was summoning a CMO contractor who worked in the Directorate of Operations. Didn't this constitute some breach of traditional protocol in terms of the division of labor between the CIA's two directorates? Shouldn't this have been handled first within the DO before getting the analysts involved? This was most certainly the case.

Had the DO been firing on all pistons on the Saudi nuclear question (as it could and should have been), the CIA's seventh floor management and station chief overseas would have already had this event covered well before it was unfolding on a Saturday afternoon in Washington—right around midnight in Jeddah, in case you were wondering. (Another shipment arriving under the dark of night. Yes, this was one more delivery to be worried about, alright.)

* * *

The thing I remember most about this particular episode was overhearing Robbie and his fellow DI analysts (several of whom had come in for the event) brainstorming yet another scenario involving the *Pakistanis*.

"No, no, no...," I chanted from the office next door where I was busy drafting the requested ops cable. It would be comical looking back on all of this—almost like "Keystone Kops"—if the stakes weren't so incredibly high. This ship had originated in *China*—not Pakistan, guys. *God damn it.*

There would be several similar skull sessions there in the DI's spaces in which I would try to advance the view that it was China, not Pakistan, that was arming the Saudis with a new ballistic missile system—one that logic dictated was most likely nuclear capable.

I should point out here that, at the end of the day, I really didn't distinguish much between the delivery system (the missile) and the nuclear capability (the warhead). But this was not a function of some set of preconceived notions that I had arrived with on my first day working on the Saudi account. It was only after figuring out all of the *who's, what's, where's, when's, why's* and *how's* of the overall Saudi WMD question, that I ultimately boiled this situation down to the cold hard fact—as I saw it.

My instincts told me in clear and undeniable terms that (given the political atmosphere of the Middle East at the time—one largely defined by the reality that Iran was likely pursuing a nuclear capability of its own) if the Saudis were looking to upgrade their borderline-mothballed arsenal of CSS-2 missiles that Prince Bandar had purchased from the Chinese in the 1980s, then common sense dictated circa 2006 that the U.S. intelligence community should be watching for the provision of a *nuclear capable* missile system.

This was realpolitik, the term political scientists use to characterize decisions made by state actors based on pragmatism, usually at the expense of any altruistic motivations. Riyadh's security needs were hardly going to diminish in the ever-volatile political environment of the Middle East. The decades-old, symbiotic energy-for-security arrangement with the U.S. had soured with tragic results, most notably the loss of over three thousand lives on American soil on September 11th and the subsequent military invasion of Iraq. But a new security partner—to the *east*—one that coveted Saudi oil fields every bit as much as the Americans had, was now waiting to take its relationship with Riyadh to a whole new level. If anything, given how Saudi crude had powered America's ascent in the twentieth century, it would have been surprising if Beijing hadn't made the offer.

While the analysts puzzled over whether *this* version Chinese ballistic missile could be "mated" to *that* Pakistani warhead, (a study had actually been commissioned with the national labs to answer this very question), there was a far simpler explanation. I referred several times—tongue-in-cheek—to a "benevolent Sunni bomb" that I suggested Riyadh might be literally buying off the shelf from China with her oil money. The DI analysts would look at me cross-eyed in response, stubbornly wondering how Pakistan could remain part of such a scenario.

I'm reluctant to mention it, but it helps illustrate some of the extraneous issues that were at play at the time. I distinctly recall having to convince one particular analyst that there was simply no way that Riyadh would be interested in a delivery system using a "drop basket" from a Saudi warplane.

"But how do know for certain?" came the response.

Trying to contain myself, I explained that it just made sense—intuitively—that the Saudis wouldn't risk their aircraft being shot down by the target country's anti-air batteries and fighter planes (Israel's or Iran's most likely), and certainly not when Riyadh had already bought and paid for an initial ballistic missile system from the Chinese. The Saudis had already made ballistic missiles their delivery method of choice. There were even Chinese missile technicians residing in the kingdom supporting the Saudi missile program—full time.

Because (speaking figuratively, as I actually had to continue) this was 2006 and countries don't typically *drop* atomic bombs anymore, as the U.S. did on Hiroshima and Nagasaki—over five decades before. They *could*, I agreed. But they could also be buying biological weapons under the table from Syria, an equally unlikely scenario for the Saudis in anyone's view.

No, at some point the endless speculation had to come back to reality. The King wanted his finger close to a button which, when he pressed it, he could unleash hell on those who might someday try to do the same to his Kingdom. Period. End of discussion.

But it wouldn't be the end of the discussion.

* * *

By "benevolent Sunni bomb" (and, obviously, I wasn't making light of this grave matter back in 2006, anymore than I was trying to make a point—just as I am now) I was referring to the age-old tensions between Iran, a Shia Muslim country, and her more numerous Sunni neighbors in the Middle East, of which Saudi Arabia is the most prominent.

Today, approximately one-fifth of the world's population (about 1.5 billion people) is Muslim. Of that population, an overwhelming 85% are Sunni. Iran, seat of the former Persian Empire, is home to the majority of the world's remaining Shia Muslim population. The divide within Islam between these two sects is a defining factor in the history of the Middle East, not unlike the Great Schism between the Roman Catholic and Greek Orthodox churches in Europe.

With both Mecca and Medina (two of Islam's holiest sites) located inside its borders, Saudi Arabia enjoys unrivaled status throughout the Islamic world as a religious epicenter for *all* Muslims. As Iran's Shia leadership in Tehran continues to push the limits of global sensibilities with its pejorative views on the state of Israel and, more recently, with the mullahs' brutal crackdown on protests relating to Iran's disputed 2009 presidential elections, the eyes of the Islamic world turn to Riyadh (on both television and on the Web) for the Sunni Muslim perspective; as articulated in the political realm by the House of Saud (particularly in relation to the Israeli-Palestinian conflict), but also (in a religious and cultural sense) as represented by Saudi Arabia's Sunni Muslim clerics.

Another factor (from an admittedly western political perspective) contributing to Riyadh's standing as a counterbalance to Tehran's ambiguous intentions, is Iran's known sponsorship of international terrorism, not only in Iraq—where it has targeted George W. Bush's bold but inherently flawed installment of a fledgling democracy—but inside the borders of Saudi Arabia as well. Iran's theocracy has long sponsored activities aimed at destabilizing the Sunni establishment in Riyadh, both openly and through violent covert means, sometimes timed to coincide with the Hajj pilgrimage to Mecca (the fifth "pillar" of Islam), an annual religious event involving well over a million Muslims from around the world. In contrast to Tehran's sponsorship of such activities, and even as the world's most infamous terrorist is himself a Saudi-born national, Riyadh's ruling elite has (on balance) been supportive of America's fight against international terrorism.

The dynamics between Saudi Arabia and Iran (in particular the religious differences these countries represent) have been evolving for centuries, ever since the fateful death of the prophet Muhammad in 632—the defining moment in history that separates these two sects. And, unfortunately, the resulting tensions from that era are arguably as entrenched today as they were in the beginning.

How, then—given its abundant natural resources and a willing partner in the form of the world's newest rising super-power—could Riyadh's newly acquired Chinese ballistic missile system *not* be part and parcel of an off-the-shelf nuclear capability?

* * *

I found myself surfing the open source online newspaper and magazine articles of the day in hopes of finding some shred of evidence—perhaps a slip of the tongue by a Saudi minister or the like—that might speak to the true nature of these many deliveries we were seeing from China to Saudi Arabia's various missile bases: Al Sulayyil, Al Joffer and, perhaps most notable, the underground storage facilities at Rawdah.

I discovered one such article containing comments from Prince Nayef bin Abdul Aziz, the lifelong Saudi Minister of the Interior. This more senior position in the Saudi government oversees a broad range of security issues ranging from the maintenance of the kingdom's police forces to passport issuance.

In 2010, Prince Nayef is also Saudi Arabia's second deputy prime minister, making him only second in line of succession to the Saudi throne behind Crown Prince Sultan. (Sultan, incidentally, is also the father of "Bandar Bush.") Nayef is the same Saudi official who, soon after 9/11, insisted that it was impossible that Saudi nationals had participated in the terrorist plot. The attacks on the World Trade Center and Pentagon had been, according to Nayef, the product of an international Zionist conspiracy. Nayef is described as a "traditionalist" in certain Mid-East media outlets, having close ties to the kingdom's fundamentalist Wahhabi establishment.

In the article I read back in 2006, Nayef was quoted as telling his Saudi audience that Riyadh was going to "great lengths" to ensure the security of the kingdom. There was something peculiar, I felt, about the context of his comments, so I forwarded the article around in email to my colleagues in the DI. I copied my CMO counterparts in the DO's Near East Division as well. Might Prince Nayef be talking out of school?

I made sure to acknowledge that Nayef might just be referring to the kingdom's domestic security apparatus. But given his proximity to the throne, could Nayef have perhaps been referring—even indirectly—to the sum total of all the many shipments we were seeing between China and Saudi Arabia?

While no one responded to my note, I was fairly certain of the answer. And I'm no less certain today.

* * *

I made sure the cable got sent that Saturday afternoon, and then headed out to a nearly empty parking lot.

This ship just wasn't going to turn, I thought to myself on the drive home from Headquarters. The boogie man of A.Q. Khan and the DI's stubborn assumptions about Riyadh's support of Pakistan's nuclear program—these red herrings just weren't going away anytime soon, no matter how many times NGA beat us over the head with the view from above.

12 / CURIOUSER AND CURIOUSER

From a bureaucratic or—perhaps more accurately—*administrative* stand-point, interactions with my Saudi WMD counterparts in the Directorate of Intelligence were also handicapped by a classification system used by the Agency for managing incoming intelligence reporting. It was a system that was simply ill-suited for the question we faced on Saudi Arabia.

Picture a pair of desks facing each other through an opaque partition. I'm on one side (the DO side), and my analyst colleagues are on the other (the DI side). But prior to our arriving at these desks (to address the Saudi WMD question), the Agency's classification gurus had already set the terms by which we would be able to *officially* communicate with one another.

Now picture a series of small holes in this partition (the "cabinet," in CIA's lexicon), through which I'm able to pass incoming intelligence reporting. These holes have labels attached to them, intended to correspond to the subject matter of the reporting I'm seeing on the DO side. These labels read (in CIA code-word, of course) "A.Q. Khan," "Missile," "Political/Intentions," etc.—together constituting, in theory only mind you, the "compartments" that contain the various perspectives of the U.S. government's HUMINT-based understanding of the Saudi WMD question.

If a report comes in to me pertaining to a new ballistic missile system the Saudis are acquiring, I would pass it through *this* hole. However, the report that comes in talking about that same new system, but that also mentions something about A.Q. Khan, *probably* gets passed through the "missile" hole, but not necessarily. And if a report comes in talking in general terms about the king's thoughts on acquiring a nuclear weapons capability, I have to get up out of my chair and give it to someone from the DO's Near East Division, because that's

"Political/Intentions" reporting, and a CPD CMO isn't allowed to coordinate and disseminate *that* brand of intelligence. (Bear in mind that NE Division's CMOs were invariably up to their eye balls in reporting pertaining to the war in Iraq and the Global War on Terror.)

Meanwhile, on the DI's side of the partition, as these reports are passed through their various holes, they're getting organized into their own separate (stove-piped) piles. And to be able to read a report from a given pile, an analyst has to be "read in" for access to that particular brand of information—imperfect as the labels on the holes (cabinets) may be. And they were imperfect—as I'll revisit later.

I recall one HUMINT report in particular that came as close to telling the whole story as we could possibly hope for up to that point in time. The problem was that (protests from yours truly not withstanding) the information was literally cut and pasted into two separate intelligence reports—in order to better conform to the classification system I've described above. I remember actually printing out a copy of the original report, along with the two newly created reports (based on the original) that I and my Near East Division CMO counterpart were directed by management to create.

When you read the original, you had a very clear understanding of the *who, what, where, when, why* and *how?* elements of the report (just as I had been trained at the Farm). The case officer in the field had written an outstanding (original) intelligence report. But when you read the two subsequent reports—the ones manufactured at Headquarters—it just wasn't the same. You just didn't come away with the same *big picture* of what was going on.

This would be the subject of many animated conversations between me and the DI's analysts and, to a much lesser extent, my CMO management chain in CPD. It was, after all, management's accepted way of doing business, and as a contractor there was little I could do to change it.

* * *

There was another report that came in, prompting a rare but memorable meeting in the front office with Olivia, CPD's chief of reports.

The meeting started with me having to explain why I thought the particular report needed to go into *this* compartment rather than *that* compartment. After agreeing with me on the administrative issue, Olivia opened the conversation slightly, allowing me to talk more candidly about what I thought was going on: the imagery of the shipments from China, my frustrations with the DI over their stubborn Pakistan fixation, etc. To her credit, Olivia listened. She seemed to appreciate (or at least understand) my fervent approach to the matter at hand.

But Olivia could have said nothing worse at the end of our meeting to crush whatever dwindling enthusiasm I still had on the Saudi account at that point. After listening to me describe (as diplomatically as I could) how clumsy CIA's working level approach was to the Saudi WMD question, Olivia told me (all too stoically) that *whatever it was going on between China and Saudi* was—I'll never forget her saying it—"above all our pay grades."

If you're not familiar with the phrase, what Olivia meant to say was that this deal between China and Saudi Arabia was all being handled by people with much more important titles than she or I. Titles like "prince," "president" and "king."

While stopping short of fully endorsing my view of things, the obvious implication of Olivia's blunt comment was that our toiling in the bowels of the U.S. intelligence community—on such trivial matters as which *pile* to put a report on—would, in the end, make no difference whatsoever.

* * *

For better, but mostly worse, what CIA's filing management system tended to counteract on the DI's side of the "partition" was any sort of tunnel vision as to how a possible Saudi nuclear capability might come into being.

As mentioned earlier, from a practical standpoint, a ballistic missile and its warhead go hand in hand. Without one, you can do little with the other. And, surprising as it was for me to hear it, there was fair consensus amongst CIA's analysts in the DI that you could—potentially—have a situation where the missiles could come from one country, while the warheads came from another.

In the case of the Saudi ballistic missile program, too few of my DI counterparts were in agreement that China was supplying the new generation of missiles. There were indications going back to the 1990s that the Saudis might be considering a variant of Pakistan's Ghuari missile, as a replacement to the aging CSS-2 arsenal from China, but this was a minority view. It was generally understood that Chinese missile technicians were firmly ensconced at the kingdom's various missile bases—living there full-time even, ever since the CSS-2 deal that Prince Bandar brokered with China back in the 1980s. The ongoing stream of satellite imagery of shipments arriving from China in the 2006 timeframe made the origins of a new delivery system virtually indisputable.

But if some of my DI colleagues and I could agree at times that China was responsible for the next generation delivery system, there would still be significant debate over the nature of the shipments we were seeing arrive in Jeddah. Was this really a *new* system, some analysts would question, or were the Saudi Strategic Rocket Forces merely "refurbishing" the old CSS-2 missile airframes? I was just as surprised by this suggestion as I was by the idea that you could get your missiles from one country, but your warheads from another.

As it was explained to me, there was the notion that rather than replacing the old CSS-2 system, the Saudis might have opted (in the midst of the first term of the Bush administration) to *refurbish* the missile airframes already present inside the kingdom.

As I questioned this "refurbishment" hypothesis with my DI colleagues, I remember not being referred to any sort of official report suggesting that this was indeed a possibility. Truth be told, there was nothing on paper to suggest that this theory was based in reality. It quickly became apparent that "refurbishment of the CSS-2s" was a concept that had long outlived its shelf-life.

I was left to my own devices to weigh the merits of this refurbishment theory. I imagined myself as a Chinese missile technician living in the kingdom. If, on some 20+ year old CSS-2 missile, I perhaps detected some corrosion on the *left tail fin*, I could then submit an order for a new (and identical) left tail fin from the manufacturer in the People's Republic of China. A few months later, assuming a replacement fin was available, it would arrive by boat through Jeddah. I would proceed to remove the old tail fin and install the new one. Piece of cake, right? Obviously, I'm using this example only to illustrate my point, but the bottom line is that one would have to assume a great deal about the reliability and quality of such a supply chain from China, thousands of miles away from Saudi Arabia and with many years having passed since the initial delivery.

That said, believe it or not, this is how some DI analysts preferred to explain the numerous maritime shipments we were seeing arrive in Jeddah at the time. Well beyond any doubts that aging ballistic missiles could be effectively updated in such a manner, I just didn't believe that the Kingdom of Saudi Arabia—the *richest* oil regime on the face of the planet—would want to cut corners with their increasingly important ballistic missile arsenal. Cost cutting, in the context of Saudi national security, simply didn't pass the gut test.

This was the same gang of princes who buy jumbo jets to fly with their mistresses to Nice for late-night soirées on the French Riviera. Rather than fixing up their old missile system (and some of the imagery analysis indicated the exact opposite—that the SRF was actually mothballing the old hardware) Riyadh was going to go top-of-the-line with any replacement. None of this patching *this* rust hole and rewiring *that* circuit box. A brand new system—had to be.

The only problem was that there was no HUMINT to validate this view; no HUMINT to confirm what the imagery was telling us—most of us, that is.

Occasionally, however, reason prevailed and the conversation with the DI would finally assume an altogether *new* missile system from China. But the dubious theorizing only continued.

"OK, if they aren't *refurbishing* the old CSS-2s, maybe they're just getting *new 2s*"—was one hypothesis, one that yet again strangely chose to discount what we were being told by satellite imagery. Nevertheless, the nuclear question would still be relevant in this scenario, because the highly inaccurate CSS-2 is (as stated earlier) also capable of carrying a nuclear warhead.

It's worth noting that, following the delivery of China's CSS-2s in 1988, Riyadh would repeatedly insist that the missiles would never be used to deliver a WMD warhead—*of any kind*. Interestingly, not only did the Saudis assure the Reagan administration of this directly in writing, Riyadh was also compelled to finally sign the Nuclear Non-Proliferation Treaty—almost two decades after its creation.

* * *

"Simplify, simplify," as the American writer and philosopher Henry David Thoreau used to say.

In this same vein, I was more of the mind that the December 2003 shipment that Charlie Allen helped to delete from the IC's memory—that this was our best source of information on the ongoing parade of shipments we were witnessing in 2006. Both in terms of what the images themselves reportedly indicated and, just as importantly, the fact that they got boxed away as quickly as they did.

The analysts at NGA never went into great detail about the exact circumstances of Charlie Allen's intervention, but the general consensus on that shipment years later (corroborated by multiple sources directly familiar with events at the time) was that the imagery from late 2003 indicated that Saudi Arabia had received one or more *CSS-5* class ballistic missiles from China.

The CSS-5 (DengFeng 21, DF-21) is a mobile, solid fuel, medium-range ballistic missile (MRBM), manufactured by China's Changfeng Mechanics and Electronics Technology Academy. The missiles, stored in temperature-controlled cylinder launch-tubes, are individually transported aboard specially designed tractor trailer trucks. The trailer is equipped with an erector launcher used to ready the CSS-5 for launch. The missile is capable of carrying up to a 500 kiloton nuclear warhead.

The CSS-5 shipment in December 2003 (the one the Saudi's supposedly returned to China under observation by U.S. officials watching from a distance with binoculars) had been a clear indication of things to come for Saudi Arabia's ballistic missile force. This shipment was either the first of many, or perhaps another in a series of such shipments that spanned most of George W. Bush's presidency—and Dick Cheney's *vice presidency*. In either case, there was no arguing the facts—at least as seen from above: Saudi Arabia was acquiring a new and far different ballistic missile capability.

Even after December 2003, NGA would continue to disseminate plenty more imagery analysis, right up to the time of my departure in April 2007 in fact. These subsequent write-ups all pointed to a new system, one with characteristics quite consistent with the CSS-5. In addition, several key Saudi missile bases were undergoing significant overhaul during this time; changes that (by all appearances) were consistent with the arrival of a new class of ballistic missile. Large launch pads at the bases, which had been used for years by the Saudi SRF as part of their CSS-2 launch training, went into disrepair or were reused for entirely different purposes.

One particular report out of NGA described a massive shipment of what analysts concluded with a high degree of certainty were "TELs" (transporter erector launchers), the tractor trailer launch vehicles described above. These TELs looked very similar to the Chinese CSS-5 transport vehicles one finds in *Jane's* military encyclopedia, although—to be fair—"looked like" should not be confused with a one-for-one match. As much as Hollywood likes to portray U.S. satellite capabilities as being able to provide the numbers of a car's license plate parked in downtown Moscow, this was not the same level of fidelity that NGA analysts were working with over Saudi. Nevertheless, this particular shipment had clearly been a substantial delivery of missile transport vehicles. That much was clear.

And yet, oddly, NGA's published analysis of the event failed to reference the CSS-5 by name. But the Chinese make and model was clearly there, in between the lines. And if you bothered to ask the analysts at NGA who had actually written the report what they thought was going on (indeed, what they *wanted* to write), they were more than happy to explain.

* * *

If concluding that the Saudis had replaced their aging CSS-2 arsenal with mobile CSS-5s (or some like variant) was only *informed speculation*—and it really wasn't if you allowed the imagery to speak for itself—the greater question was the second piece of the Saudi puzzle: Would Riyadh play by the rules with this new system and maintain a conventional (non-nuclear) capability? After all, the Saudis *did sign* the Nuclear Non-Proliferation Treaty in 1988.

Or, flouting the rules, would Riyadh opt to go nuclear? And assuming Riyadh wanted to become a nuclear power, was this really a possibility?

Not only was it a possibility, it was highly probable given the state of affairs in the Middle East at the time, a radically charged climate that continues unchanged today.

But to achieve a higher level of confidence in my estimation that the Chinese had armed Saudi Arabia with nuclear weapons, I would have to start thinking less like a CIA academic, and more like those who were making the rules in Beijing and Washington.

13 / AXIS OF NUKES

Early on, I alluded to the Socratic notion that one can really only "know" that one knows nothing. I stated up front that my claims—that what I believe—is based on circumstantial evidence and confidence in my abilities to read between the lines. Such is life in the nation's capital, of course, but particularly so in the notoriously slippery and deceptive world of foreign intelligence.

That said, I fully expect that my words here will be met by the powers that be—in Washington, Beijing, Riyadh and elsewhere—either with beneficent confession or vociferous denial. Obviously, I hope that our current president chooses the former, without delay and without regard to what will almost certainly be a long, protracted denial (or even deafening silence) from Beijing and Riyadh. Regardless, this is my story and I will stand by it.

Because of this, I'm rather hesitant to mention much of the history of the nuclear research programs and resulting weapons capabilities of China, Pakistan and (as I'm asserting) Saudi Arabia. I'm just not an expert on all that went before this shortsighted transfer of "bomb power" to one of the world's most unstable regimes.

First of all, I was not working as a WMD analyst (in the true sense of the word) at CIA, or any of a number of DC think tanks that employ experts on the subject. I was, as I've explained, a Collection Management Officer—a middleman between the government's subject matter experts and policymakers, on the one hand, and, on the other, those U.S. intelligence officers on the ground overseas with closer access to people "in the know."

Secondly, I hesitate to discuss more of the prelude to this new reality in the Middle East because, in my mind, it amounts mostly to a rehash of the rumors and misguided theorizing that I fought against in vain during my time in CPD.

All that peripheral talk about Saudi financial investment in the Pakistani nuclear program, the pointless arguing over whether Riyadh would dare shirk its responsibilities under the Non-Proliferation Treaty—just too much hot air. However, I would be remiss as the messenger of this bad news if I didn't describe more of the analytic trail related to the chief concern of this book.

* * *

The general timeline of Riyadh's interest in acquiring nuclear weapons begins back in the mid 1970s, when France agreed to sell the government of Iraq an Osiris-class nuclear reactor. Construction on the facility began in 1979, just as Saddam Hussein was coming into power. Part of the agreement between the French and Iraqi governments was that the reactor would not be used for illicit weapons purposes and, in fact, Iraq was a signatory to the Non-Proliferation Treaty at the time.

However, according to documents later provided to the U.S. government during the Clinton administration by Saudi defector Muhammad Khilewi, Saudi Arabia's King Fahd (sometime in the mid 1980s) reportedly approved a significant amount of financial assistance to the Iraqi nuclear program under Saddam Hussein. Riyadh's payback, assuming Saddam's program could live up to expectations, would be to have several nuclear bombs manufactured and ultimately transferred to the Saudi Strategic Rocket Forces.

Today, some websites in the online national security world go so far as to state that this Fahd-Saddam weapons deal had become a closely held secret in Washington. According to an unnamed "former high-ranking American diplomat," the website Global Security suggests that "the CIA was fully apprised" of this secret nuclear pact. Having only just started high school at the time these rumored events were unfolding in the late 1980s, I obviously can't speak much to their veracity. But this supposed Fahd-Saddam, *money-for-nukes* deal is definitely consistent with what I would come to learn about the high level relationship amongst Riyadh, Islamabad and Beijing—one that became more prominent by the 1990s.

Dubious as Khilewi's story may have been on the Saudi-Iraq conspiracy, he also insisted that the Saudis had begun funding the Pakistani nuclear and

Ghuari missile programs during the 1990s in exchange for a "nuclear umbrella" arrangement with Islamabad. Such was the conversation between Phil and I on a few occasions when I first started on the Saudi account. Should Saudi Arabia ever be attacked by an aggressor with nuclear weapons, the story went, Pakistan would respond on Saudi Arabia's behalf using its own nuclear arsenal.

There's no question that an avalanche of oil money from the kingdom played a critical role in Pakistan's eventual success in obtaining its own indigenous nuclear weapons capability. Without it, Pakistan would likely not have been able to finance the technical infrastructure necessary for such advanced research activity. And if those reading my view on these events are intrigued by the "nuclear umbrella" theory, I will neither encourage nor discourage them from subscribing to it.

But to the issue at hand, it is imperative to focus on the origins of Pakistan's sudden and surprising leap onto the world stage as a nuclear power. There was a puppet master at work there in the late 1990s at the Kahuta uranium-enrichment facility (and the nearby ballistic missile factory) in Pakistan. Indeed, virtually every aspect of Pakistan's newly acquired nuclear weapons capability could be traced back to the People's Republic of China.

The technology behind Pakistan's Ghauri missile had technically come from North Korea, but China's support to the North Korean program was indisputable. The more closely coordinated aspect of the relationship between Beijing and Islamabad, however, was on the nuclear research front.

Just as Chinese missile technicians had been living in Saudi Arabia in support of the Strategic Rocket Forces since the late 1980s, Beijing had been seeing to it that Chinese nuclear expertise and key logistics requirements were being provided to the nascent Pakistani nuclear weapons program during the 1990s. As much as Riyadh's oil money had helped build the walls of the research labs at Kahuta, it was Beijing that made sure that the end result would be an Islamic nuclear bomb.

* * *

In its official 2009 report to the U.S. Congress, the U.S.-China Economic and Security Review Commission went into unprecedented detail on China's covert nuclear ties with Pakistan. Under the sub-heading "History of Sino-Pakistan Military Relations" the commission's analysts wrote:

"Sino-Pakistani nuclear cooperation began in the early 1980s. This cooperation has included both civil and military nuclear agreements. In 1983, U.S. intelligence agencies reported that China had transferred to Pakistan a complete nuclear weapon design and enough weapons-grade uranium for two nuclear weapons. In 1986, Beijing and Islamabad penned a comprehensive nuclear cooperation agreement, and China began assisting with Pakistan's uranium enrichment program. Despite Pakistan's poor track record for preventing proliferation of nuclear materials and technology, China continues to support Islamabad's nuclear development."

This partnership, according to the U.S. Congress now, "began in the early 1980s." To use a choice acronym from the U.S. Navy's phonetic alphabet: *Whiskey, Tango, Foxtrot.* This report was published to inform Congress only in late *2009?!* I'm tempted to say "better late than never," but this would only make light of a severe and chronic problem in our legislative branch.

If U.S. intelligence agencies had evidence that China was helping Pakistan to acquire nuclear weapons as far back as 1983, how long would it be before Congress was properly informed of the significance of the 2003 Jeddah shipment—and all that has since followed—from China to Saudi Arabia?

We need to stop this insanity in its tracks, or it will be the end of the United States as a viable force for good in the world, I'm absolutely certain.

* * *

I remember watching the news that evening in May 1998, just after Pakistan had successfully detonated not one, not two, but *five* nuclear devices, becoming only the seventh country in the history of the world to successfully develop and test a nuclear weapon.

The televised footage showed men, women and children rejoicing in the streets of Islamabad. A camera zoomed in on one particular woman who wailed "All Pakistani women *love the bomb!!*"

A.Q. Khan, the titular head of Pakistan's nuclear program, had become a national hero overnight. Pakistan's neighbor and blood rival India had already successfully conducted its second nuclear test weeks earlier that same year. Dr. Khan (read China) had restored the celestial balance between Pakistan and India with a nuclear weapons capability all his own.

* * *

Years later in October 2003, *Washington Times* reporter Arnaud de Borchgrave would write an article entitled "Pakistan, Saudi Arabia in Secret Nuclear Pact: Islamabad Trades Weapons Technology for Oil." Borchgrave quoted a "ranking Pakistani insider [who] has proven reliable for more than a decade."

Parts of the article read more like a bad CIA intelligence report. "Future events," the source claimed, "will confirm that Pakistan has agreed to provide [Saudi Arabia] with the wherewithal for a nuclear deterrent."

The article went on to briefly chronicle how all of this made sense. That, despite the inevitable denials from Islamabad and Riyadh, Pakistan was desperate for free or discounted oil and that Saudi Arabia was highly vulnerable by that point following the deterioration in U.S.-Saudi relations which had ultimately resulted in the withdrawal of U.S. armed forces from the kingdom earlier in 2003. Borchgrave even mentioned the long standing Sunni-Shia rivalry between Riyadh and Tehran. "The Saudi rulers, who are Sunni Muslims," Borchgrave noted, "are believed to have concluded that nothing will deter the Shia Muslims who rule Iran from continuing their quest for a nuclear weapons capability."

This all made perfect sense. A member of the Saudi royal family, Borchgrave added briefly, had even attended a test firing in 2002 of Pakistan's Ghuari, an intermediate range missile capable of carrying a *nuclear* warhead.

The problem was that Borchgrave's theorizing focused only on the nuclear side of the equation, paying mere lip service to the delivery system question in an effort to portray a complete thought. And even that coverage was tainted with the same Pakistani-centric group-think that ran wild within CIA throughout my time there. With all due respect to Mr. de Borchgrave, a Saudi royal attending a test-firing of a Ghuari in Pakistan alone does not mean that any sort of missile deal had been struck between Riyadh and Islamabad—even for the implied purposes of providing a *nuclear weapons* capability. That sort of confirmation comes with hard evidence—not unlike what U.S. satellites picked up over Jeddah in 2003 when a Chinese flagged vessel made a delivery that—for reasons I can't accept—no one in Washington was supposed to know about.

In terms of the menu of options available to Riyadh in their pursuit of a nuclear capability, I subscribe to the notion that the right answer is often the one staring you straight in the face. "Simplify, simplify."

Yes, Riyadh had dumped billions into the Pakistani nuclear program and, yes, it was conceivable that if and when things got dicey with Tehran or Tel Aviv that some sort of "nuclear umbrella" might open from Pakistan to cover the kingdom.

But was this really rationale? My gut told me *no* back in 2006 and still does to this day. Just because a CIA analyst can dream it up as a possibility doesn't make it so. Nor does a published newspaper article.

* * *

Yet another theory that I would encounter in my interactions with DI analysts was that there was at least a remote possibility that Saudi Arabia's own nuclear scientists might have somehow partnered with Chinese and/or Pakistani nuclear experts within the borders of the kingdom. Perhaps some sort of covert weapons research activity was housed somewhere deep inside the cavernous underground storage facilities at Rawdah. (No, no reason in particular, just the fact that the U.S. intelligence community was aware of this massive underground military shelter.)

The King Abdul Aziz City for Science and Technology (KACST), a Saudi state sponsored research organization first established in Riyadh in 1977, was known to have a small number of researchers trained in the nuclear sciences. Was some restricted hallway at KACST possibly home to illicit weapons-related activity?

We in CP/NE eventually settled on the view that the particular activity that was of interest on the campus of KACST was in fact limited only to medical research, i.e. the study of radioactive isotopes in the treatment of certain cancers. But it remained possible to keep spinning the theoretical web, and several DI analysts would do just that, burrowing deeper and deeper into an endless rabbit hole.

The old adage that you can't prove a negative sums it up nicely.

* * *

The most logical explanation for where things stand in the Middle East today in 2010 is that, soon after the American invasion of Iraq in 2003, Riyadh began receiving the kind of nuclear deterrent that every other nuclear power in the world has today. The kind of power that if the king in Riyadh picks up the phone and calls one of his SRF generals, he can level a city and fatally cripple its suburbs.

In 2003, Riyadh could certainly afford such a capability. And sometime soon after denying that they were acquiring nuclear missiles from Pakistan (because, in fact, they weren't), Riyadh committed billions of barrels of Saudi crude to the Chinese government for just that same purpose. In the end, whether it's a custom made nuclear capable CSS-5 missile shipped directly from China, a Pakistani made warhead (using Chinese technology) taken from the tip of a Ghuari missile and retro-fitted onto a CSS-5, or—hell—even a "refurbished" CSS-2, it simply doesn't matter.

The reality, I maintain, is that President Bush and Vice President Cheney were aware of the final end state: nuclear capable ballistic missiles in the hands of Riyadh's ruling elite. And neither of these men did anything to intervene. On the contrary, the chummy relationship between Bandar Bush and the U.S. administration was to carry on well after the prince stepped down in 2005 as ambassador to the United States.

Worse in my mind, however, was the way Vice President Cheney (in both his role as manager of Bush's foreign policy and as overseer of the U.S. intelligence community) executed a perfectly hypocritical about-face in his interactions with CIA's Counter-Proliferation Division. Where he was once chomping at the bit for indications that Saddam Hussein was arming himself with nuclear weapons, Cheney was now content to just let the Saudis have their way in their radically new relationship with the Chinese. With several good years remaining to keep pumping Saudi crude (even if America would soon be taking seconds behind China) it was, *whatever Riyadh wants, Riyadh gets*.

Nuclear weapons in the kingdom had been inevitable all along given the China-Pak-Saudi nuclear nexus. The fact that Washington had once strongly opposed a Saudi nuclear weapons capability was water under the bridge by the beginning of Bush's second term in 2005. Washington had opposed Pakistan's pursuit of the bomb, too, years earlier, and look how that turned out. *Boom*.

Besides, these were different times. There was (rightly so) a War on Terror underway and the U.S. needed all the help it could get—from Pakistan *and* the Saudis. Nuclear weapons from China? *Shhh! Let 'em have 'em*. The war must go on!

Yes, this was *Dr. Strangelove* kind of thinking, to be sure. But such was the rationale behind one of the most reckless policy decisions ever made in Washington, as I'm afraid time may someday prove.

14 / SOMETHING WICKED THIS WAY COMES

There were a handful of rather significant intelligence reports that I was able to coordinate on there at my desk in the basement of CPD, reporting that I thought (even if naively at the time) contributed in some way to the overall picture. And when senior DI analysts assigned the task of briefing the President and Vice President used such a report, I was always eager to learn what—if any—feedback there had been.

There was the time that a PDB (President's Daily Brief) briefer touched on the ongoing speculation that the Saudis were anticipating some sort of return on investment from the Pakistani weapons program, after having for years bankrolled Islamabad's illicit nuclear activity. The source was a member of one of the prominent majlis councils in Riyadh, part of a network of influential Saudis who constitute a trusted advisory board consulted by King Abdullah himself.

The problem I had with the information attributed to this particular Saudi with friends in very high places was that we were hearing it through a retired CIA Riyadh station chief. This Saudi spilling the beans on Pakistan (*uh-huh*, I thought, rolling my eyes) knew he was talking to a well regarded former CIA operative. He knew that the information he was providing would almost certainly make its way back to Langley.

In the debriefing that followed at Headquarters, the retired chief of station recounted the conversation he had had in the kingdom—in Arabic of course—with his Saudi protégé. I looked on as the meeting progressed, the DI's analysts obviously quite satisfied with the underlying implications of the conversation. Never mind the distinct possibility that CIA was being spoon fed this old tired line. The analysts were happy to hear confirmation of their Pakistan scenario, even if it was dry and familiar to them; even if the story we were hearing from this old CIA codger clashed terribly from a logical standpoint with the many shipments we were seeing arrive from China. It was comfortable. It went down easy.

The feedback from the briefer who delivered the lackluster news in the Oval Office not long after our meeting with the former chief of station revealed nothing from POTUS' 30,000 foot view—as I always hoped for. But it was pretty damn humorous nonetheless. Upon hearing the identity of the majlis member who was passing this supposedly sensitive information to the U.S. government, President Bush commented that he knew exactly who the man was. He had been in the room during one of Bush's personal meetings with King Abdullah.

If King Abdullah knew this guy was talking to us, Bush reportedly observed to the briefer, "he'd have his *balls sliced off*."

There were a few other times that I was privy to such raw presidential feedback on the issue from inside the Oval—comments, mind you, that Bush himself knew might trickle down to the action officer level of the U.S. intelligence community. One briefing in particular turned (as it only rarely seemed to, given the grave implications involved) to the issue of Riyadh's nuclear weapons aspirations. Bush listened while the briefer made his points and then turned to his chief of staff saying, "Bolton, get [National Security Adviser] Hadley. We need to get Bandar on the line."

The president's response revealed nothing more than what was already known to the world about the close family relationship between the Bushes and Prince Bandar. What really mattered, of course, was what was said once Hadley actually got Bandar on the phone.

Similarly, what really mattered was what China's President Hu Jintao said to President Bush and Dick Cheney when Hu stopped over in Washington on his way to Riyadh in April 2006 for meetings with King Abdullah and Prince Bandar.

I tend to think that every "on the record" PDB briefing given to President Bush and Vice President Cheney—that touched on the Saudi nuclear issue (at least during their second term)—amounted to little more than a dog and pony show.

There was nothing the CIA could offer, based on the fragmentary HU-MINT reporting that was coming in at the time, that either of these men didn't already know better about themselves through their own direct communications with Bandar and King Abdullah. Rather than informing the president and vice president on what might be going on in the kingdom, these briefings worked in more of a *counter*-intelligence fashion; confirming for the nation's top two elected leaders what the U.S. intelligence community *didn't* know about the deal going down between Beijing and Riyadh.

* * *

The intelligence community as a whole was stretched thin throughout the Bush administration, no less so from 2005 to 2007 while I was working in CPD. The wars in Iraq and Afghanistan had been ongoing for several years by that point and the country's intelligence capabilities focused on the Arabian Peninsula were already beginning to gravitate more to developments in Yemen and Somalia. Saudi was a concern, but from almost a purely counter-terrorism standpoint.

By this point, too, CIA's Counter-Proliferation Division seemed to be finally getting over the sting of the Iraq intelligence debacle, but only so much so. The Iraq intelligence mess continued to be in the news in 2006 as the Valerie Plame/Scooter Libby scandal kicked into full swing. Perhaps these ghosts from CPD's past had something to do with the institutional inability to take a more aggressive approach to the Saudi WMD question. I believe it was much more than this, however.

There were other factors that came into play, some of them rather surreal, that really drove home the reality that I had stumbled into very strange territory on the Saudi account. I don't think the analogy to *Alice in Wonderland* was far off on certain days, one such time being when Phil informed me that someone from SIG wanted a few minutes with me to offer their perspective on the Saudi account. "Crazy Bob," as Phil called him (and warned me prior to my closed door meeting with the man), did indeed have a very unique perspective on all things Saudi.

Crazy Bob and I were suddenly alone in John's old office. He began with the standard niceties of "This is who I am…Where are you from?" And then he quickly launched into a rant that must have gone on for at least thirty minutes about "plane loads of cash" that an old Agency asset had been hired to fly either *in* or *out* of the kingdom on behalf of a Saudi prince. I had little clue what Crazy Bob was talking about.

He proceeded to tell me the names of various intelligence reporting compartments, compartments that he advised me to get access to myself so that I'd have a better grasp of the missile issue, which—lucky me—Crazy Bob was there that day specifically to talk with me about. Before Bob finished, I was even all caught up on the many vices of several prominent Saudi princes, to include one in particular who was prone to sodomizing young male aides who happened to wander into his office at precisely the wrong time of day.

There was the time that one of the DI's Saudi analysts phoned in (Phil took the call) regarding a strange encounter over at the Pentagon involving a Chinese national. Apparently the man had approached an American civilian DoD employee and began spouting off curious details about China's support of a nuclear weapons program inside Saudi Arabia. As the last in this game of *telephone*, we obviously got few useful details, but the key players that were supposedly mentioned definitely piqued our attention—to say the least.

CP/NE management sent me upstairs to brief the chief of the division, which I did best I could given the vague circumstances. He listened patiently, asked a few questions, but then of course decided that it wasn't worth writing up for the record. For all we knew, this was some crazy guy who had read something suggestive off the Internet the night before and, well—what can you possibly do with something like that?

Still, given our view in CP/NE of the ongoing developments between Beijing and Riyadh, we had a hard time dismissing it entirely as a hoax.

* * *

Similar streaks of reality made their way down to the basement, and sometimes weren't nearly as dismissible. But because some of them arrived as fragments in the Agency's operational message traffic (rather than as formal intelligence reports) they wouldn't see the light of the day with the DI's analysts—let alone be included in any official briefings to policy makers at the White House or on Capitol Hill.

There was the cable that came in from the kingdom sometime in late 2006. Reportedly, there had been more than a few Chinese males loafing around on the pier in Jeddah, accompanied by Saudi military personnel as the containers of a Chinese flagged vessel were promptly unloaded and sent on their way inland from the port. Only each of the Chinese men who were present for that night's delivery were covered head to toe in traditional Saudi national dress—or *"thobes."* You may have seen the robe-like garment on television or in the newspaper. It's what Saudi King Abdullah and Prince Bandar were wearing when Abdullah took President Bush's hand for that short stroll from the royal motorcade to Bush's private office at the ranch in Crawford, Texas, on April 25, 2005.

Back to *thobes* in a moment...On the agenda that day in Crawford (at least as told to the White House press pool) was the soaring price of oil. It is instructive to note here that *oil* was still on everyone's mind a year later in April 2006 when King Abdullah hosted China's President Hu Jintao for talks in Riyadh. (Hu, incidentally, stopped over in Washington for a chat with President Bush on his way to the kingdom—although, one must agree, Washington is hardly "on the way" from Beijing to Riyadh.) Clearly, whatever the king and Hu had discussed in Beijing only a few months earlier in January 2006 required some direct one-on-one follow-up in the Saudi capital. What with the price of oil and all the shipping activity at the Jeddah Islamic Seaport, the two men certainly had plenty to discuss.

"Thobes? Yeah I know what they are. But *everyone* in Saudi wears them," came the response from one of my DI counterparts when I mentioned it one day.

Oh, *really?* Even Chinese males standing on the pier in Jeddah as yet another military shipment from China is unloaded under the dark of night? Maybe so, but it still seems more than curious to me.

And there was another time (separate shipment) that a port operator in Jeddah made the off-handed remark that the ship arriving from China that night was, to his knowledge, "more than just rockets."

By "rockets," the port operator was clearly referring to missiles. The subsequent movement of the contents of the shipment out of Jeddah to SRF bases in the kingdom, along with the imagery of those same containers being unloaded at the bases confirmed that much for us. But what can you do with such a vague statement—"more than just rockets?" Yes, the implication is alarming, but the statement itself is no more useful in the HUMINT realm than some strange rant from an Asian looking gentleman in the parking lot of the Pentagon. It simply didn't meet the requisite threshold for reporting.

This didn't keep me from sounding a muted alarm over the Agency's online chat system, however. I couldn't resist. I borrowed another famous line from Shakespeare's *Macbeth*, one that I used to hear every so often as a kid from my melancholy father. For several days after first reading this ominous indication of something "more than just rockets" arriving in Saudi Arabia, my online chat banner read simply, "Something wicked this way comes"—a quote from the play's second witch in reference to the traitorous Macbeth.

No one in the DI ever commented on my posting, but just knowing it was there for someone to read provided at least some solace.

* * *

There was at least one other occasion that I would put my frustrations with this impossible situation in writing, but this time it was in a none-too-subtle email to Sandra, CPD's executive officer.

Sandra was essentially the office manager of CPD's front office, populated by GS-15 and mostly new Senior Intelligence Service (SIS) officers. I would imagine she was at least somewhat familiar with what was going on concerning Saudi given her close proximity to not only Chief CPD's office (an Operations Officer), but chief of reports Olivia's office as well.

After recounting in my email recent events that had transpired at Jeddah port (brought to us, as always, through imagery from NGA) and adding a clip from that day's operations traffic (not unlike some of the bits I've described above), I submitted my bottom line to Sandra: "the Saudis are lying to us on a scale of monumental proportions," my email read.

If there's a way to dig into CPD's email archives back circa late 2006, it's in there. And what won't be there is any sort of reply from Sandra.

I would run into Sandra in the hall sometime after sending this email missive. Still eager to take her pulse on what the hell was going on, I joked sarcastically as we passed each other, "Damn Saudis!"

She actually stopped and looked at me, as she appeared to recognize what I was getting at. Or maybe not. This was the CIA, after all.

"The *Saudis?!*" she responded with equal sarcasm. "They're a bunch of *freaks!*"

* * *

Buckminster Fuller, the accomplished American architect and futurist of the twentieth century, also had a way with words. As just one example:

"Those who play with the devil's toys will be brought by degrees to wield his sword."

I would have posted this as well in my online chat banner somewhere along the line, but I think the quote (due to space limitations) would have cut off right at "devil's toys…"

* * *

And there was the time that a cable came in talking about a "refrigeration" requirement in relation to a pending suspicious shipment out of China.

Now, just as I knew nothing when it came to the electronic documents project I worked on for the Silicon Valley firm years earlier in Sacramento, I really knew nothing about the logistics of transporting a nuclear warhead by boat to Saudi Arabia. While I had gotten fairly close to some Tomahawk cruise missiles as they set off for their targets in Iraq in December 1998, a nuclear device is—to say the least—altogether different. Whereas a cruise missile sometimes amounts to little more than a political statement a month or so after the fact, a nuclear bomb has the potential to level downtown Manhattan in seconds flat.

So when I saw the "refrigeration" blip in ops traffic, I took notice. I shot a note to Robbie in the DI asking whether he could reach out to the Air Force to get some information on how nuclear warheads are typically handled. For example, what are the requirements for transporting them over long distances? Nothing too technical, just something to help us better understand this mention of a "refrigeration" requirement.

But although Robbie said he would look into it, I never did hear back from him.

And it was one more delivery from China to the kingdom, down the hatch.

15 / PIRATE OF THE CARIBBEAN

I remember the first time I heard of the whole home equity lending phe-
nomena. It was during the spring of 2004. I wasn't yet even halfway through
my first year as a trainee at CIA. Over a stretch of several weeks, I was commuting to Headquarters with a fellow trainee who lived with her boyfriend just
off Lincoln Park on Capitol Hill.

Christina, a former reporter, and her boyfriend had recently bought a three
story apartment house just off the park, the kind that's common throughout
DC, but particularly on Capitol Hill. They were making a successful business
of it, as she explained to me one morning on the drive up the George Washington Parkway.

The conversation naturally turned to the topic of small business ownership and entrepreneurship. Christina described an idea of hers about maybe
someday opening a kind of "doggy day care" on steroids; a rural dog park
operation—"Trails and Tails" she called it—for which she would charge dog
owners on a per visit basis. It would be preferable to the traditional dog kennel because the dogs would be out in the fresh air getting exercise, rather than
being cooped up indoors. How this venture would play out alongside her new
career in the CIA (she was a diehard OO, by the way) was less clear, but you
could tell she really liked the idea.

I was intrigued. When she finished her pitch for "Trails and Tails," I
began describing my own dreams for someday owning and operating a small
business. I've always been into cooking, I explained. It had to be a restaurant
of some sort. Or maybe even a combination bakery and coffee shop. I especially loved to bake, I told her, suddenly giving a fair amount of thought to a

new track in life that was rather unlikely for someone who had just started the CIA's new hire program only months earlier.

"But where would the money come from?" I asked, half serious.

Boy, if Christina didn't have the answer! She went on to explain the wonders of home equity loan programs—how she and her boyfriend had tapped a substantial sum of cash from the market-based *equity* of their apartment house. Together, they proceeded to use much of the newly acquired capital to renovate the living spaces of the building into rentable apartments.

I had actually considered this already myself for financing some much needed improvements to the row house, but my understanding of the *greater* potential of such a loan—as I quickly saw it—only became clear in talking with Christina about "Trails and Tails" and (even more than my bakery idea) perhaps someday being my own boss.

The banks prefer that you use your equity loan on improvements to the collateral property—your *home*. However, Christina informed me, there's nothing keeping you from putting the money towards *other* things.

"*Really?*" I asked. Really. For instance, she and her boyfriend took a vacation that they never would have been able to afford without the equity loan. You should look into it, she urged.

Well, well, well. The cat was out of the bag. As much as my father had done to acclimate me to the world of Wall Street and investing, he had never mentioned this animal before. A thirty year fixed was about as creative as he ever got in the home mortgage department.

Not only did I proceed to take out a second mortgage on the row house during that first summer at CIA, I would eventually go on to max out on the property's total market value with a sizable *third* equity loan—less than a year later.

The goal of all this was to be directly related to the sort of business endeavor that Christina and I talked about that same spring morning. Only instead of a dog park or gourmet bakery, my wife and I would be putting our modest jack-pot towards a retail outfit called Harbor Palm.

* * *

Before the reality of business ownership out on Maryland's Eastern Shore was to break on the horizon, however, Christa and I would first spend some of our new found disposable cash on a little winter vacation.

But this wasn't to be just any winter vacation. In January 2006, Christa and I decided to fly to Turks and Caicos, the chain of islands in the Caribbean several hundred miles southeast of Miami.

As usual, my gut would have a say in my decision making; this time warning me that I was probably starting down a very slippery slope. After all, the money wasn't really *ours*.

However (as I began to rationalize), was it really the *bank's* either? I mean, when a Saudi Arabian prince wagers ten times the value of my home equity loan on a single hand of blackjack and *loses*—only to then keep right on playing!—what was this thing called "money" anyways?

If I lost the reader with this last observation, please don't hold it too much against me. It's hopefully of some consolation that I realize now—years later—just how little regard I had begun (*continued* really) to have for "the rules." I can't say I've learned my lesson entirely, but recognizing one's own tolerance for risk—be it in relation to the proceeds of a home equity loan, or in writing a memoir/exposé that attempts to tackle the weighty issue of nuclear proliferation—it counts for something in life. I'm sure of it.

Be that as it may, I've survived the consequences of my fiscal indiscretions stemming from my past interactions with the home mortgage industry. (As if the banks and Wall Street haven't themselves been equally guilty in this whole financial mess.)

And not only have I survived, you better believe we took that trip to the Caribbean.

* * *

We rented out a condo for the week right on Grace Bay on the island of Providenciales (Provo), the most developed of the Turks and Caicos chain.

The place was on the outskirts of town, so getting there and back was a bit of a hassle. As a result, we spent most of our time doing exactly what one *should* be doing while on vacation on a Caribbean island. The white sand beaches were literally right outside our door. The reality of it all reminded me of one of those screensavers you see at the office, only we were actually *there*, barefoot with the sand between our toes.

Chloe was almost a year old and crawling non-stop by this time, so she couldn't get enough of the beach. Coated in sunscreen, she played in the sand under a beach umbrella until well past her nap time.

Christa and I enjoyed ourselves, too. It was unlike any vacation either of us had ever taken. The cool white sand; blue, blue water. A good splurge really is worth it, every now and then.

Christa had time to think about her clothing boutique idea (which she had more than begun kicking around), while I was just happy to be taking a break for a few days from beating my head against the wall on the Saudi issue.

Inevitably, though (even while lounging there in the Caribbean), my mind wandered back to the affairs of Washington. I just wouldn't be myself otherwise. I had purchased Robert Baer's second book, *Sleeping With The Devil*, on iTunes for the trip. I listened to it as I waded farther and farther into the water of Grace Bay.

The subtitle of Baer's book said it all: "How Washington Sold Our Soul for Saudi Crude." Why was I doing this to myself? Why not Richard Branson's autobiography *Losing My Virginity* or, better yet, some fictional action/adventure with pirates in it?

Baer was talking to me all over again, just as he had when I read the book *See No Evil* in the guard shack off the I-15 in San Diego County years earlier. Only this time, the tale the author told was all too familiar, and much more personal for me. From his perspective as a former CIA case officer working in the Middle East and Central Eurasia, Baer told story after story of the overly cozy relationship between Saudi Arabia's leadership and America's own politicians and private defense sector executives. He wrote as well of the pervasive *consent of silence* at both the CIA and State Department—one that quite simply defies logic.

I was especially disgusted by Baer's account of the history and modus operandi of the famous Carlyle Group, the private investment firm based in Washington, DC. Founded in 1987, the firm's list of past members of its board of advisors includes former president George H. W. Bush and former secretary of state James A. Baker III. Baer expertly illustrated how this American firm's guiding principles weren't far different than those of the 41st president's long-time compadre, Bandar Bush.

Carlyle was all about the accumulation of wealth—*vast* amounts of wealth. Not at all in the competitive, Main Street American capitalist sense, either. (Certainly not *my* version of capitalism, at least.) Far from it, Carlyle excelled like few others in exploiting the unlevel playing field of financial realities, not just here in the U.S., but around the globe. Its members leveraged their exclusive relationships to master the art of siphoning obscene amounts of money from *this* government's treasury coffers to *that* businessman's personal bank account, all under the guise of fatuous defense contracts, public speaking honorariums and flat-out, bought-and-paid-for preferential treatment in connection to the day-to-day business of government.

As I listened to *Sleeping With The Devil*, it was no longer a question of what was going on between Washington and Riyadh. The detrimental effect of Washington's relationship with Riyadh's oil barons was plain as day. All one had to do was listen to Baer's words. While I'm at it—I disagree with him on other political and social issues of our times, but film maker Michael Moore had himself done much to expose the ugly underbelly of U.S.-Saudi relations with his thought-provoking 2004 film *Fahrenheit 9/11*.

What was it that was allowing this complete lack of accountability in Washington? Why were America's leaders not heeding all the warnings—even *after* 9/11?

Knowing the answer only made it all worse.

* * *

But this 30,000 foot level dystopia aside, back on *earth* (on vacation in Turks and Caicos, no less), I was trying hard to think of all the possibilities for me and my own family.

As a contractor, I had decided, I was merely a pawn in this multi-layered Washington charade. I reminded myself that even had I been working in CPD as an *official* CIA officer, my work on the Saudi account would still mean nothing in the grand scheme of things. This sobering conclusion was of course coming even before I had formed a more certain assessment of the game that was going on between CIA and Dick Cheney's office in relation to China's missile shipments to Saudi Arabia.

Sure, the pay was good working as a contractor. But there would never be any real job satisfaction for me working in government under such circumstances. On top of the futility of the issue I was working, I was also part of the "pork" the talking heads on television and too few in Congress were always complaining about. I had done it once in San Diego with Booz Allen Hamilton crunching numbers for the Navy, and here I was doing it all over again at CIA, supposedly "managing" the collection of HUMINT against the Saudi WMD target. This was not any long term career track I wanted for myself. There had to be something else. But *what?*

Knee deep in the Caribbean, I thought about all these things as a stiff head wind began to pick up.

16 / CHINATOWN

As I write this, my family and I are living in an apartment in South Pasadena, California, just a ten-minute drive north of downtown Los Angeles.

I took my daughters to lunch today in L.A.'s Chinatown. Actually, lunch was secondary to the primary objective of the trip, the purchase of a pair of hand fans: black with gold trim for Chloe, red with a floral décor for her sister Sidney. They got the idea from an animated *Barbie musketeers* movie they watched recently, in which Barbie and her girlfriend protégés wield fierce hand fans in their quest to do good.

After finding two that came close enough to meeting the specified criteria, I decided to duck into a neighborhood restaurant for a quick lunch of beef and broccoli. When the order came, my daughters were more than happy to help dad with the large side order of rice, their brand new hand fans resting close by on the table. I scooped some beef onto Sidney's plate. Chloe said she'd pass, especially on the broccoli.

What a contrast, I thought to myself. *Made in China* hand fans today, enjoying lunch with my two young daughters in beautiful southern California; nuclear capable, Chinese ballistic missiles only a few short years earlier, hunkered down there in the windowless basement of CIA.

* * *

A few days prior to the Chinatown excursion, I was surfing the Internet in search of a similar pair of fans. Had I taken the lazy way out and just clicked *put in basket*, I would have spent over thirty dollars (plus shipping) for the selections Chloe and Sidney had made for themselves while pointing over my shoulder at the computer screen.

"Just go to Chinatown," Christa suggested later that night. "It'll be a lot cheaper."

Christa was right, of course. The two Chinatown fans together cost just six bucks and change. It's likely that their quality is different than those I found online, but I doubt they're *thirty dollars* different. If there was such a difference, my two musketeers certainly didn't notice. And so, somewhere in the world, a businessman is making a much better profit off the dad who *didn't* visit Chinatown for *his* musketeers.

Maybe that capitalist businessman is in the U.S.; maybe he's even in China these days. Wherever he is, that's the free market for you. Freedom to buy from whomever you choose and—just as importantly—the freedom to sell your wares, *however* and to *whomever* you choose.

That said, *caveat emptor.* Buyer beware. As Buckminster Fuller himself would probably agree, the axiom applies as much to the purchase of nuclear weapons as it does to children's toys. But the stakes for the former, of course, couldn't be more terribly high.

* * *

I have to admit to being superstitious, or whatever it's called when you spend a few more seconds than the next guy (or gal) considering how that slip of paper in a fortune cookie makes sense in the context of *your* life.

When three cookies arrived on the tray containing the bill at the restaurant in Chinatown, I gave one to each of my daughters and then cracked mine open with, as always, undue anticipation.

This time the slip read, "Life to you is a dashing and bold adventure."

17 / WEEKENDS WITH THE PRESIDENT'S MEN

Perhaps it was adventure I was seeking that morning in February 2006 (not long after returning from Turks and Caicos) when I decided to play hooky from work at CIA and drive out to Maryland's Eastern Shore, about a two hour drive east from Washington over the Chesapeake Bay Bridge.

With my contractor salary filling our bank account faster than Christa and I could spend it, I had started to entertain the idea of investing in a piece of land. The fact that I was only just turning thirty-one at the time didn't matter in the least. I've never been one to think or act my age. I wanted something substantial, something to look forward to down the road (wherever that was leading). All of the philosophizing I had done while on vacation in the Caribbean was only spurring me on.

Months earlier, I had begun my search online by looking at available land in the opposite direction, out in West Virginia. But while the idea of being able to someday build on property with great mountain views had at least some appeal, I wasn't overly excited about it. Perhaps it was the time I spent in the Navy, or how much I had enjoyed rowing on the Potomac River as a freshman in college; I just wanted to be closer to the water. And so I looked east, towards the Chesapeake Bay.

Before crossing the Bay Bridge early that morning, I had phoned the office saying that I was feeling under the weather and that I likely wouldn't be in until the next day. This is something I never did at CIA, even when I was actually sick.

Christa would be surprised to see me home early that day, but I figured I'd explain myself when I saw her.

* * *

My first stop on the Eastern Shore turned out to be about twenty-five miles south (as the crow flies) from where Christa and I were to eventually wind up living for over two years, from June 2006 to the end of December 2008.

Cambridge, Maryland is a nice old fishing town on the Chesapeake Bay, but there was something about it that morning that didn't strike me quite right. It was probably due to the fact that I was visiting too early on a cold February morning, but I just didn't see anyone out and about. I liked where the town was on the map (in close proximity to the Chesapeake), but other than that it was pretty much dead.

So I moved on to the second destination on my itinerary, a small parcel of land I had seen advertised on the Internet in the town of Royal Oak, about halfway between Easton, Maryland and the weekend sailing and day-tripper town of St. Michaels, the "heart and soul of the Chesapeake," as the town's chamber of commerce slogan suggests.

Please don't ask what I was thinking. The Royal Oak piece of land was more like a piece of something else. There were rather dilapidated homes on either side of the property, the only sign of life in them thin wisps of smoke from a kitchen stove or fireplace. The muddy drive from the road onto my would-be retreat literally dead-ended into a dense mass of vegetation that had engulfed what *used to be* someone's home.

But none of this kept me from thinking big. Sure, I'd have to have the old dwelling chain-sawed in two and hauled away, but then I'd be left with a rustic piece of land on which I could someday build my getaway home, I remember somehow thinking to myself. This piece of land had potential, if for no other reason than I wanted it to.

With the Royal Oak property in mind, I continued my tour of the area by driving farther out on the peninsula to the town of St. Michaels. It took me about five seconds to feel good about the place as I drove along Talbot Street, the main drag through the center of town. There were a few restaurants and a number of small retail shops on either side. I pulled into the ACME super-market parking lot, one of only a few places in town that were open at that hour of the morning. I got out, found my way to a nearby coffee shop and bought a cup.

When I came back outside, I stared up at a crisp blue February sky and took a deep breath of icy cold air. But it felt good. I sipped at the hot coffee. The Royal Oak parcel was already starting to seem more like the bad idea it really was. St. Michaels, on the other hand, was where I would begin something new, far away from the dead end track I was on in Washington.

I just wanted out.

* * *

My state of mind that morning probably warrants closer examination given how things would turn out for Christa and me living in St. Michaels.

This image of me stepping out of a coffee shop into a winter morning epiphany—while true—is simply too romantic, too pure. The reality is that I was an angry young man; mad about life in a way that I both can and can't still relate to today, only a few short years later.

Not the least of my angry disillusionment was how my career was turning out up to that point. How was it that I wound up working as a *contractor* at the Central Intelligence Agency? Why hadn't it been in me to play the game down at the Farm, to get "Ops certified" as a Collection Management Officer, to finally be pursuing a more *legitimate* career (as my father would have certainly regarded it) as a patriotic civil servant of the federal government?

True, I was doing much the same work at Headquarters as many of my fellow Farm classmates were up to that point, but this would change over time as they would begin to rotate out to their initial assignments overseas. Was I meant to just remain in Washington indefinitely as a soulless (albeit well compensated) intelligence contractor?

But it was more than unhappiness with what I was doing for a living that drove me out to the Eastern Shore that morning. Chloe was a year old by then and, while Christa and I had fixed up the interior of the row house (and also installed some hardscape pavers and a nice barbecue grill in the backyard), we both felt that 14th Place in Northeast DC was no place to raise a small child. The neighborhood had come a long way over the few years we were living there, but not far enough for our comfort as parents. There were times in the early morning hours that we could hear shots being fired only a few blocks away.

In the midst of all this, Christa and I were still trying to find a steady state of happiness together as a young married couple in Washington. That week of downtime in the Caribbean a few weeks earlier had been a nice break from the routine but, like all vacations, it had quickly come and gone. Christa and Chloe were back to being cooped up in the row house with only the occasional outing to the park or supermarket to look forward to; I was back to working the Saudi puzzle—with more than half the pieces missing.

But Christa was also getting farther along with her idea of opening a small clothing boutique, something I definitely supported in theory but hadn't given much serious thought. My own day was already occupied working a rather engrossing issue at CIA. And while Christa was thinking children's clothes and women's accessories, I was still tending more towards a restaurant or coffee shop.

Unbeknownst to me at the time, however, Christa's planning was becoming fairly advanced. She would venture out with Chloe in the car seat on weekdays to investigate potential store locations, both inside the District (on Capitol Hill and Georgetown) and in nearby Alexandria, Virginia. But more than possible locations, she also started inquiring directly with several vendors in New York. Christa had a very clear vision for the store she wanted to build.

I wanted something too. It was just still out of focus.

* * *

I walked a short ways down St. Michaels' Talbot Street, noticing several real estate offices. I took down the number of the Coldwell Banker office to have a local contact on hand, and then headed back to the car.

On the drive back home I stopped for another look at the lot in Royal Oak. A few days later (I'm rather embarrassed to admit) I faxed an offer in from Washington. I was pretty sure I could take some "equity" out of the row house *piggy bank* if things progressed to the point of an actual sale.

Fortunately, the deal never went forward. As it turned out, the lot wasn't on the town sewer system (shocking, I know) and so it would have been necessary—if I ever wanted to build on it—to have a new septic tank installed. For this and related reasons, the realtor I was working with called to advise that I withdraw the offer, which I did.

As spring drew closer a few weeks later, I drove back out to the Eastern Shore over a weekend, this time with Christa and Chloe. For the hell of it, we swung by the Royal Oak lot. "It had *potential*," Christa offered, coyly. That was putting it nicely. When I look back on that Royal Oak idea, just one word comes to mind. *Moron.*

We drove on to St. Michaels.

* * *

Driving into St. Michaels this time, weeks after my first visit to the town, I was even more aware of the full potential of the home equity loan trend of the day, particularly in terms of what it meant for my desire to cut away from Washington.

We bought the Capitol Hill row house for a steal in early 2004 and, while we had already taken out one small equity loan against it, there was still plenty more available if we were so inclined. And we were so inclined.

Christa and I took a look at a house on the edge of town. Too far from Talbot Street and too close in style to something you'd find in the suburbs of Washington, Christa and I agreed. We drove to a second house which we liked more, except that it faced the baseball field of the town's high school. Finally, we drove on to 102 North Harbor Road.

102 North Harbor was a sprawling split-level home, with little curb appeal to be perfectly honest. But I immediately loved the lot it was on. It wasn't on the water; waterfront property in that part of Maryland all went for over a million dollars—well beyond our price range. However, 102 was within a stone's throw of a water *inlet* off the Miles River. (The Miles empties into the eastern side of the Chesapeake Bay, several miles to the west of St. Michaels.) So not only was the home at least close to the water, it was also on a nice quiet road that was still within easy walking distance of the shops on Talbot Street.

It so happened that there was an open house that day. Watching Chloe crawl around inside on such wide-open floor space was a pleasant contrast to our much more confined living space in Washington. The house also had a decent yard, front and back.

But more importantly, while Christa and I didn't yet know that our second child was going to be a girl, we did know that another baby Scherck was on the way—sometime before Christmas. It was great news, but it only added to our motivation to find a bigger place to live.

Before heading back over the bridge to Washington that day, we also spent some time on Talbot Street checking out some of the available retail spaces. There were several possibilities.

By this point, Christa had more than convinced me that she knew what she was doing with her clothing boutique idea. The financing was still mostly up in the air, but she had a plan.

And I certainly shared in her motivation to see it through.

* * *

Our plans for relocating away from Washington continued to progress quickly after that first day together on the Eastern Shore.

We would rent out the row house and live in St. Michaels *full time*. Yes, it would be a hell of a commute for me (about two hours each way, to and from northern Virginia), but other people did it from this part of Maryland—and from West Virginia and Gettysburg, Pennsylvania even. At the office by early morning; heading home by early afternoon—this was how not a few people balanced their workday with a long commute around Washington. I would do it too.

I checked with the bank to see just how much more equity we could take out of the row house. I was pleasantly surprised by the answer. Not only would we have enough to make a down payment on the house at 102 North Harbor, we'd also have some cash left over to pursue the store idea.

A panacea to my disillusionment with life in Washington was all of a sudden on *this* side of the horizon. Christa and I wound up closing on the St. Michaels house on June 27, 2006.

We met the previous owner and his wife in an office at a title company on South Washington Street in nearby Easton. He was an affable retired naval aviator who had attended the Naval Academy in Annapolis back before I was even born.

After an hour of signing a seemingly endless stack of documents, Christa and I were St. Michaels' newest home owners. On the way out, Jim's wife congratulated Christa on her pregnancy and told us to keep an eye out in the yard for Chloe. Deer ticks (which transmit Lyme disease) were fairly common in the area, she warned.

* * *

A week earlier, I learned something else interesting about the area during the obligatory pre-closing home inspection. Vice President Dick Cheney and his wife Lynn had apparently themselves taken a liking to the St. Michaels neighborhood, not long before Christa and I had settled on the North Harbor house.

Standing in what would soon be my new kitchen, Rick (the inspector) suddenly mentioned the fact that the Cheneys had purchased a home out on the Eastern Shore the previous September, not but a few miles from 102 North Harbor. I was a little shocked, as you could imagine.

But not only did Rick personally inspect the Cheneys' new weekend retreat, he had also advised the Vice President of the United States himself— over the phone—on which of two homes he thought "Dick and Lynn" would be happiest with. While comparing notes with her husband on the final candidates from her laptop (bearing the Vice Presidential seal, no less) Rick explained that Mrs. Cheney quickly passed him her cell phone; the Vice President had some questions he wanted to ask Rick *directly* about each of the properties.

Over the next few minutes, Rick answered questions like: which house was more spacious? Which was in better overall condition? Which of the two, if *Rick* were choosing, would he pick?

Rick offered that he'd take the waterfront property off Church Neck Road in St. Michaels, advice the Cheneys would ultimately take.

* * *

On June 30, 2006 (just days after we closed on 102 North Harbor) an article appeared in the "Escapes" section of the *New York Times* that would confirm what I had learned from the home inspector.

In the article "Weekends With the President's Men," reporter Peter Kilborn described how Cheney had actually followed an old friend from the Ford administration out to the St. Michaels neck of the woods. Secretary of Defense Donald Rumsfeld had purchased a brick Georgian style home in the area for $1.5 million in 2003. A few years later in 2005, the Cheneys would pay $2.67 million for their waterfront parcel off Church Neck Road.

Kilborn's article went on to tell the story behind the name of the Rumsfelds' estate, *Mount Misery*. He wrote:

"But there is some historical gravity to the name, too. By 1833, Mount Misery's owner was Edward Covey, a farmer notorious for breaking unruly slaves for other farmers. One who wouldn't be broken was Frederick Douglass, then 16 and later the abolitionist orator. Covey assaulted him, so Douglass beat him up and escaped."

Leave it to the *New York Times* to dig up *that* part of the story on Rumsfeld's weekend home, I thought to myself.

I would see Mr. Rumsfeld face-to-face only once in St. Michaels over the next two and a half years. It was on a pleasant Saturday evening in the summer of 2007. Christa and I were heading back home with the girls (Sidney was born the previous December) when, suddenly, a white SUV darted slightly at us as it made its way in the opposite direction through the intersection of East Chew Avenue and New Lane in St. Michaels. At that moment, I saw Rumsfeld plain as day—eyeing me with surprising intensity for a guy in his mid-seventies.

"Oh my gosh," Christa saw herself, "that's Donald Rumsfeld." Yes it was.

This brief run-in with the two-time secretary of defense came well after Rumsfeld had resigned as President Bush's Pentagon chief, only a day after the 2006 mid-term elections the previous November. The first time Rumsfeld served in the position was back in the 1970s during the Gerald Ford administration—back when I was still in diapers.

Ford's chief of staff back then had been none other than Dick Cheney.

* * *

In the weeks following the 2000 presidential elections between Al Gore and George W. Bush, Vice President-*elect* Dick Cheney was no doubt in that same chief of staff mode as he sat quietly on the sidelines at his home in McLean, Virginia. While the Supreme Court would ultimately have to weigh in to put an end to Florida's "hanging chads" controversy, Cheney began planning out Bush's first term roster almost immediately.

His old friend Don Rumsfeld—Defense. Paul O'Neil (another Ford administration alum) would go to Treasury. O'Neil had proven himself to be a successful business executive after turning around the faltering Alcoa Corporation.

Cheney also drew from a circle of talent he had groomed personally while serving as secretary of defense under the 41st president, George H. W. Bush— during the *first* Gulf War. Stephen Hadley had been one of Cheney's assistant secretaries at the Pentagon; he was tapped for the new administration initially as deputy national security advisor to Condoleezza Rice. Hadley would ultimately replace Rice when she moved on to lead the State Department at the beginning of Bush's second term in 2005.

As for Rumsfeld, there had been sort of a honeymoon period early on in the second Gulf War during which his unique way with words became the source of some amusement amongst certain members of the media and, indeed, much of the country.

"Needless to say, the President is correct," Rumsfeld observed once to a roomful of reporters. "*Whatever* it was he said."

* * *

In September 2006, SpecTal, LLC, the company I worked for as an intelligence contractor at CIA, was sold by its original owners (two retired Agency CMO's) to the much larger L1 Solutions, headquartered in Stamford, Connecticut. Sale price: $100 million.

The value placed on SpecTal by investors was a testament to the private sector's growing interest in the ever-expanding federal government contracting realm at that time. As a SpecTal employee, I was part of a new class of contracting companies that had emerged in the aftermath of 9/11, one that almost exclusively supported the U.S. intelligence community, as opposed to the more traditional DoD business market. SpecTal's founding couple walked away with $90 million and were kind enough to leave $10 million to be distributed amongst the company's employees as bonuses. My cut as a *SpecTal-ian*: $16K after taxes. Not $90 million, but not bad either.

I already knew where the money was going—a certain store that was coming soon to Maryland's Eastern Shore by the name of Harbor Palm.

The problem was, in the grand scheme of things, I really *didn't* know where the money was going. As Christa and I continued putting things in motion for the store, I just never got a solid grasp on our new budget in St. Michaels. I didn't see how—even on a decent contractor's salary and having the row house rented out on Capitol Hill—a second home *and* financing a start-up business was just going to be unsustainable over the long run.

You definitely have to go for it when starting a business; you can't be afraid to spend money. But if and when your start-up capital dries up (as ours unfortunately did in late 2008), you are simply up the proverbial creek without a paddle. If I could offer one bit of advice to anyone thinking of starting their own business, it would be this: Get an accountant. Don't think of it as an extra start-up expense, think of it as making an investment in the long-term success of your business.

This realization would come later, however. For now, there in the fall of 2006, I had made it out of Washington. And while "Trails and Tails" entrepreneurial dreams would have to wait for some, Christa and I were well on our way to opening our very own small business.

18 / LET THEM EAT YELLOW CAKE

By the time we were semi-settled in St. Michaels in the fall of 2006, the Valerie Plame affair had already played out considerably in the national media. Through television news reports and countless press articles on the whole ordeal, (the famous Valerie Plame issue of *Vanity Fair*, published in January 2004, was years old by that time), I learned that Ms. Plame and I had at least a few things in common.

For starters, we had both been Air Force brats. Plame was born on Elmendorf Air Force Base in Anchorage, Alaska in 1963. I was born in the town of Woburn, Massachusetts twelve years later while my father was stationed at Hanscom. Many years later, well into her career as a CIA case officer, Plame helped direct the Agency's newly formed Joint Iraq Task Force (JITF), an analysis unit that operated right there in the same basement office spaces where I was now covering the Saudi WMD account. Remember all those copies of Iraq WMD analysis John had me dispose of during my first weeks in CPD?

The parallels between Ms. Plame's experience working the Iraq WMD target prior to the start of the second Gulf War and my own frustrations as a CPD CMO working Saudi throughout 2006 and early 2007 were beginning to come to light. As a lead manager of JITF in 2001 and 2002, Plame's task was to gather information that would either confirm or refute the administration's hard held belief that Saddam Hussein was actively developing weapons of mass destruction—nuclear, chemical and/or biological. Plame and her team of JITF officers were assigned this task over the summer of 2001, notably *prior* to the events of 9/11. It was clear to everyone involved that the administration had already made up its mind to topple the Saddam regime.

Dick Cheney had of course been George H. W. Bush's secretary of defense during the first Gulf War in the early 1990s. Now vice president, he was in charge of not only the administration's foreign policy portfolio but all intelligence matters as well. From the very beginning of George W. Bush's presidency, Dick Cheney's interaction with CIA's CPD was, quite simply, backwards. U.S. intelligence would *not* be used to objectively inform Bush administration policymakers. Rather, it was the policy crowd (Cheney's Office of the Vice President and others at the National Security Council) that would drive a predisposed and biased demand for particular flavors of intelligence.

Cheney would personally make visits to Headquarters during the lead up to the second Gulf War to check on the progress being made by Valerie Plame and her JITF colleagues in producing incriminating intelligence against the Saddam regime. The problem, from Cheney's standpoint, was that no such intelligence existed. Quite the opposite, JITF's pursuit of Iraqi scientists, students and family members abroad was yielding nothing on the WMD front. Zero. The occasional tips that JITF did receive from overseas were investigated in hopes of finding something definitive, but each time the story told was either inconclusive or, worse, a calculated hoax.

A flash of potential success came with a report that a shipment of *aluminum tubes* had made its way from Jordan into Iraq. In a very general sense, aluminum tubes are used in the process of enriching uranium, a necessary step in the production of a nuclear bomb. However, as a subsequent investigation would later attest, the limited information available on these particular aluminum tubes was hardly sufficient to conclude that Saddam Hussein was overseeing his own nuclear weapons program inside Iraq.

Yet a second dubious leg in what would become the Bush administration's case for war had to do with reports that Niger had provided uranium "yellowcake" to the government of Iraq, ostensibly for illicit weapons use.

On this question, Valerie Plame and her husband Joe Wilson would ultimately guarantee their place in the history books. Whether following the suggestion of Plame herself, or Plame's supervisor in CPD (hence part of the controversy), Ambassador Wilson was dispatched to Niger to investigate the yellowcake story. As it turned out, Wilson found nothing on his trip to validate the claim that Niger had provided Iraq with the rumored uranium.

* * *

In the end, whatever doubts there may have been at the time regarding aluminum tubes and yellowcake, it didn't matter. In a now infamous portion of his January 2003 State of the Union Address to Congress, President Bush cited both items as evidence of an illicit WMD program in Iraq.

The United States military was on its way once more to the Middle East. Only this time the goal wouldn't be merely to push the Iraqi military back from the border with oil-rich Saudi Arabia, as had been the case during the first Gulf War under then-Secretary of Defense Dick Cheney. This time, now as vice president, Cheney was going to finish the job by going all the way to Baghdad.

And Iraq's WMD program—real or imagined—would be one of the reasons President Bush would sell to the American people for doing so.

19 / A TALE OF TWO COFFEE MUGS

During Farm training, there was this orphaned mug at the coffee mess that either an instructor or a student from the previous class had left behind. It had the recognizable (to me at least) *Dean & DeLuca* logo on it—the name of the gourmet grocery store that Joel Dean and Giorgio DeLuca opened together in New York's SoHo neighborhood back in 1977.

The second and third Dean & DeLuca stores (there are only three in the country) are in Napa Valley, California and the Georgetown neighborhood of Washington, DC. I used to jog by the Georgetown location many, many times as a freshman on my way from campus down to Thompson boathouse on the Potomac River, adjacent to the famous Watergate Hotel. I was the "stroke"—the pace setter—of the first boat of the freshmen men's lightweight crew that year.

But I would do more than just jog by on those early mornings. Throughout my time as a student at Georgetown, I would occasionally take the walk from campus down to M Street to do nothing more than stroll the aisles of Dean & DeLuca. I've always enjoyed the atmosphere of a grocery, even your larger chain supermarkets like Safeway or Vons. The fresh scents, the shapes, the colors—especially those at Dean & DeLuca. I'm a "foodie," as the term has been coined over the years. I probably get this most from my grandmother, my mom's mom. She, too, *loves* food. I cook, I bake, although not as much in recent years with Chloe and Sidney around now. Still, every now and then when I get the chance, I'm in the kitchen banging away. Spending thirty dollars (sometimes less, sometimes more) on all of the special ingredients for a recipe off the Internet—or out of a Jamie Oliver cookbook—it's a nice hobby of mine.

The only thing I took with me from the Farm—other than the crystal clear realization that I was *not* an Operations Officer—was that Dean & DeLuca coffee mug.

* * *

There would be a second noteworthy coffee mug during my time at CIA. But this one I would purchase, down towards the end of my time in CPD.

The frustration had already reached its crescendo. The dysfunction between the DO and the DI on the Saudi issue was entrenched. Coordination with the DO of the DI's sheepish PDB briefs to the president and vice president (all of which continued to point at Pakistan...*maybe*—IF Riyadh was interested in acquiring a nuclear capability) had become rather routine.

Then one day I was told by management that I would be accompanying Phil to represent CPD in a briefing down at the Old Executive Office Building (also known as the Eisenhower Building) near the White House. Phil and I would be joined by my CMO counterparts: Tabitha from the Near East area division (covering Saudi Arabia) and Katherine from East Asia (China). Interestingly, there would be no DI analysts attending. Vice President Cheney's nuclear proliferation advisor Bob Swartz, whom we would be briefing, had requested the meeting. He wanted a DO-*only* perspective on what we thought was going on with Saudi Arabia.

As a personal advisor to Cheney on the Saudi nuclear issue, this meant that what Cheney knew, Bob also knew. And vice versa. This was how the office of the vice president operated. Cheney's office was well staffed with national security experts, and (by design) the lines were excessively blurred between his own office and the traditionally self-contained National Security Council. Staffers from *both* shops all reported to Cheney whom, of course, had the ear of the President. And what Cheney thought on a particular national security issue, Bush almost invariably did as well. This was how the Oval Office operated.

Throughout much of the Bush administration, Cheney actually chaired the many "principals meetings" that served to *tee up* issues that would ultimately be decided by the better known National Security Council meetings. The two are essentially one in the same in terms of participants, save the president;

when POTUS is in the room, instead of it being a "principals" meeting, it's a "meeting of the President's National Security Council." For a vice president to, in a sense, *pinch-hit* for the president during Principals Committee meetings was unprecedented. Principals meetings are typically chaired by the president's National Security Advisor. Condoleezza Rice (during Bush's first term) or Stephen Hadley should have been at the head of the table, *not* Vice President Cheney. But this would be part of the different understanding Cheney had arrived at with Bush before agreeing to serve as his vice president.

I was at once both excited and nervous at the prospect of meeting with Bob Swartz. Were we actually going to meet Cheney? I asked. Was the vice president going to be sitting in on the meeting with Swartz, chiming in with unanswerable questions—*Socratic* style—as Cheney was widely rumored to do? *Holy shit!* What the hell was I going to say?

Phil didn't know himself if Cheney would be in the room, "but he *might* be," Phil teased. He knew I was nervous. And he knew why. "We'll find out when we get there," he added. Phil, I knew, had been around the block before with OVP.

I was excited because this *could* (as I still naively hoped) be an opportunity to cut through the Pakistani-centric analytic line. We could perhaps finally talk about China; all the many shipments captured in imagery, all of the strange activity at the bases. Perhaps this could be the beginning of a fresh, top-down look at the issue to help spur new reporting from the field. But I was also nervous. As the CPD CMO, I had no substantial HUMINT reporting to explain the Chinese shipments we were seeing in imagery from NGA—the analysis of which I knew Cheney and Swartz were mindful of downtown.

Cheney himself had personally used satellite imagery of newly constructed buildings in Iraq circa 2000—as evidence that Saddam Hussein was pursuing a weapons program—in his briefings to key members of Congress during the lead up to the second Gulf War, including then-Texas Congressman Dick Armey. There was every reason to believe in the 2006 timeframe that satellite imagery was still just as important to the office of the vice president in monitoring the activities of America's largest provider of foreign oil.

* * *

As a quick aside, there was no question that Cheney's office was similarly monitoring CIA's HUMINT reporting on Saudi alongside the imagery-based reports they were getting from NGA.

I recall one particular report in from Tokyo that made a vague but alarming reference to possible illicit weapons activity at one of Japan's civilian nuclear reactors. Almost as soon as the report was disseminated from Headquarters, Bob Swartz sent a quick shot-gun email to CPD—an email I happened to be copied on.

I could tell as I read Swartz's email that the report caught the vice president's nuclear proliferation advisor completely off guard. Swartz was looking for some clarification, *as soon as possible*.

"Quite frankly," Swartz wrote with at least a touch of concern, "I don't know what this report means."

* * *

At the meeting with Swartz then, I would be armed with little to nothing in terms of official *disseminated* HUMINT. Not a good thing if you're a CMO. Just my own hunches based on ops traffic and (more importantly in the end) the curious on-again/off-again history of the Saudi matter within CPD—one that I was now witnessing first-hand.

But intuition alone only goes so far in the national security policy realm, particularly coming from the action officer level as I was. There had to be someone in HUMINT channels actually telling the U.S. government in no uncertain terms that these Chinese shipments were part and parcel of an ongoing upgrade of the Saudi Strategic Rocket Forces. The steady stream of imagery over the kingdom alone hadn't been enough for the administration to sound the alarm bells with CIA management—for some *very strange* reason.

Was there *anything* in HUMINT channels? Bob Swartz and two other National Security Council staffers were going to want to know. If not, was any such information possibly forthcoming as to the nature of these shipments from China?

Needless to say, the answer from CPD would be "no" and "most likely, no."

* * *

After checking in through security that afternoon in late 2006, the four of us made our way up to the reception area just outside Vice President Cheney's personal office in the Eisenhower Building.

Upon our arrival, I noticed several large, unframed poster-board-sized photos of Dick Cheney from various events he had participated in over the years as vice president; photo-ops with foreign dignitaries, with President Bush, a few only of Cheney himself—they hung on the wall here and there in the same room where two or three of his personal assistants worked. This was the same room that visitors would pass through on their way to meeting with the Vice President of the United States.

I instantly thought back to my high school days as an intern in the California governor's office, where similar type photos of Pete Wilson hung on the walls there in the state house in Sacramento. Standing there outside Cheney's office, I recall being rather relieved that I didn't see a shot of the vice president glad-handing any Saudi royalty.

Bob Swartz greeted us almost immediately and showed us into the conference room adjacent to the vice president's reception area, across the room from the closed doors of Cheney's private office.

I remember Swartz explaining to us as we entered the conference room that the office space we were standing in had once been home to the old Secretary of the Navy up through World War I. Swartz proceeded to show us an old desk which, as he opened the drawer, we learned had been somewhat the target of not a little bit of vice presidential *graffiti*. Through a small sheet of plexi-glass, cut custom to line the bottom of the drawer, you could see the hand-written signatures of Cheney's predecessors in the office. Swartz showed us our seats at the conference table, a piece of furniture every bit as old (and no doubt as historic) as the credenza we had just been shown.

On the opposite side of the table sat Mr. Swartz, flanked by two other Cheney aides—or perhaps they were NSC staffers, I don't recall. And, as I mentioned, Vice President Cheney himself didn't bother much to distinguish between the two. One was David Stephens, whom I would encounter during my second incarnation as an intelligence community contractor at the National Counter-Terrorism Center. (A few notes on NCTC later.)

Mr. Stephens made it a point to tell everyone up front that he would have to leave sometime before the end of the meeting for some *other* commitment. He didn't say what or when exactly, just that at some point he was going to have to excuse himself. Strange, I remember thinking, on a topic like *this?* What could have possibly been more important that afternoon, even at the NSC? Stephens' colleague, a savvy young woman whose name I don't remember, did manage to make it through the entire meeting as I recall.

On my side of the table there was myself on the far left sitting next to Phil. To Phil's right was Tabitha, and on the far right was Katherine.

Curiously, I don't remember Katherine saying a single word throughout the entire meeting from the East Asia standpoint. Whether this was due to the fact that she (to my knowledge at least) hadn't coordinated on any intelligence reporting that spoke specifically to the question at hand, or if there was perhaps something else going on over in her neck of Headquarters, I may never know.

Phil, with his many years of experience working in CPD, started things off on our side. In typical Phil fashion, he began to coolly and methodically paint a picture of the DO's collective view (myopic though it was) of developments relating to Saudi Arabia's ballistic missile program. He spoke as CIA's authoritative expert on the matter, which he effectively was at the time despite the fact that his full time job was targeting the aftermath of the dismantled A.Q. Khan network in Pakistan.

There had been the vexing shipment in 2003, Phil mentioned first. Phil paused briefly to see if Bob wanted to delve further into that topic. Bob did not. Phil noted that Steve (the analyst whom Vice President Cheney had directed be assigned to CP/NE in the aftermath of that eventful shipment) had since moved on in his career, back to the DI. In actuality, Steve was serving as Secretary of State Condoleezza Rice's PDB briefer during this time. (The president and vice president, I had learned, aren't the only high-ranking U.S. government officials to receive the *President's* Daily Brief.)

The imagery of Chinese shipments arriving in Saudi Arabia since at least 2003, Phil continued, appeared to be related to a considerable overhaul of the Saudis' ballistic missile capability. This was difficult to argue. However, despite persistent efforts by the DO to target assets for the collection of HUMINT on the issue, Phil concluded, there was just no real progress to report.

Once Phil finished his introductory summary, there wasn't much else said throughout the duration of the meeting. Phil had said it all: the CIA's Directorate of Operations—right along with the office of the vice president—knew something was underway with Saudi Arabia's Strategic Rocket Forces. Unfortunately, however, the DO was not in contact with anyone overseas who could report on the matter. There were a few questions from the other side of the table to clarify Phil's overview of things, which Phil, Tabitha and I gave brief answers to. Katherine remained noticeably quiet.

The one thing I distinctly recall mentioning came when the conversation turned to the subject of the dramatic changes that were taking place on the missile bases in conjunction with the shipments, as seen by U.S. satellites: Al Sulayyil, Al Joffer and (of particular interest) the underground storage facility at Rawdah. Obviously, NGA's bird's eye view couldn't reveal what was going on underground at Rawdah, but there was plenty of activity at the mouth of the tunnels leading into the cavernous subterranean bunker to pique everyone's interest.

"And the addition of new anti-air batteries at the bases," I said, implying that the Chinese shipments were a game-changer. "As the imagery has been indicating," I added. "It's unprecedented."

Because it was unprecedented. Beijing had been assisting Riyadh in fielding Saudi Arabia's conventional ballistic missile arsenal since the late 1980s. Why all of a sudden the need for enhanced air defenses against—in all likelihood—the Israelis and Iranians? I expected there would be at least some sort of follow-up from Swartz's side of the table.

Instead, my comment would be answered by a knowing stare from the woman sitting across from me. Swartz popped off an unrelated question and the room was off to a completely different topic. In that instant I saw that the woman sitting beside Swartz knew exactly what I was getting at, but there would be no further discussion of satellite imagery. Certainly not in our meeting.

I wasn't thinking it at the moment, but as I've looked back on this visit to Cheney's office, it was rather curious that Bob Swartz didn't invite the imagery analysts from NGA to his all-too-brief skull session with the DO. Never mind that Michael Hayden (the director of CIA at the time) was sending email missives to Agency employees on the importance of *collaboration* amongst "our intelligence community partners." The individuals that Vice President Cheney had monitoring the Saudi issue there in the Eisenhower Building were part of a far different strategy, one with a very different objective.

Swartz and Co.'s conversation with us DO action officers that day was stove-piped for good reason. The meeting in the vice president's conference room had simply been our turn to offer up what was known *officially* in HU-MINT channels about China's many shipments into the port of Jeddah, Saudi Arabia.

"Nothing?"

"Nothing, Bob."

Check.

* * *

The meeting wrapped up quickly. Swartz added something brief to his guided tour of our historic surroundings and then asked whether any of the four of us were interested in visiting the White House *gift shop*.

Swartz was actually quite a cordial guy, the circumstances of our meeting with him notwithstanding. He'd be happy to show us to the shop, assuming it was open. I was a little embarrassed, as apparently I was the only one interested in checking out the White House chotsky.

It wasn't so much a store as it was a *broom closet*. But it had all the sorts of things, I remember thinking, that a U.S. Navy ship's store offers: pens, portfolio cases, *coffee mugs*, etc. Only instead of it being the crest of USS Princeton or the aircraft carrier Enterprise, it was the famous White House emblem. I bought a mug.

And then the vice president's nuclear proliferation advisor saw us on our way back to Headquarters.

* * *

In December 2008, well after this visit to the Eisenhower Building, Christa and I would be packing up our things in St. Michaels for a reluctant return to Washington. The economic downturn of the day had taken a toll on our already dwindling start-up capital. We were being forced to close the store.

As I randomly picked and sorted through some less essential household goods there at 102 North Harbor, I paused for a moment in the kitchen. I decided to throw away that White House coffee mug.

On the other hand, the Dean & DeLuca mug still sits in our kitchen cupboard here today in southern California. I'm sentimental like that.

20 / OFFICIALLY UNOFFICIAL

Around Thanksgiving 2006 (about five months prior to my dismissal), CPD management asked whether I would be interested in doing some temporary duty at the station in Riyadh. It would be an opportunity to visit the country I was covering from afar at Headquarters in northern Virginia. I declined for a number of reasons.

First and foremost, the timing was not good. They were going to have me fly out for several weeks in January 2007. Christa was due with Sidney that first week of December. As it turned out, the due date was spot on. Sidney Alice, our second daughter, was born on December 2, 2006.

And while I didn't mention it because I very much preferred to keep talk of Harbor Palm to a minimum at work, I knew Christa was going to need me those first few months of 2007 to help prep for the store opening. The build-out was already well underway, courtesy of the landlord who was renovating the old Victorian building that Harbor Palm would occupy. But there would be plenty more to do in terms of placing new fixtures and organizing all the new equipment; everything from clothing hangers to mannequins to wrapping paper.

The second reason I didn't see a need to go to Riyadh was that I didn't think any good would come of it. There was nothing I could do in person there in country to get different answers to questions that were already (supposedly) being asked of assets in Saudi and elsewhere. If anything, I'm not exactly the friendly used car salesmen type. There's a lot of give and take involved in the handling of an intelligence asset—too much for my taste. My presence in a meeting with a source might actually have been a hindrance. I had dropped out of the Farm for this very reason, after all. Know thyself.

Yet a third reason for my reluctance was that I continued to feel somewhat of an outsider at CIA as a contractor. Yes, former U.S. military special forces types were commonplace fighting the wars in Iraq and Afghanistan by that point in time, but somehow those guys were different. They were (and continue to be, as most of them freely admit) *mercenaries*—in the traditional combat sense. CPD management wasn't going to have me fly all the way out to Riyadh just to sit at a computer terminal, I had to assume. I would be pulled into at least a few meetings in town. And the prospect of this didn't sit well with me.

Somehow, I felt that a meeting with a foreigner overseas on a matter as sensitive as nuclear weapons under the control of Riyadh's ruling elite—that such a matter ought to be handled at the point of contact, by *official, active duty* intelligence officers of the U.S. government. Not a *retired* official, and certainly not a hired gun CMO such as myself. Indeed, this is a debate that continues today at the CIA and other government agencies including the State Department. Where should the line be drawn between *official* and *contract*? That line just isn't defined clearly enough, in my opinion, particularly in the national security arena.

Perhaps my thinking would have been different had I instead been working as an intelligence analyst contractor supporting the Coast Guard and DEA with their counternarcotics operations off the Florida Keys. But this whole Saudi deal was something else entirely.

* * *

I would find myself in this gray area a few other times during my two plus years as a CIA contractor.

There was the trip to Europe, which I *did* take. I know, I know...but I decided to go because I knew I was meeting with an *American* on this particular occasion—an American who happened to live and work in Saudi. I just saw it as different somehow.

There was also the time I took a trip to the west coast to meet with a contact (another American) in the Los Angeles area. This individual traveled frequently to the Middle East and happened to be in touch with a number of people of interest to those of us tracking the Saudi question. Fond as I am of California, I had no problems making this trip either.

The funny thing about the California trip was that I had a hard time finding a hotel at the allowed *per diem* rate. I did eventually find a room at a reasonable price, but it was hardly your traditional "hotel California." For two nights there in the fall of 2006, it was as though I was in the Navy all over again—sort of. My room was actually a *stateroom* aboard Britain's old retired Queen Mary, today a hotel ship permanently moored to a pier in Long Beach.

She's rumored to be haunted. Fortunately, I didn't encounter any ghosts during my stay.

21 / MY WAY

Little did I know on this trip back to California in 2006 that I would be returning as a full time resident with Christa and my two daughters just three years later.

As mentioned earlier, I'm writing this—in the early morning hours when Chloe and Sidney are fast asleep—from our two bedroom just outside Los Angeles. My day job these days is watching the girls, which works out just fine because (as has too often been the case) I need some time to figure out what it is I want to do with the rest of my life.

Christa, meanwhile, is holding down a job on Hollywood's trendy Melrose Avenue. It's actually not far from Hollywood Presbyterian Medical Center, the same hospital where she was born. The store she's at isn't quite Harbor Palm; she misses the satisfaction of managing her own store. But she's not complaining given the state of the economy.

Not only that, working in the Hollywood neighborhood has some unique perks. She's met or at least seen in person not a few of the town's acting professionals, the ones most of us only read about in the gossip columns or see interviewed on television while promoting their just released film. Christa is convinced now that the more media savvy of the bunch actually phone ahead in advance to the *paparazzi* to inform them of their impending arrival at the store—or wherever else they're going to be that day. That way, there'll be plenty of camera shutters snapping away as a certain primped hotel heiress makes her way from her $90,000 car into the boutique, welcome fodder the following week's glossy mags. I couldn't believe the conspiracy when I first heard it.

Just the other day, Christa helped a more down to earth customer, the actress Candice Bergen. This was the same Candice Bergen who played the character of Murphy Brown on television years ago—whom former Vice President Dan Quayle took issue with for seeming to send the wrong message about the importance of fathers in raising children. (Bergen's character was a single mom on the show.) This had quite possibly been the basis for questions the press wanted to ask Quayle in Houston during the 1992 Republican convention—when reporter Ed Bradley was trying to push past a certain young pesky delegate from California.

Today, of course, I wouldn't be caught dead at a political convention of any sort, Republican or Democrat. I actually made it a point to register as an Independent since moving back to California in 2009.

Ironically enough, the congressman representing South Pasadena, Representative Adam Schiff, helped establish a national security "study group" in March 2003, "in an effort to explore emerging national security issues with other Members of Congress."

I'd be interested to hear from the congressman as to how that went for him and his colleagues in the House.

* * *

Christa occasionally brings home copies of complimentary magazines that get stacked in the café of her store, monthlies filled mostly with advertisements for everything from perfume and cologne to the opening of the latest Hollywood nightclub.

The March 2010 issue of *LA Confidential* had a short article on fashion designer Tom Ford, talking about his first time as a movie director and producer of the film *A Single Man*. "And it helps with self financing for absolute creative freedom," he was quoted in reference to his personal financial investment in the film. "I need my day job so that I can finance my movies."

Well look at that, I thought reading the article. I *also* had a day job that was helping to pay the bills as Christa and I were trying to get our retail store off the ground back in early 2007. Only my job wasn't designing for a successful men's fashion line; mine was apparently to only *look* busy as a CMO in CIA's Counter-Proliferation Division as Dick Cheney and his accomplices slowly did nothing about China's ill conceived energy-for-security arrangement with the Kingdom of Saudi Arabia.

Don't get me wrong, the day job paid off. With the help of some real estate equity—something I would definitely do differently if we ever do it again—Christa and I managed a "soft" opening of Harbor Palm in late March 2007.

In the end it was Christa's creative talent that made Harbor Palm what it was. Every last discriminating detail, right down to the size and color of the safety pins we used to attach a Harbor Palm price tag to the store's clothing items—it was all Christa. The girls and I joined her on several of the buying trips she made to the shows in Chelsea for fall and spring lines—but again, it was Christa making all the final decisions. But this didn't keep me from being a very proud cat on Harbor Palm's opening night.

We hired a local caterer to serve a little champagne for our guests on what unfortunately turned out to be a chilly spring evening in St. Michaels. We probably should have served hot toddies in hindsight. Of the two hundred or so invitations we sent out, there were about fifty or so local business owners and residents who kindly stopped by to say hello and wish us well.

Our very first sale went to an older husband and wife couple who ran a bed and breakfast several blocks away on Talbot Street. They bought a napkin holder from an assortment of Dransfield & Ross tabletop accessories that Christa had picked out for the home furnishings section of the store.

The holder is a ceramic monkey that stands about four inches off the table. Its extra long tail is what holds the napkin. Wearing a dark green jacket and what looks like a Shriner's fez hat and tassel, he sort of looks like that Rodin sculpture, *The Thinker*, or *Le Penseur* as they say in France. Oddly, the couple bought only the one monkey. The other half of the set is today packed away somewhere in a box in our apartment here in South Pasadena—probably still wondering where his brother went.

But the funky monkey napkin holder in the upstairs home furnishings room of Harbor Palm was about as close as Christa got in her buying decisions to the kind of merchandise that dominated most of the other retail stores along St. Michaels' Talbot Street. Whereas other stores played it safe with t-shirts, flip-flops and Martha's Vineyard knock-off apparel lines, Harbor Palm specialized in bringing the latest in women's fashion (from New York) to

Maryland's Eastern Shore. Christa has always been a little ahead of the curve with her fashion sense and so her store would make quite the splash, if only short-lived.

As a result, the store was in a class all its own on Talbot Street. And by that I don't mean to sound snooty or condescending towards the other shops in St. Michaels. Many of them have been there for years and some have no doubt successfully weathered the rough downturn in sales U.S. retailers have suffered since late 2008. But it was clear to me from the beginning that Christa's eye would cater to a more discerning clientele in that remote part of Maryland across the Chesapeake, pleasantly many miles from the daily grind of Washington.

The Inn at Perry Cabin is a hotel in St. Michaels that accommodates a more affluent crowd. We were always happy to see a Perry Cabin border make their way to Harbor Palm. And when they came, they would very often stay thirty minutes or more, sometimes returning the next day. They loved the store, and Christa and I greatly appreciated their business, not just from a business perspective but also from the standpoint of knowing that our overall concept was working. All the capital I had pooled for the endeavor, all of Christa's fashion sense—it was all coming together with great result by the summer of 2007.

And it wasn't just the Perry Cabin weekender type who enjoyed Harbor Palm. The St. Michaels area is the weekend and summer destination for many prominent Washingtonians, New Yorkers—people from all over America in fact.

Probably the best sale I helped with in the summer of 2007 was to a lady who had flown into the nearby airport on her family's private jet. After buying over a thousand dollars in clothes, she's walking out the door when she notices one of the necklaces Christa had placed on a mannequin.

"How much is *this?*" she asks me in a sweet Tennessee accent. Two minutes later (necklace around her neck) her driver was helping her to her car.

Two *hours* later she was very likely about to land somewhere in Tennessee, or wherever that nice accent was from.

* * *

But all this satisfaction of owning and operating our own business was still ahead of us that night in March 2007 when Christa and I hosted the house warming of Harbor Palm. There was still a lot of work to do and much more inventory had yet to arrive, but the cash register was working and the new fixtures and cash wrap looked great. We were up and running!

But what made that night special was that my mom and grandmother made it to town for the opening. My godmother Lorri surprised me as well by driving up from her home in Durham, North Carolina.

No, none of it was really *ours*. Christa and I were only leasing the retail space—a building I would have much rather owned, obviously. And all of the start-up inventory and operating expenses were being financed out of the ether somewhere between the grossly exaggerated equity of two real estate properties and the terribly fat interest payments I was making on mortgages for the very same homes.

But what was mine that night—what was *real* to me—was having my daughters there with me as I showed the place off to my mother, grandmother and aunt. Yes, I was still working as a contractor at CIA, but now my family and I were cutting a new path for ourselves, wherever that path might lead.

And even as I look back on what happened with the store (and that home of ours away from DC on North Harbor Road), I remain just as optimistic about that new path as I was on opening night.

President George W. Bush escorts Saudi Arabia's Crown Prince Abdallah (right) to his private office on his ranch in Crawford, Texas, April 25, 2005. At left is Vice President Dick Cheney and obscured in background is U.S. Secretary of State Condoleezza Rice. Saudi Prince Bandar bin Sultan is in view between President Bush and Crown Prince Abdallah. (Photo by Rod Aydelotte-Pool/ Getty Images)

President Barack Obama, seated with President Hu Jintao of China, hosts the Nuclear Security Summit April 12, 2010 in Washington. (Photo by Ron Sachs-Pool/Getty Images)

22 / NOT DOWN WITH FFT

Francis Fragos Townsend, or "FFT" as she was referred to in the CPD front office emails I was sometimes inadvertently left on (I particularly liked those), served as an assistant to President Bush for Homeland Security and Counter-Terrorism from 2004 to 2007.

Unlike Bob Swartz—who had come to the Bush administration from one of the country's national labs (Los Alamos as I recall)—I knew who Fran Townsend was. She was frequently quoted in the papers representing the administration's views on various CT issues that made their way to the media's attention.

FFT was a lawyer by training. Rudy Giuliani had recruited her early on to join his organized crime unit in the U.S. Attorney's Office in Manhattan. In February 2007, having it seemed just visited the vice president's nuclear proliferation advisor, there was a new invitation to go downtown. This time our host would be the president's CT czar.

And unlike the meeting at the vice president's office, FFT wanted to see everyone. DO and DI together, from CIA. She even wanted to see the imagery analysts from NGA. Having been less than satisfied with our visit with the Cheney side of the house, this was going to be interesting.

Once again, I thought, I would have little to contribute. But, *boy*, was it going to be worth the drive from Headquarters to watch the analyst pack from the DI push their strained "maybe *Pakistan?*" position with the imagery analysts there in the room to remind everyone of the latest shipment from China. And, adding to the occasion, this meeting was going to be held in the White House, not in the adjacent Eisenhower Building. FFT was, after all, an assistant to Bush, not Cheney.

This dual house approach to the Saudi question confirms what many have said and written about the very unique operation Dick Cheney ran as vice president. The multi-tasking policy factory he managed in the Eisenhower Building next door to the White House was nothing less than *its own* White House. And in the case of Saudi, the Cheney White House actually had a trained nuclear expert monitoring the situation. As savvy a woman as Fran Townsend was working for Bush on CT issues, she was no nuclear expert. She was a lawyer whom the president respected a great deal. George W. Bush trusted her counsel.

The president, I concluded, had decided to have FFT check in with the relevant intelligence community reps on the Saudi matter, an issue Bush was only hearing on (from the U.S. government side) through Dick Cheney. God only knows what Prince Bandar was saying around this time, by then retired from official duties as Saudi ambassador to the U.S. Washington's relationship with Riyadh had soured even more by this point in Bush's second term.

Bush, as I saw it, would have his lawyer conduct a sanity check of the picture he was getting from his vice president. Fran was going to take our pulse, if you will.

What did we know and, more importantly, what *didn't* we know?

* * *

While I made it on the list of those whom FFT wanted to meet with on a Monday morning in February 2007, this would not be a meeting I would make.

That previous Friday evening, home for the weekend in St. Michaels, Christa and I were in the kitchen cooking dinner, a half drunk bottle of Chardonnay on the counter. Sidney (not yet even three months old) was napping in her crib.

Suddenly, our *au pair,* Michelle, enters the kitchen from the other room where she and Chloe had been watching television together. She's propping Chloe up at the shoulders because "there's something wrong," Michelle tells us with a frightened look on her face. Chloe was having a hard time breathing. She was choking for air! *Oh, my god.*

I instantly snapped out of my wine buzz and laid Chloe down on her back on the kitchen floor.

Christa and I had both taken CPR training in the Navy, so we arched her neck a little to open the airway in her neck. But something was *really* wrong. We couldn't tell what. Chloe's little two-year-old body had seized up, her only movements came from her eyes, staring helplessly up at her mom and dad. And her tiny mouth, lips quivering slightly as she couldn't breathe.

We quickly started peppering Michelle with questions. *Had Chloe swallowed something?! Did she eat something?!*

Seconds passed—still no sign that Chloe's breathing was returning to normal. Christa grabbed the phone and called 9/11.

I was on the floor with Chloe in my arms. "What about those little stickers Christa's mom sent?" Carrol, being the good grandmother, had sent a Valentine's Day gift package that included a bunch of those little puff stickers. Some of them were little circles—*shit!*—just the right size to get stuck in Chloe's throat!

"Did she *swallow* one of those?" I asked Michelle, desperate for an answer—*any* answer. No, no, Chloe hadn't swallowed anything, at least that she knew of.

Christa fortunately was well into her conversation with the 9-1-1 operator. The paramedics were on their way.

Christa started relaying questions from the operator: had we laid Chloe down on her back? Yes, yes, damn it, she's on her back!! OK, calm, calm...

She's *still not breathing!!* My frantic imagination started getting the best of me. One of those stickers were lodged in the back of her throat, I was suddenly convinced. I looked inside her mouth and saw nothing. But it's back there, I was certain.

I began feeling around in the back of her mouth for a foreign object with my index finger. That *damn sticker*—I was certain I'd find it. But I felt nothing.

Chloe gagged a little at the sensation, actually a welcome sign as her body was still tight—"locked up" as Christa described back to the 9-1-1 operator.

The next seconds were a dizzying nightmarish blur. Chloe was still having trouble getting air. Christa had finished passing information and was in tears as the operator waited on the line for the paramedics to arrive. Michelle was suddenly at the edge of the kitchen holding Sidney who had woken from her nap—screaming.

"Get Sidney *out of here!*" I remember yelling at Michelle. I wasn't bothered by the noise so much as the thought that our baby girl was just feet away with her sister there choking on the floor.

Jesus Christ, was our little girl going to be alright?

I began digging deeper into the back of Chloe's mouth looking for that sticker. I knew it was in there. My index finger was deep into her throat now. I could feel the nail scratch into the tender flesh...

* * *

The paramedics finally arrived.

And no sooner had they arrived—two of them now circling Chloe on the floor as I backed away—than Chloe began breathing again. Her arms started to move. They were able to stand her up.

"She just couldn't breathe," I told them, feeling the greatest sense of relief I've ever felt in my life—and may *ever* feel.

Chloe had gone from lying motionless on the floor to standing—and bloody marvelous coughing and crying—within mere moments. It was the most wonderful sound.

I remember the look she gave Christa and I as though asking, "Why did you have your hand in my mouth, Dad?!"

"Looks like she's doing much better," one of the paramedics assured us. "But we're going to put her in the ambulance just to be safe."

I looked at Christa who was holding Sidney. Yeah, that made sense.

"Can one of you ride with her to the hospital?"

"I'll go," I said. Christa would follow with Sidney in the car.

The first stop was Memorial Hospital in Easton where Sidney had been born just two months earlier. We were there all of two hours before the doctor on call decided that, to be safe, Chloe really needed to spend the night under observation at the University of Maryland Hospital in downtown Baltimore.

Baltimore—as in almost *two hours* away? Yes, the doctor insisted, in case it happens again.

The most the doctor in Easton could say was that Chloe might have suffered an allergic reaction to something she had eaten, a question we had already exhausted.

Christa headed home with Sidney as Chloe and I boarded yet another ambulance, this time headed over the Chesapeake Bay Bridge to the hospital in Baltimore. And it was certainly the right thing to do. Not because Chloe relapsed—she didn't—but because we just didn't know.

By morning, as Christa arrived in the car with Sidney, the University of Maryland doctor was confident that Chloe had suffered what's called a febrile seizure. The Mayo Clinic's online definition describes it much better than I can:

"A febrile seizure is a convulsion in young children that may be caused by a sudden spike in body temperature, often from an infection. Watching your child experience a febrile seizure can be alarming. And, although a febrile seizure may last only a few minutes, it may seem like an eternity to you." – (www.mayoclinic.com)

It really had seemed like an eternity. And the drive over the Bay Bridge that night seemed almost as long as Chloe lay on a stretcher between me and the paramedic who was riding with us in the back of the ambulance.

The medical equipment around us began shaking violently as we went over each successive bump of the massive span of bridge over the bay. This was the same bridge I drove over during the work week, to and from CIA. But that night was so very different. Even though everything would be alright in the morning, it was a rough ride.

My nerves were frayed sitting in that ambulance, staring at my little "Clo." Her seizure, the stress of setting up the store with Christa, the insanity at work. It all crashed down on me. I broke down in tears. More of a sob, really. The kind you see on television every so often, usually of people overseas—not Americans—mourning their plight in the aftermath of some awful earthquake or tsunami.

"Is she your first?" the paramedic asked knowingly as I regained my composure. I nodded.

He nodded right back.

* * *

Needless to say, I didn't get any sleep that night. I got a full night's sleep that Saturday and Sunday night back in St. Michaels, but still felt cruddy when the alarm clock rang at 4 AM the following Monday morning.

When we were living out on the Eastern Shore, I was always on the road by 5 AM. That way I was in the office in CPD no later than 7 AM. Seven to three, that was my day for much of my two and a half years working as a CMO at CIA.

But that particular Monday morning was no ordinary morning. There would be my regular commute, but then the plan was for the whole Saudi gang to head downtown to the White House together.

Phil was finally back to Pakistan full time again, so he wouldn't be going this time. To Phil's great relief, management had backfilled the Saudi targeting position with a new officer, Steve #2—*Cheney's* Steve having been the first. So it would be Steve #2, myself, Tom (the Saudi ops desk officer) and several analysts from the Directorate of Intelligence.

I would call these DI analysts out by their first names to distinguish among them here, probably the proper thing to do. But I would be sorely tempted to launch back into how some of them—incomprehensible to those of us with our eye on China—continued to cling to their Pakistan fixation, a simply untenable analytic line given what satellite imagery was telling us. (Wouldn't you say, *Robbie? Wayne?*)

This motley crew then—from several very different corners of the U.S. intelligence community—was supposedly going to head to the White House that morning to get it all on the table with Fran Townsend, the president's Homeland Security/CT czar. It would be like standing around some dirty dog dish talking about how no one ever gets around to cleaning it properly, I imagined.

I turned the alarm off and got out of bed. I was about to make some coffee as I did every morning for the drive in, but before I could hit the 'on' switch I decided to call the office.

I left a message on someone's answering machine, I forget who. One of my daughters was still sick from earlier in the weekend, I explained. I was going to miss the Fran Townsend meeting unfortunately.

I went back to bed, relieved. Relieved that I wasn't going to be part of the three-ring circus in FFT's office. But mostly just happy that Chloe and Sidney were sound asleep in their beds.

* * *

Several times while working at CIA, my former college professor Faruk Tabak and I would meet for beers afterhours at a bar in Washington.

Over a few pints of Guinness we would talk about the current state of international affairs. They were grim. Almost daily suicide bombings in Baghdad. Gruesome video recordings of heinous beheadings in Afghanistan. These were terribly turbulent years of the George W. Bush presidency.

There was no Guinness to be had the last time I met with Professor Tabak, this time in his office on the Georgetown campus. He was putting the finishing touches on what would be his final book, *The Waning of the Mediterranean, 1550–1870*.

I revealed to him some of my frustrations working an especially slippery issue at CIA. He was intrigued, but not shocked. On a happier note, I told him about how satisfying it was for my wife and I to have our own business up and running outside the maddening world of Washington.

This decision to cut away and start something new didn't surprise him in the least. "This is the system," he said, referring to America's capitalist economy, a hand lightly punctuating his thought in the air. Of course you want to get out and make money for yourself, he observed. It's the American way.

Sadly, less than a year later in February 2008, Tabak suffered a cerebral hemorrhage after visiting with family overseas in Ankara. He was just in his mid-fifties when he passed.

I owe a debt of gratitude to Faruk Tabak for having given me such a better grasp of the ways of the world.

23 / CROSSING THE LINE

I simply have nothing nice to say about Bonnie, my last supervisor in CP/NE. And the reason has little to do with the fact that she was the one to ultimately fire me from the Saudi CMO post in early April 2007. While she delivered the "pink" slip that morning, she was just so completely detached from the important work we were doing there in CIA's Counter-Proliferation Division. In a word, she was indifferent, a sentiment shared by most everyone else in the office, contractor and staff alike.

Best I can recall, she had been an art history major in college. How she wound up working in intelligence was anyone's guess. I genuinely hope (for her sake) that she has since found another career track because I can't see how she could possibly find any real happiness as an Agency "lifer."

Sometime not long before my second daughter was born in December 2006, Bonnie was transferred internally to CP/NE from another section of CPD. Before long, she had me give her an overview of the Saudi account, which I had been covering for about a year up to that point.

As I sat down in her office, I told her up front that much of my view of things was based on the imagery analysis, the one thing she seemed familiar with as I spoke. I explained that the issue, for whatever reason, just wasn't getting any traction with collectors overseas. But by the time I started getting into the details, she was entirely disinterested.

I very much doubt that any of the rudimentary information I provided really registered with her that day. China's delivery of CSS-2 ballistic missiles to the kingdom back in 1988 could probably as easily have been a dozen Russian fighter jets for all she cared.

* * *

Sometime after this, about two months prior to my departure from CPD, Bonnie directed me—in no uncertain terms—to cease in my interactions with counterparts at NGA.

Bonnie's office was out of earshot from my cubicle, but I sat immediately opposite a woman who served as sort of the perennial second-in-charge of the group of CMO's I was assigned to in CP/NE. The woman's name was Sandy, not to be confused with the front office's *Sandra*. On both a personal and working level, Sandy and I got along just fine.

But unless she came in during the morning with an iPod blasting in her ears (or perhaps some other distraction), there's no way Sandy couldn't have listened in on at least a few of the phone conversations I would have on a semiregular basis with the analysts at NGA. This was almost certainly how Bonnie and management above her were aware of my incredibly irresponsible behavior.

If Bonnie asked, Sandy would have been hard pressed to say that I wasn't still every so often talking shop with Joe, my contact at NGA.

Fast forward now to less than a month prior to my final day in CPD. A tipper report had come in for Headquarters review concerning the pending arrival of yet another Chinese ship into Jeddah.

By this time, confusing as things were in terms of CP/NE's working relationship with SIG, I understood that because the pending report dealt strictly with *ship's movement* information (when a ship was scheduled to pull into a given port) that SIG would take responsibility for ensuring that it was coordinated and disseminated accordingly.

Several days went by, however, and the report was still sitting in SIG's cue. No one in SIG had yet gone to the trouble of checking to make sure that all of the *I*'s were dotted and *T*'s were crossed in the report and—most importantly—that the information was deemed reliable from Headquarters' perspective. So I sent Stephanie in SIG an instant message online to remind her that the shipment was set to arrive in Jeddah soon and that the report would be of assistance to others in the intelligence community, particularly NGA. I remember this chat session with Stephanie ending rather abruptly on her end, but I still came away thinking that she planned to get it out in time.

But more time went by and then it was just a day or so before the ship was set to arrive in the kingdom. Rather than ping SIG again, I decided to just cut to the chase and communicate informally on the substance of the report directly with NGA. This sort of coordination had been going on between CP/NE and NGA Saudi analysts since back when the first Steve was getting his hands dirty with the issue.

With Steve #2 standing over my shoulder as I drafted the message to Joe at NGA, I provided the general details of the shipment as described in the pending intelligence report. "Yeah, send it," Steve agreed, not thinking twice about it. Such tippers had been useful not a few times in the past for NGA to gauge which segments of time to pay closer attention to in the nightly dumps of imagery from U.S. satellites over the Arabian peninsula. And this time was no different. *Click*, off my note went to Joe at NGA, in his office in the old Navy Yard in southwest DC.

As sensible as this seemed at the time, my gut was telling me that I had really crossed a line. Bonnie's directions had been crystal clear only a few weeks before: Jonathan, do *not* communicate anymore with NGA. Do you understand? Yes, I understood.

If memory serves, the report was finally released from SIG, but it was disseminated on the very same day as the shipment's arrival in Jeddah, useless to the guys at NGA—along with everyone else tracking the maritime activity of the Red Sea's busiest port.

But it just didn't matter anymore. A few days after sending that note to NGA, I began to quietly clear out my desk.

* * *

What I'm about to describe was at once both shockingly surreal and sobering in a grave sort of way. Having heard little to nothing during my time working Saudi from CIA's counterparts over at the Department of Defense, a startling message came in one day.

The text of the message was innocuous enough. Apparently a U.S. defense attaché operating in country had been gifted a few trinkets from his Saudi military counterpart. The Saudi happened to be a member of the Strategic Rocket Forces. Interesting.

The militaries of the world are of course no different than most every other professional organization. The U.S. military has its many symbolic uniform patches and organizational crests and, as I was about to find out, so too did Saudi Arabia's SRF.

The U.S. attaché indicated that the SRF officer had provided him with a writing pen and men's wristwatch, both ostensibly as a sign of professional respect or perhaps simply as a gift. But there was a curious military crest contained in each item, the attaché noted. Did anyone at CIA happen to know what this new SRF crest was supposed to mean?

I really didn't have a response when I opened the first JPEG photo attachments. They were, as the message described, a watch and pen not unlike those you'd see in a corporate gift shop or, as I was thinking, a U.S. Navy ship's store.

But the attaché's concern became clear as I opened up the additional photo files. The end cap of the pen, the silken lining of its case and the face of the watch all shared the same graphic: a pair of crossed missiles, some Arabic script and, shockingly, the universal *atomic* symbol—that little diagram of several elliptical electron orbits traced symmetrically around a centered nucleus. It was plain as day there in the attaché's digital picture, right under the glass face of a rather expensive looking timepiece.

Was this a prank? I immediately started asking myself, and later Steve and Tom once I had forwarded it to them. Is this an elaborate hoax? If it is, it's a damn good one, we all agreed.

The pictures looked authentic and there was certainly nothing suspicious about the amplifying information that had accompanied them from the attaché. Even so, maybe the SRF officer was put up to this somehow. After all, it's pretty easy to have just about anything you want made up these days if you have the money, and the world's graphics design and jewelry pros were no exception. It doesn't matter if your order is *legit* or not. It's just business in the end.

But my gut was telling me that the objects pictured were indeed the real deal. The way the attaché described receiving them, the look of the items and, most strikingly, the styling of the crest. All of this, and of course the fact that this was the very road I had been going down in my mind for some time by this point. The internationally recognized atomic symbol over a pair of ballistic missiles—what more could one possibly say? The analysts in the DI withheld comment until we heard back from an Arabic linguist.

The military detachment name and unit number specified in the crest suggested that it was quite possibly legitimate, although there was a difference of opinion as to whether it necessarily represented a *Saudi* military unit. Of course there was a difference of opinion, I thought. Did the attaché's own words not suffice?

I put some follow-up questions together which got sent back to the military attaché on the ground in Saudi:

- Could he confirm that the SRF officer was in fact assigned to the unit designated in the crest?
- What SRF base was he assigned to?
- And what did the atomic symbol represent *specifically*?

But if and when CPD ever heard anything back on this, I would never know. My time there in the basement was getting very short.

* * *

Two weeks before my dismissal, CPD's deputy chief of reports, Julie, sat in on one of CP/NE's CMO group meetings.

"And thank you for all your hard work over the last..."—her hand waved in the air at some vague span of time.

Staring straight at me as she said this, Julie may likely have been referring to my past eighteen months on the Saudi account. She offered a smile, too, though faint. I nodded, acknowledging a comment that seemed directed at no one else.

But my upper lip stiffened a little as I stared back at her. I did not return the smile.

* * *

My last morning on the Saudi WMD account in CPD's Near East Branch began as it typically did, with a trip to the cafeteria for a cup of Dunkin' Donuts coffee (if the line wasn't too long), a bran muffin and some fresh pineapple.

But after an hour or so back at my desk, having read through the overnight message traffic and having started in on the online *Wall Street Journal*, I sent fellow contractor Scott an instant message. Would he mind taking a short walk with me? I needed to vent.

I didn't say much to Scott that morning in the hall outside CP/NE, but I said enough for him to understand that things between me and management had taken a turn for the worse. I didn't see how things could continue much longer.

As I'm getting this off my chest, a fellow SpecTal contractor just happened to walk by in the hall. He was doing the same job I once did as a SpecTal "program manager," serving as our company's point-of-contact with the customer—CIA's CPD. He nodded coyly at me and continued—as I would only later find out—on his way to *Bonnie's* office.

When I got back to my desk, an instant message was flashing on the computer screen. Bonnie wanted to see me in her office. I knew exactly what was coming.

She had me close the door and began briefly recounting how she had asked me several weeks prior not to continue corresponding with NGA on Saudi matters. Bonnie spoke to me and my SpecTal colleague alternately as she explained that, because I had continued to do so, I was going to have to leave my position in CP/NE. Immediately.

The thought didn't even cross my mind to protest. Not with Bonnie. She was just the messenger. As I later found out, she actually rotated on from her position only a short time after. The answer to how management knew that I was staying in touch with NGA was obvious. The cubicle wall between me and Sandy was awfully thin.

No, the only thing I could think to say—and I had a hard time getting it out to be honest—was that I felt I had done the right thing. In short, incomplete sentences I explained to Bonnie's deaf ears that there had been a report about an impending arrival at Jeddah, that it would have been helpful to analysts at NGA…Oh, why bother.

I made a few quick stops to say "I'm outta here" (and not much else) to some of the people I had worked with over the past twenty-seven months in CPD—including eighteen on Saudi. Tom wasn't around, so I missed saying goodbye to him. But Steve #2 was at his desk. He had a puzzled look on his face as I told him I was leaving in a few minutes. I didn't want to get into it.

Back at my desk one last time, I shut my computer down and grabbed my coffee mug and the portable water heater I had used so many times to make tea there at my desk, just as I had learned from Foxwell during my interim as a trainee in Central Eurasia division years earlier.

Finally out of the vault, I was in the corridor leading to the elevator. Who do I run into on the way out but Phil, the very guy who had shown me the ropes (such as they were) on the Saudi situation back when I first started on the account. The fatalistic joke we had shared over the previous eighteen months about someday possibly getting hit by a "milk truck" (*getting the ax*) finally paid off. I was just too wrought up to say much more than a few words.

"*Milk truck* came," I said. No explanation necessary as I avoided direct eye contact. I was about to lose it. Phil was sorry to hear it and seemed a bit stunned himself.

We shook hands and then I made my way to the elevator.

I was numb that entire drive home back to St. Michaels. But I do remember not going straight back to the house on North Harbor Road. The au pair would have the girls for another several hours still.

I headed to Harbor Palm to tell Christa what happened.

* * *

Ed, one of SpecTal's executives at the time, asked me afterwards what precipitated my sudden departure from CPD. I responded with the words "it was getting very political," realizing instantly how bush league this must have sounded.

Ed was a well regarded retired case officer. He knew full well that *everything* at CIA was political—it's the nature of the work. And here's this thirty-something kid, telling him that the reason for his removal from a CMO account was "political." But what other way was there to say it? Besides, Ed wasn't interested in an in depth explanation; it was a done deal by that point.

I found out later that Janet, the CP/NE Branch Chief, had called a branch all-hands up at the front of the vault not long after my departure to inform everyone that I had in fact been removed from the Saudi account and that—just to clear up any rumors that might be going around—this happened due to my failure to abide by CPD policy in its dealings with outside agencies, specifically NGA.

Of course, Janet said nothing of the fact that such sharing of information with NGA had not been unheard of in CP/NE—particularly in relation to the Saudi matter, even well prior to my arrival. Nonetheless, Janet concluded her announcement by saying that, due to his indiscretions, Jonathan Scherck would never be allowed to work in CPD again.

When I heard about Janet's rather explicit announcement months later (over beers with some former colleagues) this really broke my heart—but only so much. By that time I was well aware of the fact that this was all so much bigger than me.

But it didn't help matters that SpecTal quickly found a replacement to cover the Saudi CMO slot. A real superstar, apparently, as I later found out. *Utterly incompetent.* Not my words, mind you. I've never met the person.

Not surprisingly, CPD management would keep my replacement on until well after both Steve and Tom had themselves moved on from this debacle.

* * *

In the end, those twenty-seven months working in CPD had been a crash course on the surreal Machiavellian world of global energy politics and nuclear weapons.

Over time, any doubts I had in my initial understanding of what transpired at the highest levels between the Bush administration and Riyadh (and between Riyadh and Beijing) would yield to a certain and profound disappointment in a president and vice president whom I had put much faith into during those first months following 9/11.

But this reality would hit home well after returning to St. Michaels on that day in early April 2007. With two beautiful daughters in my life and a store on Maryland's Eastern Shore to help my wife run, I still had—happily so—a very full plate.

24 / BEACHED

As busy as we were with the store during that first summer, there were still a few times that Christa and I were able to take some time off with Chloe and Sidney.

One day we decided to visit Ocean City, Maryland's largest Atlantic beach destination. At a minimum, I figured we could let the girls get their feet wet in the ocean and play in the sand. Christa was less enthused with the plan given Ocean City's more *touristy* reputation, but was happy just the same to break away for the day.

We were driving east along highway 50 towards the coast when Christa got a call from American Express. The credit card company was calling about a customer from Virginia who had visited Harbor Palm over the previous weekend. She had charged over six thousand dollars to her card for the purchase of some fine bed linens. Could Christa please verify the transaction? AmEx wanted to know.

Oh, it was real, alright, Christa assured the account manager. We were actually still giddy about the sale even as we were getting into the car earlier that morning for the drive to the beach.

The home furnishings Christa selected for the upstairs of Harbor Palm were all premium. Ann Gish, one of the store's bedding lines, was no exception. Ann Gish styles go by names like *Aquamarine Dupione Stripe* and *Chocolate Pumice Monaco*. These are some serious pillow cases.

Along with the rest of the "upstairs room" (as Christa and I referred to it), the bedding sold at Harbor Palm catered to a very particular St. Michaels clientele, a customer that often has the luxury to pick and choose the best times of the year to live in that charming part of Maryland's Eastern Shore.

* * *

When we finally got to Ocean City…well, let's just say it didn't remind me of Grace Bay in Turks and Caicos.

But I set up the umbrella, laid out the beach blanket, and took out the shovels and buckets for Chloe to play with—Sidney, too, although Sid wasn't even a year old yet at the time.

Chloe could have stayed and played in the sand at the edge of the surf all afternoon, but after ninety minutes or so, Christa had had enough. And, to be honest, I had as well.

Before packing it in for the day, my cell phone rang. The number read "703," which I knew to be northern Virginia's area code. I had no clue who it could be.

It turned out to be a young woman by the name of Hilary, from my old company SpecTal. I had met her once or twice during my time working at CIA. She always seemed quite pleasant in person.

Hilary's reason for calling me out of the blue over the summer of 2007— months after I had been ejected from my CMO position in CPD—was that she wanted to know whether I would be interested in a new position supporting the embryonic (at that time) Office of the Director of National Intelligence. The position would be mostly administrative in nature, not involving the more substantive work I had been doing as a CMO. Nevertheless, Hilary politely explained, it was an option and SpecTal would happily submit my resume for consideration to the government hiring manager if I was interested.

I don't know for sure what Hilary knew of the circumstances surrounding my removal from the Saudi account. But beyond whatever excuse CPD's chief of reports Olivia had provided to CIA's contracting officer to justify my dismissal, Hilary obviously didn't know what I knew.

Still, when I answered with a flat "no," she didn't press the issue, which I appreciated.

"I totally understand," Hilary replied.

Well, she didn't *totally* understand, but I knew what she was getting at. The call ended.

I looked at my two daughters playing nearby and then over at my wife. Christa totally understood.

25 / WORTH THE DRIVE

By the end of that summer in 2007, after taking a much needed six month hiatus from one terribly dysfunctional corner of the U.S. intelligence community, I regrettably succumbed to financial realities and would take yet one more federal contracting job in northern Virginia. This time (my final stint in the IC) I would be working at the National Counter-Terrorism Center (NCTC), less than a ten minute drive up the road from CIA Headquarters.

NCTC was an all new level of U.S. counter-terrorism bureaucracy in the post-9/11 era, one that was still in its early stages when I started there in November 2007. Somehow (beyond my comprehension) the conclusion of members of Congress and decision makers in the Bush administration had been not only that the CIA and FBI needed to be working more closely with each other on CT matters, they also now needed to be working with two *more* independent bureaucracies: NCTC and the newly formed Department of Homeland Security.

The federal government's existing counter-terrorism capabilities already residing in FBI, CIA and the Department of Defense—well before the World Trade Center towers fell in 2001—really would have to work harder and smarter now, as they tried to make sense of all the sniffles and burps of two newborn (and unbelievably costly) layers of Washington bureaucracy. With two young mouths to feed, a start-up business to support and my Top Secret clearance still in hand, it so happened that I was looking for work as a contractor at *both* of these agencies there in the late summer of 2007.

I would have just as easily wound up working at the Department of Homeland Security except that NCTC beat her to the punch and hired me first.

* * *

Over the course of my brief time working in the Information Sharing and Knowledge Development Directorate (ISKD) at NCTC, I would come to recognize that my job description boiled down to a single sentence—and little more: Get management here at NCTC to make *biometrics* a priority.

If this sounds strange to you, don't fret. It's quite simple actually. Believe it or not, I didn't have a lick of biometrics training myself when I took the NCTC position, and I was able to quickly catch on just fine.

In the movies, when the cops happen upon the murder weapon, they're almost always able to "dust for prints"—fingerprints. The only thing you need to know about fingerprints in the "biometrics" world of the federal government and the Global War on Terrorism (as it was more aptly called back in the George W. Bush years) is that your (the reader's) prints are different from mine. And mine are different from those of the Egyptian Ahmed Mohamed Hamed Ali who, in August 1998, facilitated the bombing of the American embassies in Dar es Salaam, Tanzania, and Nairobi, Kenya.

I had been hired by NCTC management as only the second contractor to help coordinate the Center's efforts in the biometrics realm. Yes, other parts of the federal government had already been working in biometrics for years but, as I mentioned, the powers that be in Washington had decided to dump a great deal of taxpayer dollars into creating a new expert entity in the field. Move over FBI (an agency having advanced fingerprint analytic capabilities that went back decades to the days of J. Edgar Hoover), NCTC's new Terrorist Identities Datamart Environment (known by the acronym "TIDE") was the federal government's new kid on the biometrics block.

TIDE was mandated by Congress to be the U.S. government's new *consolidated* database on all "known or suspected" international terrorists. As the Center's website states, TIDE "supports the U.S. government's various terrorist screening systems or 'watchlists' and the U.S. Intelligence Community's overall counter-terrorism mission." The problem in the fall of 2007 was that the U.S. military and FBI were in possession of various biometric data (i.e. terrorist fingerprints, facial images and eye scans) that TIDE simply did not have in its holdings in any useful and accessible form.

During the first few weeks of my mostly uneventful tenure at NCTC, I met with the senior government manager overseeing TIDE operations, a career government civil service officer by the name of Russell E. Travers. Travers, serving as NCTC's deputy director for Information Sharing and Knowledge Development (ISKD) at the time, stated quite matter-of-factly in reference to my stay as a contractor in his directorate that I was going to "see some waste" during my time working at NCTC.

Was Mr. Travers referring to me? I asked myself sitting there in his office. By "waste" was he referring to the $200K the federal government had expended that fiscal year to see to it that I would only be keeping a seat warm in NCTC office space? Unfortunately, I would come to conclude during my twenty-one months there at NCTC that this is precisely what Travers was saying to me. To say that biometrics wasn't even on the radar of NCTC leadership in late 2007 would be a gross understatement.

Up to that point, the TIDE database had been almost completely biographical in terms of the information it contained. There was the occasional JPEG mug shot that the government had acquired either in person or perhaps from some open-source outlet but, by and large, the government's centralized database for international terrorists did not provide biometric data on terror suspects; information that was becoming increasingly available as the U.S. military's engagement of such individuals was expanding exponentially on the front lines of the War on Terrorism.

The other point to highlight here is that biometric data (infinitely more useful in identifying a given individual than, say, a terrorist's surname or passport number) are tremendously useful in screening the ebb and flow of people over America's borders. At places like JFK Airport in New York or at the land border between the U.S. and Mexico just south of San Diego, the ability to scan a suspicious person's fingertips and quickly compare the results to fingerprint records known by authorities to belong to a watch-listed individual—this is an incredibly powerful weapon in the War on Terrorism.

The problem in late-2007 and (I hate to say) even still at the time of my departure from NCTC in the summer of 2009, was that TIDE remained incapable of ingesting and processing such critical data. It wasn't for lack of trying on my part, or any of the several more contractors that would eventually be hired on to try to rectify the situation. The problem had to do with NCTC's civil service leadership failing to make biometrics a priority in the development of an upgraded TIDE database.

The technical development of a next-generation TIDE system had been an ongoing parallel effort, one managed by the federal contracting juggernaut Boeing. TIDE II (as it was called when I was at NCTC) was a multi-million dollar software development project that absolutely needed to be joined at the hip with the push for a new biometrics capability at NCTC. Sadly, support for this new capability just wasn't gaining steam. NCTC's management was strangely content with mere fixes to the existing biographic-based database, only the "low-hanging fruit" as several of them inexplicably preferred to settle for.

The dysfunction I had witnessed in CPD was plain as day all over again there at NCTC, albeit in a less insidious form. Nevertheless, was the federal government not spending tens of millions of taxpayers' dollars on an effort that—with only a few strategic personnel decisions here and there—could have easily been accomplished in two years' time?

Bear in mind, there were already companies at the time in the American private sector that specialized in building these sorts of information management systems, lashing biographic information to corresponding biometric data—names and passport numbers to peoples' faces and fingerprints. Indeed, Deputy Director Travers had himself acknowledged the need to incorporate biometrics into NCTC's business process *years* earlier in a statement he made to the National Commission on Terrorist Attacks Upon The United States in January 2004.

In the "Future Developments and Future Challenges" section of his comments submitted for the record, Travers cited technical development efforts at the time, noting that TIDE:

"will fulfill not only a watchlisting mission, but will also be used as an analytic tool. This database will begin to incorporate biometrics to form true 'identities,' rather than using a purely name-based system."

And yet there we were in 2008 and 2009, *over four years later,* myself and my fellow biometrics teammates on one side in ISKD supporting NCTC management, the software developers at Boeing ready to build the solution on the other—all of us waiting idly for NCTC's leadership to simply levy the requirement, to commit (both on paper and in countless meetings on the matter) to this powerful new way of tracking "true identities." It was an obvious course to take, one that was known all along.

But the biometrics requirement—as explicitly called for even in an official White House directive signed by President Bush in June 2008—would instead be viewed at the bureaucratic level of the U.S. intelligence community as only a "nice-to-have" capability. Far from being an imperative, the transition to biometrics was strangely regarded as *optional* by federal bureaucrats whom either didn't fully grasp the benefits of the technology or, worse, simply didn't have the initiative to see it through in a timely fashion. And this would be just fine, apparently, as there was simply no accountability on the matter at NCTC, or even within the now familiar (from my time working the Saudi issue) Office of the Director of National Intelligence, responsible for oversight of the Center.

The end result of all this foot dragging was that, as the Department of Homeland Security was moving forward with its new biometrically enabled screening system at the nation's borders, NCTC was being left in the dust. And while NCTC has since gotten its act together and gotten more up to speed in its ability to store and process biometric data, a considerable amount of time and money was needlessly wasted over many years.

I'm just at a loss as to why it had to be this way given Travers' comment to me early on in my time at NCTC. If it was known that "waste" was going on, why the hell didn't someone step up and do more to make biometrics a priority? Clearly, the Center was in many ways a redundant addition to the intelligence community, but now that it was bought and paid for by Congress (and ultimately the American taxpayer), why was so little effort being made to ensure that NCTC was fulfilling its stated goals?

And so, not long after arriving at NCTC, I was very often by mid-afternoon of the workday anxious to make that long but worthwhile drive back over the bay bridge to St. Michaels, where life made sense once more.

* * *

If I may, the failure highlighted herein of Vice President Cheney in his role as principle foreign policy advisor to President Bush aside for a moment, I want to mention one of the real highlights for me while working at NCTC.

It came totally unexpected in December 2008, little over a month before he would be succeeded in office by President Barack Obama. President Bush made a surprising farewell visit to NCTC. And had I known I was going to be meeting a sitting U.S. president that day, I most certainly would have worn a coat and tie for my picture with him.

Now, you're damn right it crossed my mind to get a quick word in with him personally on the whole Saudi affair. When he had supposedly said years earlier that the Saudi King would have a man's *balls sliced off*—as the PDB briefer relayed from his meeting earlier that one morning in the Oval—had W. really meant that? I amused myself with this question (ever so briefly) as the President of the United States approached.

As I shook his hand, I said the only thing I could think of when shaking the hand of the leader of the free world. "It's an honor." He smiled, looked me straight in the eyes, but said nothing.

On his way out of the room he paused near the group I was standing with and observed with not a little bravado, "Ya know, every day as president has been joyous." His Texas swagger was in full effect as he hinted (I felt at least) at his belief in a higher being, something I share with the man. You have to see him in person, he's quite a charismatic presence, regardless of your political views...and regardless of what I thought of his decision to look the other way on Saudi.

"Some days are up, and some days are down. But every day as president is joyous," Bush intoned before walking away.

26 / OVER DINNER

Our habit of taking walks—first with our dog Prada and then with Chloe in the stroller—around Capitol Hill's Lincoln Park continued during the time we lived on the Eastern Shore in St. Michaels. Only now we added another family member, our baby daughter Sidney.

These evening walks would be just as pleasant. The stress of working the Saudi account had begun to recede, but of course it had been replaced by new stresses. I was still commuting to and from DC as I had when I was at CIA, only now I was at NCTC. And, honestly, as great as it was for Christa to be running our own retail store, I was beginning to have a feeling in my gut that we didn't have as much working capital on hand as we were probably going to need, especially if store sales started to sag for whatever reason.

While I wasn't physically working at CPD any longer, my mind would often drift back to the issue—back to the madness of my time in the basement of Headquarters—whether on the drive to Washington or walking the girls and Prada around St. Michaels. Over and over again, I would think of the many angles of my CPD experience, including the administrative procedures I had to follow as manager of what little intelligence came in on the Saudi matter.

In hindsight, it often seemed that someone with a perverse sense of irony had been responsible for assigning the code words to the pair of "compartments" created during this particular time for the Saudi account. The virtual receptacle for cable traffic pertaining to operational matters had been dubbed SUPERCELL. The corresponding compartment for any resulting raw intelligence could have come from W. himself: DECIDED. I mean, in retrospect, this was all a sick joke. SUPERCELL? More like SUPER*SOLD*. DECIDED? Most certainly.

* * *

As I think back now, yet one more headache that prevailed during these years comes to mind. A big one.

Mary Margaret Graham, a career U.S. intelligence officer who served as deputy director of National Intelligence for Collection from 2005 to 2008, had been a major factor on all things Saudi for our small band in CP/NE. I never met the woman, although I did pay several visits to her executive assistant in a futile attempt to get Graham to correct what I felt, at the time, had been possibly just a frustrating oversight.

Today, I can't say with certainty that it was calculated, but what Graham did, in finally signing off on the creation of these much needed compartments in the 2006 timeframe, was to restrict the subject matter to be contained in DECIDED to only those raw intelligence reports that pertained to—and *only to*—the *delivery of ballistic missiles* into Saudi Arabia. If a report so much as touched on another topic, the argument could be made (and it was) that it didn't belong in DECIDED.

There just wasn't a whole lot of HUMINT reporting available to begin with on the actual delivery of ballistic missiles into the kingdom. We certainly weren't getting anything on the China end at that time. And regarding the expedited nighttime handling of the shipping containers into and then quickly out of Jeddah port (remember the Chinese men in thobes report?)...folks weren't saying much about what was inside the containers during these small windows of time either. The only chance we had to see (or hear) that these shipments constituted nothing less than a new world order for the Strategic Rocket Forces was when they were getting unpacked—ever so carefully—at the various Saudi missile bases inside the kingdom, and by then it was too late.

And so the "dots," as it were—the Chinese men in thobes report, the indication of a refrigeration requirement for a particular shipment, the "more than just rockets" quote attributed to a Jeddah port operator—this human intelligence (and I defy anyone who was insisting otherwise at the time to argue today that these sound-bites of information weren't of value) would just have to do without a proper home, according to Mary Margaret up in the Office of the

Director of National Intelligence, several bureaucratic rungs above those of us actually trying to work the target in CIA.

I took issue with the narrow definition contained in the "Mary Margaret Memo" almost as soon as it came down to us in CP/NE. I can't remember the number of emails I wrote or the number of conversations I had with my CMO management complaining about how counterintuitive the DECIDED guidelines were. Assuming lightning struck and we actually got something, where would we put a report on, say, a nuclear warhead or even a *conventional* warhead—in transit to the kingdom? After all, the Saudis would have to put something on top of all those new missiles they were getting from China.

Crickets. Nothing but silence from ODNI on this question which, I was told, CPD management had raised on more than one occasion. Mary Margaret Graham, who had earned two prestigious government service medals (the National Intelligence Medal of Achievement in 1996 and the CIA's Donovan Award in 2001), was now, in 2006, inexplicably content to just let all of this arguably significant information fall to the cutting room floor. If a report in from Riyadh or Jeddah didn't pertain *specifically* to ballistic missiles entering Saudi Arabia—gosh, we're awfully sorry, but CPD just doesn't have a place to put it.

And there they very likely sit even today, in the form of electrons on archive computer servers at CIA. *More than just rockets. Suspicious Chinese technicians wearing Saudi thobes at Jeddah port.* Bits and traces of the big picture, all collecting virtual dust.

* * *

Not to be outdone, the name decreed from on high by Mary Margaret's office for the overall Saudi WMD "cabinet" containing its two aptly named compartments would be, I must say, rather imperious amongst its more pedestrian contemporaries at the Agency. EMPOWER. Enough said.

Coincidence or not, this was a done deal already. We were just cogs in the intelligence bureaucracy on a dead account. Just going through the motions.

* * *

As my family and I were rounding the corner onto Water Street near dinner time one evening, I quickly saw that a motorcade was making its way towards us in the opposite direction. And as it drove closer I could see that, whoever it was, this motorcade was rather considerable for the small town of St. Michaels. There were several unmarked minivans up front, the limousine and then (the telltale sign) a large black Suburban bringing up the rear.

As the shiny black limo passed by, I saw none other than the vice president. Dick Cheney was sitting right there in the far back passenger's seat, not but three feet from where I stood.

"That's Dick Cheney," I said under my breath.

If his bullet proof window had been rolled down just a bit, I could have reached over and tapped him on the shoulder. "Hi there, Dick," I could have said. Alas, it was more like two ships passing in the night.

As Cheney's motorcade passed out of sight, me and my gang continued our walk up onto Talbot Street. After walking a few blocks along the main drag, I knew almost immediately where the vice president's motorcade had wound up.

The restaurant Bistro St. Michaels is widely considered to be the best in town, the only close contender being Town Dock. Bistro is the kind of restaurant that a couple can easily spend $100 on a single outing, not including the bottle of wine and tip. Cheney and his party had good taste that evening.

With Sidney in the stroller and Chloe and Prada just ahead of us, we made our way along the sidewalk in front of Bistro passing three or four U.S. Secret Service agents who were posted out front. Cheney had already been whisked to his table. His limousine was parked across the street near the end of Grace Street where it dead-ends into Talbot. The Secret Service had left just enough room for the more low-key Scherck *stroller*-cade to cruise on by. Christa and I grinned at each other.

We continued along on our walk home past Bistro, past Gallerie Français (a neat little lithograph store) and then finally past our very own Harbor Palm. As usual, the display windows of our store looked fantastic. Christa always made sure they did.

* * *

We never did get to have dinner at Bistro. Come to think of it, my family and I never even made it out on a boat around St. Michaels during our time there. That has to be a crime in someone's book. St. Michaels is one of the most popular sailing destinations on the Chesapeake, second only to Annapolis. But two small daughters—both under the age of four at that time—and working to get a small business off the ground will do that to you.

That evening I had come within only feet of the man who had been the *real* "decider" in the decision to turn a blind eye on the Saudis' oil-for-nukes deal with the Chinese. And yet we were poles apart on whether such complicity was warranted.

Playing devil's advocate on Cheney's and President Bush's behalf, the overriding factor could have been that the U.S. had only so much political capital to expend on the Middle East at a time when the first priority was to see the toppling of the Iraq regime to an acceptably stable conclusion. The planting of the flag of democracy (as it was advertised)—which I and millions of Americans didn't argue with at the time—*that* was the priority...along with dismantling Saddam's dangerous weapons program, that is.

Assuming Bush and Cheney's realization about the Saudis' nuclear weapons intentions coincided with the troubling shipment into Jeddah in December 2003, there was no alternate course of action by that point, not with the ongoing prosecution of the Iraq war and the subsequent Neo-conservative hopes for democratizing that country—as Paul Wolfowitz and his gang of fiercely proactive brave new world pols over at the Pentagon had been scheming even well before the game-changing events of 9/11. The "shock and awe" campaign to finally remove Saddam Hussein from power had already begun on March 20, 2003, months prior to the alarming arrival from China. Washington would have to pretend that this all just wasn't happening.

Riyadh's support of Bush's decision on the Iraq front may well in the end have tied his and Cheney's hands when it came to the Saudis' newly discovered security arrangement with Beijing. Forceful protest of the missile deal might have been entertained by the two men, but perhaps the king had Bandar tell Bush to not even think about it. Saudi Arabia was going to arm itself in the face of regional instability and Iran's Ahmadinejad, regardless of any objections from Washington. But I maintain that if this theoretical scenario is indeed how things played out, it was still reprehensible in the end to have remained silent as the whole mess unfolded. If not the United States to stand up against the proliferation of weapons of mass destruction in the world, then who?

Without question, if President Bush had made the difficult decision to challenge both Riyadh and Beijing on this devilish deal, (and it would have to have been both), the United States government may likely have lost official Saudi support for the war in Iraq and the increasingly involved campaign against international terrorism. Worse, the U.S. economy back at home may have been held for ransom as the king in Riyadh could have decided to cut the flow of oil from the kingdom, thus punishing Bush for intervening in his sovereign right to a nuclear arsenal all his own.

Worse still, perhaps China might have been tempted into the fray, deciding itself to flex some military muscle in the Taiwan straits. After all, the Non-Proliferation Treaty notwithstanding, it was now Beijing's prerogative here in the post-Cold War era to broker its own brand of energy deals with the oil rich countries of the world. Who was President Bush anyways, with blood on his hands in Iraq, to say that President Hu couldn't barter for Saudi crude using China's own stockpile of nuclear missiles?

Beijing—Washington's partner in what will undoubtedly prove to be the most important international bilateral relationship of the twenty-first century—could have as well easily toyed with Western financial markets by perhaps announcing aggressive retaliatory measures aimed at calling in the U.S. government's sizable debt to the People's Republic. *So, Washington wants to play the role of international policeman again, eh?*—the thinking could have gone in Beijing—*Let's see how long that lasts when America can't even pay the interest on her debt anymore.* Such steps would have been (and would be no less so today) rife with crippling complications for America's chief banker, but China would have sent a most powerful message.

* * *

As grim as some of these scenarios might seem, wouldn't such factors arguing against a more forceful stance have been outweighed by the more immediate obligation to get it right on the issue of nuclear weapons proliferation?

After all, this had been—in principle at least—one of President Bush's primary reasons for going to war with Iraq.

Wouldn't Bush have actually redeemed himself after the American people learned that he had no clothes with his justifications for the war against Saddam? I think this absolutely would have been the case. But Bush, at Cheney's urging I'm convinced, allowed political expediency to rule the day. And as a consequence, George W. Bush would get no redemption song for his handling of China's fateful shipments to Saudi Arabia.

This wasn't to be for reasons that I both can and can't begin to imagine. It's possible that my view of things is skewed chronologically, that Bush and Cheney were aware of Riyadh's nuclear intentions prior to the telltale shipment late in 2003. Perhaps it was President Clinton and his National Security Advisor Sandy Berger who had first learned of the possible deal even before Bush and Cheney took office in 2001; the secret may have been passed from the 42nd president to the 43rd.

It may be that Vice President Cheney, particularly following his days working as an oil executive at Halliburton, had a keener sense for the kind of catastrophic impact a crisis in America's relationship with the Saudis might have had if Bush had put his foot down on the missile deal with Beijing. Perhaps even I (opposed as I am to the course Cheney endorsed through this *Catch-22*) would have been made more a believer by whatever Top Secret forecast there may have been at the time out of Treasury or the Federal Reserve: an irrevocably crippled U.S. economy and, by that point, a military hung out to dry as its fuel thirsty F-14 Tomcats sat grounded indefinitely on the decks of American aircraft carriers in the Gulf.

But I take this devil's advocacy much too far.

Sometime before or at the time I am assuming—late 2003, *after* the start of the second Gulf War—even under these worst of conditions, President Bush would have had the opportunity to turn the page in America's history of addiction to foreign oil. Canadian oil production could have been spiked to help compensate for at least some of the shortfall resulting in a loss of Saudi production. Over the short run, America's own strategic oil reserves could have been tapped as well to buy some time for Washington to get it right in its stance on Beijing's proliferation activity.

The result would have been dicey times for the American people, no question about it. It would have been the oil crisis of the late 1970s all over again in the United States. But when it was all over, America would have been stronger for it. We could have finally turned the corner in our senseless dependence on Saudi oil.

Better still, perhaps American industry would have been kick-started into producing—on a grand scale at long last—*renewable* energy-based transportation alternatives, an ultimate fix that has been possible for years except, of course, for Washington's love affair with the world's oil barons. But, again, this was not to be.

* * *

Barring a future Congressional inquiry, the American people will likely never know the details of the discreet communiqués that took place amongst Washington, Riyadh and Beijing during this time.

Was the White House initially told that the king was merely considering a deal with Beijing, only to later be informed that an agreement had been reached? Or was it known to be a fait accompli from the beginning, perhaps part of some back channel negotiations in connection with the war in Iraq or, potentially, the evolving nuclear standoff with Iran?

I just don't know enough to say precisely, even as one of a small group of people working the issue for the U.S. government. But I am no less certain because of my working level perspective that a deal was ultimately closed. And whereas Dick Cheney had been instrumental in crafting the trumped-up charges against Saddam Hussein, the White House would say nothing about the very real crime going on just south of Iraq on the Arabian Peninsula.

Thus, the Bush administration's hypocritical approach to weapons proliferation in the world would come full circle.

* * *

While Christa and I missed out on Bistro that night, we did make it to another restaurant in the area that Cheney visited on at least one occasion,

Mason's on South Harrison Street in Easton. I have no idea what Dick Cheney selected from the Mason's menu on his visit—the local *Star Democrat* article didn't say. But I had the beef, Christa had the fish.

I do know, however, who Cheney's dinner date was that evening. He was none other than the vice president's old friend from the Ford administration, Donald Rumsfeld; the very same man to return to the Pentagon as President Bush's secretary of defense, only a short time prior to the start of America's second and hopefully final war in Iraq.

27 / SHIFTING GEARS

We were at times loose with our spending while living out on the Eastern Shore, no question about it. There were months that Harbor Palm was doing quite well as a retail start-up, and with no clear separation between the store budget and our own household budget, it was easy to fool ourselves into, for example, dining out more than we probably needed to. My version of a sole proprietorship budget was unfortunately one that blurred the line between business and pleasure. Too much so.

In August of 2007, store sales more than exceeded expectations. I don't recall exactly, but the figures a year *later* were far, far below those first-year totals. I didn't mention it immediately to Christa, but as August 2008 sales came to a dismal close, I began considering the distinct possibility that we would have to call it a day. We just didn't have the working capital on hand to weather a retail downturn for much more than a few months. And, as the country was about to find out, the worst was certainly yet to come.

By mid-September 2008 I submitted one last desperate application for a loan to the local Talbot Bank. When I still hadn't heard back a week later, I gave them a call. Things were getting really tight in the credit market, the bank's rep explained. It was a no go. I knew this was going to be the answer even before making the request, but Christa and I had invested so much of ourselves into making Harbor Palm a success, I wasn't about to just roll over and call it quits.

The downward trend in sales continued through September and October. I broke down and asked my own mom for a last minute loan to try to keep things going, if only through Christmas of that year. It was as though we'd had the wind knocked out of us.

While I greatly appreciated my mom's generosity, it was too little, too late. Harbor Palm, like so many other small businesses across America at the time (and well into 2009 and beyond), was going to fall victim to the Great American Credit and Home Equity Crisis that had begun engulfing the nation's economy over the summer of 2008. People weren't spending because bank accounts were dry; credit cards were maxed beyond their limits. Worse, American homeowners were beginning to discover that their homes weren't worth as much in the market of real life as the banks were only pretending they were on paper. This was a toxic combination, one that continues to sort itself out today in 2010.

Over the course of a few two-hour commutes to and from work at NCTC, I settled on the only course of action sensible to me at the time. It wasn't a question of whether to jump ship from the Eastern Shore, buy how soon?

* * *

The home in St. Michaels went on the market the first week of November 2008. I wasn't about to continue the long commute to work in northern Virginia if there would no longer be that silver lining of Harbor Palm to make it all worthwhile.

I, more so than Christa, had really enjoyed the small town atmosphere of St. Michaels over the previous two and a half years, but I wasn't a glutton for punishment. When the bay bridge backed up at the toll plaza for an hour (and sometimes more) on a hot summer's day, it was hard to argue that this commute I had somehow committed myself to was anything short of insanity. I had reached a breaking point.

But I would run into some snags in my attempt to quickly rectify this unique strain of road rage. The row house on Capitol Hill was still rented out to several congressional staffers and, while they did politely consider my predicament, they just weren't willing to up and leave several months short of the end of their lease. I understood completely, but was frustrated nonetheless.

Their inflexibility prompted some short-lived but still agonizing reflection: what if we had never left Washington? Wouldn't we have been much better off financially had we not rolled the dice with a store? Couldn't we have just put a little more money into the row house—to make it more comfortable? Yes, it was small a small place, but that's what "living within your means" is all about, right?

I knew the answers, and for a few days I only got madder.

But that's just not how life works, I somehow started to remind myself. You can't look back like that. You *can*, of course, but there's really no point to it. When you see something you want in life—as I had that first visit to St. Michaels on a cold February morning—you have to go for it. Better to do so and fall short (as all the proverbs go) than to do nothing and wonder what could have been in life. It really is true. Besides, there was too much to take care of at the time.

While I continued looking into short-term living arrangements in Washington, Christa also accepted what needed to be done. She got busy planning how she would off-load the store's remaining merchandise. The store fixtures (the racks, cash wrap, etc.) which we had invested a fair amount of money in only two years prior, would eventually get sold through an online auction that, fortunately, went a long way in offsetting the original cost.

But, obviously, there would be many things that we just couldn't do anything about. Chief among them was the three-year lease I had signed for the retail space Harbor Palm occupied. It wasn't set to expire until December 31, 2009, a full twelve months beyond the time I had decided would be the store's final days.

When I called the landlord on the drive home from work one day, she would hear nothing of it. She immediately suggested modifying the lease so that Harbor Palm could occupy a smaller part of the building, but I explained that this simply wasn't going to work. The reality was that we had reached the end of our financial rope.

"There's just *no money* for a new season of inventory," I clarified, not knowing what else to say.

In hindsight, this would be one of my biggest regrets about our time in St. Michaels. As much as we had helped the owners by leasing one of their empty Talbot Street buildings over the preceding two years, the bottom line was that I was breaking my contract with them. In the end, my signature on those lease papers meant nothing.

* * *

Imperfect though our departure was from the Eastern Shore, all that remained was the question of where my family and I could hunker down back in Washington while we waited for the tenants to vacate the old row house on 14th Place.

Donna and Tom, the same friends on Military Road in Northwest DC who had welcomed Christa and me years earlier when I was first starting at CIA, were there for us yet once more...and for Chloe and Sidney, I might add.

By New Years 2009, Harbor Palm had closed for good. The St. Michaels home was up for sale and we were once again living back in the nation's capital. I didn't know what the future held for us, and I sure as hell didn't see myself lasting much longer as a contractor in the intelligence community. And yet, crazy as things were, it sure was nice not to be making that long commute to and from northern Virginia anymore.

28 / LIGHTS, CAMERA...

The sting of what happened in CPD still hadn't faded. As we waited those first months of 2009 for the row house tenants to quit their lease, it was becoming clearer than ever that my decision to move out to the Eastern Shore had been as much about what I wanted for me and my family (a big home, a small business of our own, etc.) as it was about the worsening cesspool on the banks of the Potomac.

But there would be no more running away from Washington at the end of the work day. After over two years of making that long drive over the Chesapeake in and out of that town, I decided that I would instead *write* my way to some peace of mind. And so, as Christa and I began to fall behind on payments for the house on North Harbor Road, this is exactly what I began to do.

At the end of the day, it would be the experience of having gone to so many movies with my father as a kid that prompted me to channel all of this jaded anxiety, all this disgust—into a *screenplay*.

* * *

We had been living back in Washington for less than a week when I went online to order *Movie Magic Screenwriter 6.0*, "the most popular screenwriting software used by Hollywood professionals," as the Internet advertisements claimed.

It cost almost $200, which was suddenly a lot of money again given our more modest financial situation. But this didn't deter me. *Put in basket. Click.* I was on my way to writing my first screenplay.

I was still at NCTC at the time and we of course still had our hands full; Chloe was three at the time and Sidney had just turned two. I really don't know how Donna and Tom put up with us those three months, to be honest. Between work and taking care of the girls, the only time I had to write was in the early morning hours.

I would get up at 3 AM, head downstairs and start typing. On the weekend I would change it up a little by taking off with the laptop to the nearby Starbucks across from the Tenleytown metro station on Wisconsin Avenue. I kept up this routine the entire time we were living there on Military Road. By the time we were able to move back into the row house in early April, it wasn't quite finished, but I was getting close—so I thought.

Always in a rush to just get things done, I hadn't taken the time to read any books on how to actually write a screenplay. However, I did have a general sense for how many pages a feature length script is supposed to be—about 110, and no more than 120. And I had the overall plot down: this mid-thirty something CIA analyst by the name of Andy Sherpa (I merged the CMO and DI analyst into one) was fighting an uphill battle, trying to get to the bottom of whether Saudi Arabia was acquiring nuclear weapons—all the while contemplating just calling it quits and heading back to California.

I especially enjoyed adding all the extra directing elements that serve to guide the actual shooting of a film. Everything from camera angles to how long a particular shot was supposed to last—it was all right there in my script. The problem was (as I would only later learn) I was attempting to write what's known as a "shooting script," something that doesn't come until *after* the original script is finalized and ready to be produced. But of course I didn't know this yet. I was too busy getting my vision down on paper for the next *An Inconvenient Truth*. And, unlike global warming, this movie was going to have a purpose that no one could reasonably argue with.

I even gave some thought to the soundtrack. The greatest mega-rock band ever is of course Ireland's U2. The group's lead singer Bono had written a track (number four) for their aptly titled 2004 album *How To Dismantle An Atomic Bomb*. Audiences were going to hear Bono's lyrics up against the Edge's roaring guitar as the movie's closing credits began rolling over footage of a nuclear mushroom cloud advancing, frame by frame, *in reverse*. The end of the film would thus be the moment just *prior* to detonation—as I had things all planned out in my script.

But as I finally typed the words "fade out" there at the end, I began to have my doubts that I had done it the way they do in Hollywood. The *Movie Magic* software was good, it made sure that my character names were centered and capitalized properly and that the margins on the page were correct as my story moved from dialogue to action sequences, and back to yet more dialogue. But did I really have a *screenplay* in my hands? I went to the Internet and searched on "scripts" and "screenplays." I was rather disappointed to discover that my feature debut film— I called it *Tilting At Windmills*—was probably not quite ready for the silver screen.

I finally read two scripts of movies that I had really enjoyed in recent years; George Clooney's 2005 *Syriana*, based on the books I had read (and listened to) years earlier by Robert Baer, and the Cohen brothers' chilling thriller *No Country for Old Men*, adapted from author Cormac McCarthy's novel by the same name. The latter won the best picture Oscar in 2008, and rightly so. Actor Tommy Lee Jones' opening narration, in which his character Sheriff Bell (a near retired southwestern law man) puzzles over the heinous crimes of the day, so artfully captures the anomy of the post-modern era.

Speaking on his inability to understand the evil he confronts in his line of work, Jones' sheriff offers somberly, "You can say it's my job to fight it, but I don't know what it is anymore."

* * *

Looking back on my reasons for trying to write this out for the big screen (beyond my love of movies), one of them was that I was still dependent on *the system* there in Washington. As a result, I had to be careful in how I went about bringing all of this to light.

Say what you will about education and work experience, I will tell you for a fact that a significant number of federal contractors working in the intelligence community and department of defense got their jobs—and retain them—by mere virtue of the security clearances they hold. Don't have it at the time of application? *Sorry pal.* Lose it for whatever reason once you're in a position? *Thanks for playing.*

I just hadn't yet come to the realization that if I was going to put this story out to the public, I was going to have to pull the curtains *way* back. I would ultimately have to write this book. But still working (and now living again) in the Washington fishbowl as an intelligence contractor provided just enough fear for my security clearance—my livelihood no less—for me to still want to play it safe. Writing a fictional movie script that followed the trials and tribulations of a frustrated CIA analyst seemed one way to do just that.

And safe it was. The script does contain Chinese shipments to the Arabian Peninsula, and there's a CIA "seventh floor" boogie man doing the bidding of a wartime administration. The analyst tries in vain to do the right thing. But there's also a coup brewing in Riyadh, as well as a whole lot of dialogue—too much dialogue for a movie script, really.

For example, upon seeing the successful detonation of the first atomic bomb at the Trinity test site in Los Alamos, New Mexico on July 16, 1945, Robert Oppenheimer cryptically remarked, "I am become death, the destroyer of worlds." This is actually a loose translation of the Bhagavad Gita, an ancient Hindu text.

My own father used to attribute this quote to Oppenheimer, but also—erroneously—to the Bible. From the time I was a young boy, my dad would parrot the words every so often. He had a very dark sense of humor at times. When I heard them, I would think for a moment of how (the odd grammar aside) the words so perfectly convey the utter sense of hopelessness one must feel at the sight of an atomic bomb detonating before one's eyes. I put the quote in my script, a CIA source in China uses the words in reference to one of the shipments bound for the Middle East.

And CIA's Publication Review Board reviewed and approved my screenplay in just about two weeks.

* * *

While on the topic of government review boards, the following is provided to add context to my decision to proceed as I did with the publication of *Patriot Lost*:

The manuscript for this book was officially received by CIA's Publication Review Board on April 12, 2010. On April 26, 2010, I sent an email to the board requesting an estimated completion date. Dave at PRB responded that "their standard review goal is 30 days."

On May 12, 2010 (over 30 days later) I sent the following email:

Dave,

Having not yet received response from PRB either electronically or in regular mail, please note that I intend to move forward with the next steps of publication of Patriot Lost by the end of the week.

However, I will continue to be prepared to accommodate the board's feedback if and when it's received.

Thank you,

Jonathan Scherck

Later that day, I received the following response—not from Dave this time, but from a Richard at PRB:

Mr. Scherck —

The PRB's review of your manuscript remains ongoing and we will notify you immediately upon the conclusion of our review. Until the time that we have ensured that there is no classified information contained within the writing, you do not have approval to share it with anyone else. We trust you will continue to abide by your contractual obligation and promise to safeguard classified information by allowing us the time to make a careful review. It is our intention to complete this as expeditiously as possible.

Richard/PRB

I'll let the reader judge for himself the reply I sent a few hours later:

Richard,

I have read your email. Please provide an estimated date of completion now that PRB has exceeded its stated 30 day goal.

Since you raised the issue: please be assured that I am more than mindful of the "contractual obligation" I entered into as an employee in CPD. That said, I trust PRB is equally mindful of my rights as a U.S. citizen, rights that I'm confident a third party would deem paramount in this particular case to my obligation to abide by any judgment rendered by PRB or others.

30 days was more than sufficient in my view. I look forward to your response at your earliest convenience.

Jonathan

On June 5, 2010, having received no response of any kind, I submitted *Patriot Lost* for publication. (See *Note from the Author.*)

* * *

The curious title I had chosen for the script, I should note, wasn't as odd as it may sound.

The instant messaging system at the Agency had this feature that, when you were in a "chat" with another user, his or her online status would be displayed: "I am available," or "I am away from my desk." But you could also go in and edit your status message to read however you wanted.

My colleague Phil almost invariably had one of two personalized messages attached to his chat windows. One of them referenced the famous Spanish writer Cervantes' 1605 tale of Don Quixote. Were we perhaps "tilting at windmills" working there in CPD? Phil asked rhetorically.

Phil's other personalized status message (which I saw increasingly in chats with him towards the end of my time at CIA) was far less nuanced: "The skeptics are getting restless."

* * *

By early summer 2009, we were again living in the row house on Capitol Hill. Christa had been working since January in Georgetown as the manager of the women's apparel store White House Black Market.

As in Cheney's *White House* and the global *Black Market* for nuclear weapons—I would darkly joke to myself a few times while driving home from NCTC past the entrance to CIA Headquarters in northern Virginia. I know, I know—how juvenile of me. How can I make light of such a grave national security scandal?

I can hear it now: *The kid lost it! Move along, now, just another CIA conspiracy theory here. Nothing to see...*

Or, if you're so inclined...come along and join the skeptics. It's alright, I too never saw myself in this boat. But now that I'm in it, I'm as convinced as ever of my view of things.

* * *

Right around this time, while heading home from work from NCTC, I ran into someone I hadn't seen since last passing him in the hall at CIA years before.

Who do I see standing waiting for the elevator there in the lobby of the Liberty Crossing office building but Steve—as in *Cheney's* Steve.

NCTC shared office space at the time in the same building as the office of the director of National Intelligence. I instantly assumed ODNI was where Steve was headed as I made my way past him to exit the building one afternoon. By the time I recognized him and thought to maybe say hello, however, I was already halfway across the lobby.

Along with Phil, Steve helped me ramp up on Saudi early on in 2006 when I was first starting on the account. He did this by sending several emails (some via Phil) containing synopses of developments in the kingdom as they related to the Strategic Rocket Forces over the years, as well as some background information on Riyadh's financial support of the Pakistani nuclear program. But what's interesting looking back on all of this is that, while Steve's emails were somewhat helpful, there was never an actual face-to-face meeting with him on the matter.

To be fair, as Phil once explained to me, Steve was awfully busy with his briefing duties downtown. I would imagine that getting peppered every morning with questions from a woman as sharp as Condoleezza Rice would more than keep your day full at the office. But there were obviously problems with getting the needed data dump only through email on a subject as involved as Saudi.

In terms of their substance, most of the emails that Steve relayed were duplicative of the information Phil had already shared with me, circa 1998–2002 information, pertaining mostly to the Saudi-Pakistan linkage. If Steve had anything more up to date—perhaps other material he had compiled while working in CPD—now *that* would have been helpful.

But whether it was because no such information existed or if he failed for whatever reason to share it, I never saw anything in Steve's emails to help flesh out the Saudi-*China* angle, the very reason Steve had been assigned in the first place to monitor a possible Saudi WMD situation. Consequently, Steve's virtual turnover did little more than reiterate much of the group-think I would later encounter with counterparts in the DI.

* * *

The last time I saw Steve had been in passing in the halls of CIA Headquarters. We both stopped for a brief chat. Phil had introduced us once or twice before.

"So are you going to be hanging around with us on [Saudi] for a while?" Steve wanted to know.

I responded that I was finding it to be an interesting account, but that it was a tough one to get your head around. "We'll see how it goes," I said.

What I wanted to ask Steve at the time was how and why he had been put on the Saudi matter in the first place, immediately following the troubling Charlie Allen shipment. Had Steve really been re-assigned from the DI at the request of Vice President Cheney, as Phil once explained? But this was not the time or the place.

Seeing him again as I did a few short years later in the lobby of Liberty Crossing, Steve and I made brief eye contact but said nothing to each other as I brushed by. Honestly, I was surprised that he even recognized me (as it clearly appeared) brief as the encounter was.

I don't recall ever using the phrase seriously in my life, but I swear if Steve didn't look like he had seen a ghost.

As Steve got into the elevator, I pushed my way out the door and headed home.

29 / FREE FALLING

At this point in my tale—working in my third incarnation as a federal contractor—I would much prefer to say that sometime over the summer of 2009 (having realized that I could no longer continue playing the hours game at NCTC), that Christa and I put the row house on the market, packed up the U-Haul once more and headed back to California with our two young daughters. I could have written about how Christa and I lived briefly with her parents in Upland (about forty miles east of Los Angeles) before I found a new job outside the suffocating rat race of the Washington beltway.

However, unless you haven't been paying attention up to this point, you know that this is not how my life has gone since getting out of the Navy in the summer of 2001.

The way things actually went was that by early July 2009, I was in fact done with working as a contractor in the Washington area. *Done. Finished.* Will not drive to northern Virginia a single time more to sit in my cubicle for eight hours of the day.

I gave notice to both my NCTC and SAIC management chains, but in doing so did not reveal the fact that I had no real plans, something I'm doing only now in writing this. I told everyone at work that I was following my wife to the Raleigh, North Carolina area, where Christa had accepted a promotion position with Chico's FAS, the company that owns the White House Black Market chain of women's clothing stores.

This was a lie on several levels. The easy part to set straight is that Christa couldn't have been farther from getting promoted within the conform-or-be-fired corporate world of Chico's FAS.

The other fact that I chose not to disclose to my employer (for the simple reason that it was none of anyone's business) was that Christa and I had been going through a real rough patch coming out of our time on the Eastern Shore. My own frustration with working as a contractor went from bad to worse as I lost that sense of purpose that the store and second home outside of DC provided. Meanwhile, Christa was putting a lot of time and energy—too much, I argued—into her job managing the White House Black Market store in Georgetown. We were just completely out of sync, both in terms of our marriage and as parents to Chloe and Sidney. Enough said.

Even though almost every marriage has such troubles, and often far worse, I hesitated to include this part of my story here given the grave nature of the other half of this book. I very much want my indictment of the Bush administration on the nuclear proliferation matter to stand on its own. And I truly believe that my view of things, on balance, will do just that. I would not have written this book otherwise.

But as I stated in the introduction, I felt that my personal experience surrounding my time at CIA was important not just for my own family's understanding, but for the public to understand who the author is of this chilling exposé—one that brings this previously undisclosed high crime to light.

It's because of this that I opted to go back on my original promise to my wife and briefly acknowledge here the marital problems she and I were having at the time. Indeed, this part of the story was the only thing standing in the way of our inevitable return to California—as a *family*.

* * *

The very next day after calling it quits at NCTC, I loaded up the Volvo with a bunch of clothes, diapers, etc., and headed south from Washington with Chloe and Sidney in the back seat.

The three of us would spend little over a week with my mother in Cary, North Carolina before I found a rental in the small town of Fuquay-Varina, about thirty miles south of Raleigh. Christa remained at the row house on Capitol Hill, still working in Georgetown. I had not told her I was leaving with the girls.

After getting situated in Fuquay, I enrolled Chloe and Sidney in a nearby preschool. Christa and I still weren't on good terms yet at this point. As I continued the *soul searching* (or whatever you call it trying to figure out what's broken in a marriage), I began a half-hearted job hunt. I wanted something totally different from what I had been doing working in the intelligence community.

I knew I enjoyed the entrepreneurial life, but all that start-up capital we had burned through with Harbor Palm was long gone. But there had to be *something* in the private sector, I hoped, that I could still get excited about. Maybe I could go to work for a local bank, or work as a project manager for one of the big regional home builders. Surely, my Navy experience would mean something, even if it was years old by that point.

I was in for the proverbial rude awakening. In case you didn't know, the recession that started nationwide sometime towards the tail end of the Bush administration had yet to hit the Washington, DC metropolitan area—even by the summer of 2009. And if the current cast of characters at both ends of Pennsylvania Avenue keeps it up, any sort of sweeping economic downturn probably won't affect the job market of our nation's capital until maybe 2020 or so—when China finally calls in all the debt our government has been accumulating all these years.

Before leaving Washington, I knew the job market in the "outside world" of North Carolina (and elsewhere around the country) was tight, but I was expecting to have at least a few responses from prospective employers. I would get not a single call back from any of the employment inquiries I submitted during that first month of job hunting there in the Tar Heel state. With cash running low, and with Christa and me still working things out, I very reluctantly reached out to my old friends in the "beltway bandit" world of federal contracting.

Sure enough, despite what had to be my worst job interview *ever*, (my heart just wasn't in it, for reasons that are obvious by now), I landed a job at the U.S. military's Joint Special Operations Command (JSOC) at Fort Bragg, about an hour's drive south from the rental I had taken in southern Wake County. Ironically enough, Fort Bragg is adjacent to the town of Fayetteville, North Carolina where my father was born in 1944.

The pay at JSOC was far less than the premium salaries I had been receiving at both CIA and NCTC, but I wasn't about to complain. And to his credit, the civil servant I worked for (ever so briefly) at JSOC actually engaged the DoD contracting officer to ensure that my salary was commensurate with the responsibilities I would have in the position and—much more of a factor in this case—consistent with the drastic difference in cost of living between the Washington metropolitan area and North Carolina.

For less than sixty days, beginning late in September 2009, I would go to work as (once again) a financial manager for the Department of Defense. I had sort of come full circle from my days working at the Navy's GCCS-M program office in San Diego. I would be doing much the same work at JSOC as an Excel spreadsheet jockey: writing cables to document the expenditure of American tax dollars to this or that vendor in the private sector; building a rudimentary knowledge of the hardware and various capabilities that the money was going to support. The problem was (not surprisingly) I wanted nothing to do with any of this anymore.

The office I was in at JSOC actually supports programs that I very much believe in. Of all the dollars that Congress appropriates for the myriad of DoD efforts, those spent on the programs under JSOC's purview are easily among the most critical. But even this didn't matter to me anymore.

After working on a total of four federal contracts in my life now (two with DoD and two in the intelligence community), it's been my experience that the old saying, "you can lead a camel to water, but you can't make him drink" has a corollary: "You can pay a federal contractor good money to sit at a desk and do work, but if he gets up and leaves, he's not a contractor." It's not as catchy as the camel and water line, but no less true.

* * *

By November of 2009, Christa and I were well on our way to sorting things out. I made another U-Haul reservation to collect the household goods that remained in Washington, and somewhere along the line we managed to get the row house on Capitol Hill rented out. As chaotic as all this may seem in retrospect, Chloe and Sidney took it all in stride. And, of course, they were quite the happy campers seeing mom and dad together again.

The final call was an easy one. It might be difficult to understand given the tough job market across the country, but by Thanksgiving 2009, we were all back in California. Christa, Chloe, Sidney and "Prada" (very likely the only Afghan Hound to ever attend the CIA's Farm) flew out from Raleigh Durham International Airport in mid-November. And, after quickly wrapping things up at JSOC, I followed them out a week later in the all-too-familiar U-Haul.

Finally, on November 23, 2009 (Christa's and my eighth anniversary, no less) I crossed the border from Nevada back into the Golden State.

30 / DON'T TREAD

In a sense, the writing would quite literally be *on the wall* in terms of whether I was ultimately headed back to California. As if writing a screenplay for a movie wasn't a plain enough sign (*my* version of a screenplay at least), amidst my abrupt flight from Washington I even purchased this rather peculiar silkscreen wall-hanging.

Christa wound up not being a fan when she eventually saw it on the wall in Fuquay, but I liked it nonetheless. I got it while making a pit-stop off the I-95 on one of the drives south to North Carolina. It was about thirty by thirty inches in size and was mostly rust orange, white and black in color. Pictured was San Francisco's Golden Gate Bridge with a series of palm trees in the foreground; northern and southern California, all in one shot.

But the best part of the canvas was that on the right hand edge, reading vertically from bottom to top, were the faded-out words "Don't Tread." "On me," the rest of the famous saying, was apparently deemed extraneous by the artist, which I appreciated.

The origins of "Don't Tread on Me" (the phrase emblazoned on the historic Gadsden flag, under the likeness of a rattlesnake) can be traced back to none other than American founding father Benjamin Franklin. Starting with a letter to the editor of the *Pennsylvania Gazette* in 1751, Franklin suggested that the American colonies should "thank" London for its policy of exiling British felons to America by sending a shipment of venomous *rattlesnakes* right back at them. After all, America would be no Australia.

In 1754, a few years later in the midst of the French and Indian War, Franklin had sketched a picture of a dissected snake (to represent the thirteen colonies) to help make his point that only by *uniting* could the colonies overcome

British monarchial oppression. The cartoon ran in newspapers throughout the American colonies with the blunt caption, "Join, or die."

Finally in 1775, with America on the verge of winning its independence from the British crown, Franklin wrote anonymously in the *Pennsylvania Journal* in favor of adopting the rattling reptile as the new national mascot, notably in lieu of the Bald Eagle which Franklin regarded as "a bird of bad moral character." Citing the fact that the rattlesnake is indigenous only to the Americas, Franklin argued the following:

> "She never begins an attack, nor, when once engaged, ever surrenders: She is therefore an emblem of magnanimity and true courage. ...she never wounds 'till she has generously given notice, even to her enemy, and cautioned him against the danger of treading on her."

By this time, some of the country's first Marines were already painting the snake on their war drums right next to a newly coined motto. Before long, the words could also be found flying under the popular serpent on the American colonies' red and white striped First Navy Jack: Don't Tread on Me.

I loved it. More my taste than my wife's, that silkscreen hung on the wall of the family room in Fuquay-Varina our entire three months of limbo there in North Carolina.

Alas, my picture would not make the trip to California with us.

* * *

When I gave my mom a copy of the script I had written, she asked why I had chosen to write the story as a screenplay. I immediately thought to remind her of the time when I was still a junior officer in the Navy. She and my father had asked me what it was I *really* wanted to do once I got out of the service.

I had never considered directing films a legitimate possibility for me, especially given the track I was on by that point—a Georgetown education, four years as an officer in the Navy, etc. But somehow I answered my parents' question candidly and off-the-cuff: "I would want to be a director—a movie director."

I would later joke with a writer I met in Hollywood (who didn't think much of my script, by the way) that it was as though I told my parents that I was gay that day. My mom looked over at my dad, my dad looked at my mom, they *both* stared at me. Are you *serious?* read the look on their faces.

* * *

Most filmmakers these days are more than just a director or writer. It's common for successful directors to also be credited as the writer and sometimes even producer. James Cameron, for example with *Avatar*: Writer, director, producer. Wow.

Despite my altruistic hopes for it, my script *Tilting At Windmills* would be no *Avatar*. Soon after finishing it in the spring of 2009, I hurried to enter it into Francis Ford Coppolla's "American Zoetrope" screenwriting competition. Such competitions offer the opportunity—though slim—for novice screenwriters to get discovered by Hollywood. Winning submissions *sometimes* (though hardly often) get made into feature length films. Out of 2,600 entries, *Tilting* didn't even place in the top 100. I would enter it into two other competitions, hoping that perhaps lightning would strike. But nothing.

Once we were semi-settled in the Los Angeles area, I finally broke down and bought a book on screenwriting by Syd Field, renowned as the original guru of how to write for the big screen. It's a great read. In very simple, straightforward terms he lays out the fundamental structure of successful screenplays. Act I. Act II. Act III. You set the story up, there's conflict, and then the story has a resolution. At the heart of every good film, Field explains, is a strong, dynamic character; and that character, along with everyone else, *must* "arc"—or undergo some sort of metamorphosis between the first and final scenes.

This was all stuff I was at least somewhat familiar with having studied a few novels back in high school and college, only this time the format was that of a screenplay. Field's guidance rang equally true in relation to a few theatrical pointers I picked up from a Shakespeare workshop I participated in one summer in Sacramento.

Save the Cat, was the second screenwriting book I would read. It was brought to my attention by a fellow aspiring screenwriter whom I met while working a Christmas party at Pasadena's ritzy Langham Hotel. (Catering gigs were easy to get when we first moved back to California in late 2009—and we needed the money.)

So there I was—I kid you not—prepping for publisher Larry Flynt's 2009 *Hustler* (as in the adult magazine) Christmas gala. "You really ought to read *Save the Cat*," my screenwriting protégé suggested, as he and I polished wine glasses and poured ice water for the arriving guests. And, yeah, let's just say Santa's elves that night were a little different from the ones I remember as a child.

In reading this second book on screenwriting, the light finally went on—and stayed on this time. *Tilting At Windmills* would never be made into a film. It just wasn't a movie script. Yes, it looked like a script, but it wasn't structured as a screenplay. The characters didn't all "arc" from beginning to end. There was way too much dialogue. The main character's *life* wasn't at stake.

But my stubborn German/Polish genes weren't about to take "no" for an answer. I may not have written the next *Citizen Kane*, I concluded, but I certainly had a story that I wanted to see get out. For my own personal gratification—as some sort of vindication for the course I had steered through my young adulthood? Yes, this was probably true.

But much more than this, I believed that what I witnessed at CIA was a story that Americans *needed* to hear. This turn of events needed to see the light of day because, in the final analysis, our government's intelligence apparatus had failed to tackle a problem that, over the long run, will allow no margin for error.

* * *

I started near the top.

Lawrence Bender is one of Hollywood's best known producers: *Reservoir Dogs*, *Good Will Hunting*, the recent *Inglourious Bastards*—just to name a few.

But Bender is also listed on the "Who We Are" page of the website for Global Zero, an international non-profit organization formed partly in response to President Barack Obama's well-publicized call early in his administration for a world free of nuclear weapons. I wrote Mr. Bender the following letter just weeks after arriving back in California:

December 11, 2009

Mr. Lawrence Bender
Lawrence Bender Productions
Beverly Hills, CA 90211

Re: Global Zero

Dear Mr. Bender:

I am a former CIA employee who worked a Middle Eastern WMD issue from January 2005 to April 2007. I'm also a fan of much of your work, *Good Will Hunting* in particular.

Through some research relating to the Global Zero initiative, I understand you have a documentary in development about nuclear weapons proliferation. While technically I remain bound by a non-disclosure agreement, I did submit material based on my experience to CIA's publication review board and the DNI's public affairs office this past spring. Both offices have reviewed and approved *Tilting At Windmills*, a drama/spy thriller inspired by real events.

My goal is to see *Tilting* produced as its own feature project. It's about a CIA analyst trying to do the right thing as a cog in the U.S. intelligence bureaucracy even as the George W. Bush administration (i.e. Cheney and Co.) turns a blind eye to China's oil-for-nukes dealings with the Kingdom of Saudi Arabia. At a minimum, I think the material could be of interest to you as it has the potential to better inform the Global Zero campaign.

I look forward to hearing from you at your earliest convenience.

Sincerely,
Jonathan Scherck

I didn't just mail this letter, I slid it under the stairwell door to Lawrence Bender Productions, on the corner of La Cienega and Wilshire in Beverly Hills. "Personal for Mr. Bender," I wrote on the envelope. "RE: Global Zero."

It took over a month to get a response from Bender's people, and it wasn't much of a response. If I wanted to provide my script for review, the email read, they would happily take a look. I forwarded the file of *Tilting At Windmills* in an email the next day.

I have yet to hear back from Mr. Bender.

＊ ＊ ＊

In re-reading this letter and thinking about how much I wanted someone in the industry to do *something* with the story, I realize now how detached I had become from my former Washington self. On the one hand, I was being careful to note that the story had been reviewed by some board in Langley, but on the other I just didn't give a shit about keeping it all boxed up anymore.

While it was true that CIA's publication review board had posed "no security objection" to the public release of my script, was it really appropriate for me to be shopping it around in such naked terms? "Even as the George W. Bush administration (i.e. Cheney and Co.) turns a blind eye to China's oil-for-nukes dealings with the Kingdom of Saudi Arabia," as my letter read. I really had turned a corner in my thinking on the dismal situation the Bush White House had ushered America into with China and Saudi Arabia. On some level, I had passed the point of no return in my quest to see this crime against truth in democracy broadcast to the American people. Suddenly, it was no longer about playing by the CIA's rules, but by *my* rules.

This former Halliburton oil exec from Wyoming had the audacity to hijack America's foreign policy, flagrantly violating his Constitutional obligation as vice president to keep Congress abreast of the wicked reality of Saudi Arabia's evolving relationship with China. To what possible end? To avoid an oil crisis that may have rivaled that of the Jimmy Carter era, but that also guaranteed nuclear weapons in the hands of self-appointed princely quasi-statists? To *avoid* being consistent on an issue that the administration had only recently hyped as its primary justification for going to war with Iraq?

And don't dare suggest that Saudi assistance in the War on Terror at the time warranted such irresponsible complicity. This had been the country of birth for the majority of the September 11th hijackers. Did this count for nothing in weighing whether to intervene?

Had it even only been in the form of an otherwise flaccid demarche from the State Department, at least this would have been something. A United Nations-like stern letter of admonishment from president to king would have at least put America on the right side of one of the biggest challenges facing the world in the modern era.

And to hell with that Non-Proliferation Treaty that Dick Nixon had signed on behalf of the American people. This was little more than an antiquated wish list that the world had long since all but ignored.

* * *

Sometime not long after the non-response from Mr. Bender (and two or three of his peers in Hollywood), Christa and I were on the couch early one morning watching some TV together. Christa was still working on Hollywood's Melrose Avenue and I was already well into writing the first draft of this book. Sidney and Chloe still hadn't woken up yet. This was one of those rare moments of peace in our South Pasadena apartment.

I would have much rather been watching the Charlie Rose interview of General David Petraeus that I had recorded from the night before, but Christa really wanted to watch some reality show on the Bravo network. Guess which one we wound up watching?

One of the characters on this particular "reality" episode suddenly started talking about how he really wanted to get his book published, to "show the world [his] creative side," he said.

I turned to Christa and muttered, "I want to get *my* book published so that people *understand* me."

Without skipping a beat, Christa looks over at me and shoots back, "Then you shouldn't be trying to be a creative artist." She was of course referring to the script I had written.

Like I said, every now and then Christa knows me better than I know myself.

* * *

My hopes for seeing this cosmically stupid complicity revealed for what it is on the big screen obviously found the right outlet ultimately. But before I would even start writing the first words of this book, I had a critical question to answer for myself: was I willing to risk violating the confidentiality agreement I had entered into as an employee of the U.S. intelligence community?

Contractor, or not, I had signed not a few pieces of paperwork prior to going to work in the Counter-Proliferation Division as a CMO. In doing so, I acknowledged that I understood that working in the realm of national security comes with a commensurate level of responsibility to safeguard the information one comes in contact with.

Not surprisingly, answering this question a short drive from the Pacific Ocean was much easier than when I was still working as part of the U.S. intelligence community in northern Virginia. As much as I wanted to at the time, it's just not wise in life to bite the hand that feeds. Especially *that* hand. But now that I was finally out in California, I was no longer wearing that yoke of silence. Not on an issue as black and white as this.

The utmost concern in my mind—that I might be divulging classified information—was unjustified, I would finally decide. In my heart, when I began writing *Patriot Lost*, I believed that whatever "state secrets" I might be divulging in my story were secondary to the far more important need to bring this scandal to light. After all, our democratic principles of government had been trampled on by the Bush administration. The American people needed to be informed. I would be respectful of the CIA's restrictions on releasing classified information outside of the standard review process, but at the end of the day the story absolutely had to be told.

And I'm not being coy here with this question of what would and wouldn't constitute "classified" information in this terribly unique case. As is typically so with such high profile tell-all missives out of Langley, it would be a subjective review process by CIA's publication review board. It was going to be less a question of whether "they" would allow me to divulge *this* or *that* aspect of CIA's work culture (along with details on the organization's past relationship with Dick Cheney's Office of the Vice President), and more likely a question for policymakers (within the Obama White House itself, perhaps) as to whether they wanted to let this Bush administration skeleton out of the closet.

As sure as I was of the political dynamics of my situation, there was still some method involved as I sat down to write this all out. If I were to write a book this time, would I be able to do so while still passing the CIA's principle litmus test? After some apprehension over how to write this high crime out as a book, would I be revealing any sensitive information on CIA's sacred *sources and methods* in the process?

A) Sources: Could I write a book that told the story of why I believed the Bush administration had turned a blind eye to Saudi Arabia's acquisition of nuclear weapons without compromising the identity of any human sources I had come across while working the Saudi account?

Yes. As I've explained, there weren't any regular, long-term sources to speak of during my time working Saudi. Just the one or two-time blasts from certain sources in key positions overseas whom we very much wanted to hear more from, but (for whatever reason) never did. And I have exercised great caution herein not to divulge any identifying information relating specifically to those sources.

B) Methods: Could I write a book that told the story of why I believed the Bush administration had turned a blind eye to Saudi Arabia's acquisition of nuclear weapons without revealing any of the methods used in the CIA's handicapped efforts to answer the Saudi nuclear question?

Yes, I believed so. But in the end I decided that I would leave this to CIA's publication review board, just as I had with the script I had written.

That said, I didn't feel that anything I could write would be any more revealing than the many books that have been written about the CIA on a multitude of subjects over the years, or even—much more specific to the Counter-Proliferation Division—the many articles that have been written in magazines and newspapers about the Valerie Plame scandal.

So this was my thinking as I ultimately concluded that it would be acceptable to write a full blown book about my time following the Saudi nuclear question. I wouldn't be revealing any sensitive sources because, odd as it sounds, we really didn't have any. And methods? Nothing new here.

I should clarify: nothing new, that is, in terms of "CIA methods used" in the *traditional* sense. Because in the final analysis, it may well be that I'm guilty of pushing the envelope a bit in calling out Mr. Charlie Allen by name as an accomplice in this whole affair. Indeed, there may have been other individuals even more directly involved than Allen in seeking to ensure that realities there on the Arabian Peninsula would not be properly known to all relevant parties in Washington.

Even so, I think we can all agree looking back now that the act in question—this misguided contempt for speaking truth to power, as it were—was less a *classified* matter than simply a criminal one.

Likewise, as to the liberties I have knowingly taken herein in discussing otherwise classified imagery analysis, I am no less convinced. The events captured by U.S. spy satellites flying high above the Arabian Peninsula can hardly be considered in their proper context as an *American* state secret. Surely, those many illicit Chinese shipments into Saudi Arabia pose far less a threat to America's national security than to the people of the Middle East.

That said, had I received a more timely response from CIA's publication review board, be assured that I would have taken note. Of course, whether I would have complied or not with the proposed redactions is another question entirely.

* * *

To those reading this who think I am deluding myself, that I am guilty of something worse than treading perhaps too closely to CIA sources and methods equities, allow me to pre-empt your criticism.

If it is White House *executive privilege* that concerns you, the idea that there simply exist matters of national security on the world stage—matters of life and death, fundamentally—that just can't be handled safely at the bureaucratic working level (even by intelligence analysts within the secure walls of CIA), I must respectfully disagree. I would offer that state secrets held in this regard by men and women at the highest levels of our government are inherently flawed in some way.

Particularly in free societies such as our own, the withholding of information from government agencies that were created for the sole purpose of analyzing the very same sort of information is itself an indication that the long term public good is being compromised for some short term gain.

In the case of Saudi Arabia's perilous nuclear aspirations, I imagine that the short term advantage was calculated (albeit poorly) in terms of the Bush administration's legitimacy, particularly following the realization on the part of the American public that the commander-in-chief had taken the country to war on false pretense. I think the perceived need to create a regional Sunni Islamic counterbalance to Iran's Shia Islamic nuclear ambitions was also very likely a factor. And perhaps a sense of inevitability prevailed as China's rapid ascent as the globe's newest superpower was factored into Cheney and company's overall calculus. And it goes without saying that oil was at the heart of it all, as has always been the case with America's flawed relationship with the Saudis.

Whatever the rationale, I maintain it was horribly reckless and nearsighted. To quote Oppenheimer, the father of the atomic bomb:

"If atomic bombs are to be added as new weapons to the arsenals of a warring world, then the time will come when mankind will curse the names of Los Alamos and Hiroshima. The people of this world must unite or they will perish." - J. Robert Oppenheimer, Acceptance Speech, Army-Navy "Excellence" Award, November 16, 1945.

Incidentally, I wrote Oppenheimer's words in right at the end of my movie script. They were to appear at the close of *Tilting*, just as the hellish mushroom cloud began folding back on itself towards a more peaceful initial state of being.

To those who still don't approve of this exposé, we'll have to agree to disagree. But, say what you will, I'm still a patriot.

* * *

And say what you may about my desire to get this story out, can any American now watch the footage of Dick Cheney and King Abdullah embracing in

Riyadh during the waning months of the Bush administration and not want to vomit? Figuratively speaking, of course—although there were a few times down towards the end of writing this that I felt physically sickened by the words I was typing.

Come to think of it, I wouldn't be at all surprised if film maker Michael Moore won't himself be compelled while reading this to visit the nearest bathroom to unload some disgust of his own.

31 / FORCES AT PLAY

It was a frustrating and rather ironic coincidence that my experience on the Saudi WMD account at CIA began and ended over a matter of satellite imagery of Chinese shipments arriving in the Jeddah Islamic Seaport. But at the end of the day, I know this was probably little more than a coincidence. And if it was indeed more than that, my premature exit from the Counter-Proliferation Division still means nothing in the grand scheme of things.

After all, this terrible error in judgment by the Bush White House had been the result of decisions being made several rungs up the bureaucratic ladder, on the *other* side of the Potomac; several steps up beyond my "paygrade," as CPD's chief of reports once acknowledged to me.

That said, after moving on from life as an intelligence contractor, after returning with my family to California, and having finally now written the book version—how am I so certain that Saudi Arabia has the bomb?

Because I'm confident in what I believe.

Not because any one source clued us in, as I've explained. There would be no single irrefutable intelligence report to blow all the thick smoke from our spaces there in the basement of CIA. Had there been, I'm confident this story would have broken long before, either in the form of one hell of a hastily arranged White House press conference, or (more likely) a jaw dropping front page story in the *Washington Post*.

I believe this all went down not because I personally ever saw satellite imagery that proved beyond the shadow of a doubt that the new Chinese missile arsenal on the ground in the kingdom was indeed armed with nuclear warheads. NGA couldn't say this itself at the time, I don't think. But if they could have, this would have been just one more job for the Charlie Allens of the intelligence world; another all-too-true revelation that NGA would have been prohibited from putting out to the U.S. intelligence community.

But at the same time, what NGA fortunately was able to provide (consistently over several years, in fact) was expert and unvarnished analysis of a substantial overhaul of Saudi Arabia's Strategic Rocket Forces, ranging from comprehensive preparations for a new missile system, to the system's actual arrival from China by boat, to an unmistakable transformation in the SRF's on-base training patterns. No, U.S. satellites couldn't see everything from above, but they saw more than enough. Forces within our very own government had suppressed valuable satellite imagery, critical information that would have put the U.S. intelligence community on more solid ground in its approach to China's proliferation activities.

I believe what I believe also—perhaps most importantly—based on my understanding of the underlying forces at play between the CIA and Vice President Cheney's office. This view has been validated by events as they've unfolded publically over the years between Beijing and Riyadh, Riyadh and Washington, and (albeit less conspicuously) between Washington and Beijing.

I developed my awareness not as a student in a graduate school classroom or as a senior fellow at one of Washington's "think tanks." My grasp of what happened there somewhere between Headquarters and the office of the vice president is based on having thought about little else every working day of my life for well over a year at CIA. Even years later now, hardly a day goes by that I don't give it thought. It's simply too intertwined with the course America is taking in the world today.

I was living this question on a daily basis along with my CPD co-workers. Then, after being fired for doing my job, I continued watching the news along with the rest of America: Bush and Cheney both making final trips to the Saudi kingdom late in their second term; the hugs, the hand holding.

And then, with the change in administrations, the way Saudi Arabia's King Abdullah draped an ornamental gold medallion around the neck of yet another U.S. president only shortly after he took office in January 2009. The writing was on the wall. Just another coincidence—in the case of President Obama—this bowing to the Saudi king? Just due to the fact that the United States has been so dependent on Saudi crude all these many decades now?

No. By the start of the Obama administration, it would be far more than even Saudi Arabia's vast energy resources demanding Washington's careful and continued attention.

* * *

Since the end of the Cold War, the argument has been made by some observers of CIA's analytic product that undue emphasis has been placed on satellite imagery at the expense of the Agency's core Human-intelligence collection capability. In other words, that what intelligence analysts *see* from above is given as much weight (at times more so) as what they *hear* through CIA's recruited human assets.

Perhaps my claims will be countered by this sort of thinking, that I'm guilty of putting too much stock in the imagery analysis that was produced during the timeframe I've described. I don't know as I write this and, frankly, don't much care either. In the case of Saudi Arabia's acquisition of nuclear weapons from China, such an argument is ultimately moot because there simply was no consistent and reliable stream of HUMINT to be factored in.

Beyond any didactic debate over IMINT vs. HUMINT, the national security apparatus of the Bush administration (under the direction of Vice President Cheney) did what needed to be done behind closed doors in the Old Executive Office Building and on the seventh floor of CIA Headquarters to hinder the creation of a HUMINT "smoking gun" on the issue of Chinese nuclear weapons in Saudi Arabia. It may have been active measures such as directing a station chief to eliminate Saudi WMD as a collection priority—i.e. just *don't* ask the question of any assets in the know. Or it may have been less conspicuous, perhaps a meeting involving only Cheney, a few National Security Council staffers and a higher-up from CIA—resulting in a sort of filter whereby no hard HUMINT on the subject would ever see the light of day outside CIA. The revealing intelligence report mentioned earlier that literally got sliced in half at the request of management still looms large in my mind as a likely example of this ill intended oversight.

The unseemly forces at play on this issue were just as pervasive with President Bush in the Oval Office. It was no secret that family relations between the

Bushes and the House of Saud were strained almost immediately at the beginning of George W. Bush's first term. Having voiced support for Israel's Ariel Sharon early on in his first term over the summer of 2001, Bush was reportedly forced to fall back in line with his father's (and Riyadh's) more pro-Arab stance on the ongoing Palestinian conflict. Serving yet again as intermediary between Riyadh and Washington, Prince Bandar is said to have used a veiled threat in private discussions with the younger Bush to cut the flow of Saudi oil to the U.S. had Bush chosen not to moderate his public support of Sharon.

Relations warmed slightly when Bush finally delivered a more nuanced statement on the heated situation in the Levant, but this rapprochement with Riyadh would be short lived. Bandar Bush's personal relationship with the U.S. president had been quickly set aside for more pressing matters, and Riyadh's ruling elite had once again reminded Washington of what the relationship was really all about.

Only months later, as the Bush administration's response to 9/11 began to unfold, and as a second war in Iraq was made an even greater priority by Vice President Cheney, Saudi crude would continue to be the overriding factor in Washington's narrow-minded calculus—at great expense to the legitimacy of the Non-Proliferation Treaty that had gone into force on March 5, 1970. As a matter of national policy, the Bush-Cheney White House decided to simply look the other way on China's oil-for-nukes deal with Riyadh.

Consequently, it became acceptable at the highest levels of our government—with President Bush, Vice President Cheney and at least some of Cheney's principle national security advisors (certainly those having daily interactions with senior CIA leadership)—that the nation's HUMINT collection capability was malfunctioning on the Saudi nuclear question. (I'm convinced this was the reason behind the Fran Townsend pulse-checking appointment that I failed to make; Bush wanted to make sure that CIA was still deaf and dumb on the issue.) And, naturally, there would be no pressure to correct the problem, as there had been in the case of Iraq during the frantic sprint to the start of Cheney's second Gulf war in 2003.

As I've said, the gap in reporting on Saudi was due in large part to the emphasis placed at the time on intelligence reporting to support the War on

Terror. Iraq and Afghanistan—those were the priorities. Yemen and Somalia wouldn't be far behind. The next big event, either stateside or targeting U.S. interests abroad: Where would it be? When would it be? What form would it take?

But this factor, while significant, goes only so far in excusing the unseen chokehold that was hampering the collection of HUMINT reporting on Riyadh's nuclear intentions.

* * *

The analysis of fresh incoming satellite imagery during my time on the account continued to indicate that Saudi SRF bases were in the midst of a major overhaul. New materials were arriving from China every few months via the port in Jeddah by the container-load. These weren't insignificant shipments. According to NGA's analysis these were massive shipments, shipments that base personnel prepped for the arrival of weeks and months in advance. This wasn't one or two shipping containers at a time, but *dozens* at a time. Convoys of flat bed trucks had to be carefully coordinated under the cover of night between their arrival in Jeddah and their subsequent stops in the kingdom, beginning in the town of Ta'if.

Operational training routines, as seen from above, deviated from patterns that had been established many years prior. This was not the Saudi SRF of old, nursing a fleet of late-model Chinese CSS-2s through a decade and more of semi-readiness. Imagery indicated that Saudi military personnel assigned to the various SRF bases were no longer drilling for launch of the conventional CSS-2, but were rather now training to operate a far different sort of capability.

These new missiles weren't the type to be erected on Saudi launch pads. Riyadh's new and supremely improved capability was mobile, riding on the backs of massive TELs. These WMDs had the added benefit of being solid fuel propelled, meaning there would be no wait time for an impending launch. The time-consuming liquid fueling requirement prior to launch, characteristic of the old CSS-2s, was now obsolete.

But even given all of this, there were unfortunately no indications from imagery alone that this new mobile Chinese system was necessarily equipped with nuclear warheads. As helpful as NGA was in assessing Riyadh's new capability, the imagery (like any form of intelligence) did have its limits. In the end, it would be good old fashioned human inference that would put all of this activity as seen from above in its proper context.

What the imagery analysis did highlight, indirectly or not, was the stark lack of concern by the Vice President and his proliferation advisors at the National Security Council. How was it that Cheney's office had gone from being personally engaged on the topic back in 2003, to being interested on only an ad hoc basis through aides and, worse, dispassionate surrogates—now suddenly descending by mid-2006 from a newly created National Counter-Proliferation Center? (Yet another astounding—and pricey—irony, in my view.)

To be fair, NCPC (the DNI's counter-proliferation counterpart to the National Counter-Terrorism Center) was at the time still in an early organizational phase, taking marching orders from Ambassador John Negroponte's just as new Office of National Intelligence. An apt analogy here would be the coach of a second rate high school football team being suddenly put in charge of Tom Brady and the New England Patriots in their first game of the AFC playoffs. It just doesn't turn out very well.

CIA's participation in NCPC-coordinated Saudi efforts in 2006 and early 2007, alongside our experienced intelligence community counterparts, didn't produce good results either. "Kick-off" meetings would be followed by reminder emails which would eventually be re-read months later to the tune of "Whatever happened to…?"

The bureaucratic gridlock I was experiencing on the Saudi issue at the action officer level of the U.S. intelligence community was symptomatic of an overarching problem that has plagued our nation's capital for far too much of its history: the failure to communicate. There are as many reasons for this problem as there are policy issues in Washington.

I will never know for sure why I, a CMO contractor, was dispatched to participate in these Saudi WMD interagency working groups. It was abundantly clear to me then as it is now that if this was an issue that CIA leadership really wanted to address, that I would have more likely attended these meetings as a back-bencher to more senior civilian Agency staff. The intelligence "gaps" identified in these meetings would have been socialized at a higher level of CPD and with divisional counterparts elsewhere in the DO.

This absence of senior level CPD involvement could have been more on par with the collaboration I was seeing on the Iran nuclear issue during this time. At a divisional all-hands meeting one day, CPD's chief spoke at length about how, in his estimation, we (CIA) had only about two more years to get a fix on what was going on inside Iran's nuclear program. Where was this same sense of urgency on the Saudi question? Why was not one word said at this event about all the shipments we were seeing into Jeddah?

The answer is simple. There was no sense of urgency at my level because Chief CPD didn't consider it a priority. It wasn't a priority to him because it wasn't a priority to the director of the CIA (at that time General Michael Hayden). And it wasn't a priority for Director Hayden because the White House (read Cheney) wasn't telling him to make Saudi WMD a priority.

* * *

But if this was the ugly state of affairs in the executive branch of our nation's government, you might ask, what was Congress doing to stay abreast of the issue?

There would be two separate briefing trips to Capitol Hill on the Saudi issue during my time on the account. Both occurred sometime in the latter half of 2006. One was with former Speaker of the House Dennis Hastert, the other with Senate Majority Leader Bill Frist.

I did not participate in either of these briefings on the Hill, as I was not asked to go. Instead, a mid-level civilian CMO above me in CPD accompanied the same group of DI analysts that made it to the Fran Townsend meeting at the White House (without me), but who were noticeably excluded from the DO only meeting with Cheney's Bob Swartz, which I did attend.

The feedback I got from CPD's representative to the Hill briefings was that she had said very little (nothing then, substantively speaking) and that the DI analysts had done most of the talking. This was the same CPD manager I had once told emphatically (in probably too loud a voice there in the basement vault), "This [Saudi] is an intelligence failure!"

"No, it's not," she responded dryly, without addressing any of my frustrations that day. And then she proceeded to walk back to her office. So it was safe to assume that both Bill Frist and Denny Hastert—leaders of the country's legislative branch at the time, mind you—had been spoon fed the same old and tired "maybe Pakistan" drivel.

32 / WYOMING'S OWN SVENGALI

Through some research into the Cheney factor that was once again conspicuously trickling down behind closed doors at CIA—this time on the country south of Iraq, I discovered that the former Wyoming congressman (even before 9/11 and well before the 2003 Jeddah imagery was buried) had arrived back in Washington from his days as CEO of the oil and defense contracting firm Halliburton knowing exactly how he was going to approach his role as Bush's vice president.

According to records held at the United States District Court for the District of Columbia, early on in the Bush administration the Comptroller General of the United States David Walker filed a suit on behalf of the General Accounting Office (GAO), Congress' principle governmental investigative body. Legal documents describe a request by Congressmen John D. Dingell and Henry A. Waxman (ranking members of the House Committee on Energy and Commerce and House Committee on Government Reform, respectively) for the GAO to conduct an inquiry into the "conduct and composition" of the National Energy Policy Development Group (NEPDG), chaired by the vice president. The defendant in the case? Richard Bruce Cheney.

Acting on the request, the GAO began in spring 2001 to query the office of the vice president for the following:

"a complete list of all NEPDG members and staff, and an identification of any members or staff who were not full-time employees of the federal government; a complete list of all NEPDG meetings, including the date, location and attendees of each meeting; the criteria used to determine which non-federal entities would be invited to the meetings and an identification of

233

the person or persons responsible for extending invitations under those criteria; an accounting of the legal authorities pursuant to which the NEPDG was organized and was conducting its business; and an accounting of all direct and indirect costs that the NEPDG was incurring."[†]

After much back and forth over the following months between Cheney's office and GAO, there remained no definitive response from the courts; Congress' questions—whatever their motivation—had not been answered.

When I first read the names of the members of Congress making the request (Waxman and Dingell), I must admit that my eyes rolled back a bit. These men are among the most liberal in the House of Representatives. They've been in Washington forever. I remember hearing NBC anchorman Tom Brokaw utter their names on the nightly news on almost a weekly basis as a kid during the Reagan years. Waxman was first elected to Congress from his Los Angeles area district in 1975, *the year I was born.* And Mr. Dingell, a Michigan Democrat, is the longest serving congressman in America's over two-hundred year history. He was first elected in 1955, just eleven years after my father was born.

These obscenely long tenures in Congress aside, it's apparent that these men together were rightly trying to pre-empt what they believed would be an insular, veiled approach to policy-making by the former Halliburton CEO. Indeed, Senators Levin and Lieberman would themselves ultimately get involved in this wrestling match with the vice president, claiming that the nation's energy policy was already the subject of pending legislation in Congress.

Even though I and many Americans were unaware of *Walker v. Cheney* as it made its way through the courts in Washington early on in the Bush administration, it represents a remarkable precedent set by Cheney only shortly after he took the oath of office in January 2001. The fact that it had been called out by a couple of long-time liberal congressmen was, ultimately, quite irrelevant.

As Cheney's counsel David S. Addington wrote in a prescient rebuttal to the GAO's complaint, the request by the representatives from California and Michigan amounted to an inspection by the legislative branch:

---

† *Walker v. Cheney*, United States District Court for the District of Columbia, Civil Action No. 1:02cv00340

"into the exercise of authorities committed to the Executive by the Constitution, including the authority to 'require the Opinion, in writing, of the principal Officer in each of the executive Departments, upon any Subject related to the Duties of their respective Offices,' to 'take Care that the Laws be faithfully executed,' and, with respect to Congress, to 'recommend to their Consideration such Measures as he shall judge necessary and expedient.'"

Then Addington got to the point.

"It appears that the GAO may attempt to intrude into the heart of Executive deliberations, including deliberations among the President, the Vice President, members of the President's Cabinet, and the President's immediate assistants, which the law protects to ensure the candor necessary in Executive deliberations necessary to effective government."

In the end, Cheney's office never would be compelled to disclose the rudimentary details that Congress had requested on the nature of the administration's energy group. Congress and the GAO had lost and Addington's argument had set the parameters for what would be the most secretive and influential vice presidency in the history of the United States.

It was a precedent that would help shield the Cheney way of doing business in Washington throughout his two terms as vice president. It was an m.o. consistent with the way, even as a young congressman from Wyoming, Cheney had opposed the mostly popular reforms being pushed by Senator Frank Church, the former Army intelligence officer from Idaho who had gone on to serve four terms in the U.S. Senate. Over the years, Cheney's was an increasingly impaired philosophy of democratic government, one that would further embrace the "dark side," as Cheney once observed of himself, following the events of September 11th.

Brent Scowcroft, the national security advisor to George H. W. Bush, was famously quoted on his view of Dick Cheney as vice president:

"The real anomaly in the [George W. Bush] Administration is Cheney. I consider Cheney a good friend—I've known him for thirty years. But Dick Cheney I don't know anymore."

And according to Scowcroft's own account of events at the White House immediately following the terrorist attacks of September 11th, Vice President Cheney would notably seek out the advice of Princeton University's Bernard Lewis. Lewis is touted in some academic circles as an expert on the Middle East. My own personal view of Lewis the academic happens to be less favorable based on some of the views I adopted while studying abroad under Faruk Tabak—along with some additional Middle Eastern civilization history courses I took as a student at Georgetown. As Scowcroft pointed out:

"And Bernard Lewis says, 'I believe that one of the things you've got to do to Arabs is hit them between the eyes with a big stick. They respect power.'"

* * *

But there will be no blaming 9/11 on the reckless mindset that contributed to the "effective government" (to use Addington's words) that said nothing as China quietly armed Saudi Arabia with weapons of mass destruction.

33 / OVER BEERS

I've stayed in touch with several of my former colleagues from my time in CPD. All of them have been careful not to reveal any specific details that have come to light following my departure in the spring of 2007, as one would expect from a group of professional active duty intelligence officers.

But while such details (particularly as they might shed light on some complicity in this whole affair by certain CIA analysts or even perhaps some in the DO) could well have altered my accounting of events during my time in CPD, I am convinced that my bottom line would remain unchanged. At the same time, there's been an unspoken but clear understanding of how this series of unfortunate events between China and the Saudis ultimately concluded by the close of the Bush administration in early 2009.

Over the last round of beers we all had together at a bar up the road from Headquarters (while I was still working at NCTC), one of us stated the obvious: President Bush and Vice President Cheney had blinders on when deciding to give Riyadh and Beijing a pass in this whole ordeal. Washington, to the world's great detriment, just doesn't do long term strategic thinking very well. We all heartily agreed.

* * *

In an interview in July 2009 with Harry Kreisler of U.C Berkeley's Institute of International Studies, Robert Baer discussed his latest book and made the following comment:

"…And then, at the same time, the CIA started hiring contractors, and if you look today, the CIA has acknowledged that fifty percent of its personnel budget goes to contractors. They're people that come in whose sole motivation is to continue their contracts. And so, they don't want to take risks, they don't want to go to weird places, they don't want to lose their contracts for their company. Their motivation becomes profit, solely profit, as opposed to a patriotic mission, which believe it or not, inside the CIA you had the place driven by patriotism. A CIA officer, coming in, often started at a salary less than a Washington DC policeman. So, we're talking about patriotism, we are talking about excitement – the people came in. And that all started to go away in the nineties, and that's why I left. I left because I wanted to do a second act in something else, writing or in the oil business, I didn't care. I had no idea."

I'm really torn reading this transcript. Obviously, I couldn't agree more with the last part where Baer talks about wanting to do a "second act." This was exactly my motivation when I called it a day at Fort Bragg.

But in regards to the generalizations Mr. Baer makes about hired-gun contractors, I think he misses the mark a bit. I could change the derogatory slightly and make the claim that many career government intelligence professionals are only interested in making it up to the next rung of the promotions ladder, one step closer to the Senior Intelligence Service or (if that had become unlikely) a safe government pension to supplement whatever's left of Social Security by the time they hit retirement. The Agency's staff officers, I could continue, are motivated less by doing the right thing than by a deep-seated need to be part of the "in" crowd, in this case one of the world's most prestigious and exclusive professional club—the CIA. Yes, there are some who are driven by patriotism, but such spirit is often muted by a White House that opts for the path of least resistance at the expense of the long term good. True allegiance to the Constitution in some corners of Headquarters is, in trying times, tentative at best.

And I beg to differ with Baer's inclination to, in effect, demonize an American private sector that pivoted to capitalize on new business opportunities presented by the global War on Terror. This is, after all, the United States of America. We are a capitalist society. The desire to accumulate wealth is at the heart of every true private sector enterprise. I have personally worked on no less than four federal contracts in my life. In each case, the government customer was at all times free to pursue some sort of modification to the contract if there was some cause to do so: if the work-load no longer warranted full contract support; if, upon further review, it was deemed that private contractors were not appropriate for a given task due to the sensitive nature of the work involved. I just don't believe that the private sector vendor—even Cheney's former employer Halliburton—is to blame for the waste I've witnessed while working on each of the these federal contracts over the years.

From civil servants hiring far too many contractors to do the work of only a few, to contractors being paid premium salaries to perform work that your average savvy high school grad can manage—our government's ballooning deficit and the resulting U.S. debt was *not* caused by the private sector. Make no mistake, it is ultimately the government manager who creates the market for the additional analytic support, the more user friendly command and control interface or the pricey consulting advice on how to better motivate an agency's work force. It is the *civil servant*, from Capitol Hill all the way down to the most junior administrative assistant at the U.S. Department of Education—he is the reason that Washington is drowning in red ink.

* * *

I've heard it said, and I tend to agree, that those who aspire to the highest office in the land can really only hope to achieve one thing during a single four year term. They should choose wisely based on their own vision for the country (and based on what's best for the country at the time) because it will take all of their power—even as President of the United States—to get that one thing accomplished. For President Bush that one thing will be measured in terms of his aggressive response to 9/11.

Regardless of who wins the next presidential election in 2012—Republican, Democrat, Independent or otherwise, it is my hope that he (or she) sets his sights on the out of control spending that has plagued Washington since the 1930s, since the days my grandmother and great aunt traveled from Massachusetts to Washington to take secretarial positions in FDR's fast growing federal bureaucracy.

No, I'm not an economist. I have no expert understanding for how we go about tackling the monstrous debt we've accumulated as a country since the era of the New Deal. Furthermore, I unfortunately count among those who played the credit market too loosely, thus contributing in some small way I suppose to the financial collapse of 2008 and 2009.

But on that point, if you'll allow me to rationalize for a moment, I give myself a break for the fact that I was attempting to build something new with my credit—credit that was flowing all too freely at the time from exactly the wrong places. Still, the aim with the Harbor Palm retail venture had been to create new business that may have someday produced a handful of permanent jobs in the state of Maryland. And, as some economists are quick to emphasize, had our small business stayed afloat it would have continued to generate increasing business tax revenues not only for Annapolis but for the federal government as well.

But contributing to the government's tax base was obviously the last thing on our minds in opening a store. Christa and I just wanted to make money while doing something we enjoyed. Plain and simple. Our objective with Harbor Palm was to be financially independent someday. Maybe not rich, but free to be our own boss while living a comfortable life, both for ourselves and two young children. This is a goal I still aspire to today, particularly now that I have moved on from the field of government contracting. There's nothing wrong with wanting to be well off, able to afford the nicer things in life—to be able to provide for one's children and grandchildren even.

That said, the troubled waters we see today between Main Street America and our democratic institutions of government in Washington were not, I don't believe, caused by the capitalist makings of the American Dream. The problem Americans face with their government today in 2010 lies rather with those who do not assign blame where it is due, with government bureaucrats high and low who refuse to address waste where it exists and, worse, seek to create yet more potential for waste in the form of an ever expanding federal bureaucracy. The problem lies with those members of Congress on the House Financial Services Committee who, only a few years prior to the country's mortgage and credit crisis, decided that homeownership is somehow something that *every* American is entitled to. And so they relaxed mortgage lending rules to a point that, well, just about any American who wanted to own their own home could do so. And this all ended very badly for the U.S. economy, as we all started learning together in the fall of 2008.

The problem lies with the U.S. Senator (Republican and Democrat alike) who lobbies much too hard to keep a costly decades old defense program up and running in his home state, regardless of the most recent Pentagon study that insists that the system in question has outlived its usefulness to America's military. This isn't only bad for America's balance sheet, it's detrimental to the overall effectiveness of our nation's armed forces. Lean and mean isn't just a cliché. Opposed as I am to the proliferation of weapons of mass destruction, I'm not so naïve to think that there aren't problems looming on the horizon that will require Washington to still carry a "big stick."

Such examples of fiscal waste, fraud and abuse (as we all know too well) go on and on. It will take more than a four year presidential term to see any measurable improvement in Washington's spending problem, but it will be worth it in the long run. The private sector will adjust to the new realities (as it always has) and in the end the United States—both its private and public sectors— will be stronger and more efficient because of it.

* * *

Since its birth at the Constitutional convention in Philadelphia in 1787, our country has embraced capitalism, questioned it and—several times now— returned to it as the basis for American private sector activity. Going to McDonalds, paying a mortgage (or rent) for the roof over one's head, picking out an engagement ring (whether .2 carat or 2 carat), going to a professional baseball game, joining the local gym, traveling to Tuscany, buying prescription medicine, buying diapers for your children—all are examples of what is fundamentally *private* life.

Politicians in Washington are prone of late (once again) to confusing this aspect of American life with the *public* good. The result is massive government spending, ballooning deficits and a national debt that makes you (me at least) want to take a pitchfork to Capitol Hill and give 'em a stern talking to. It's not that there aren't select areas of civic life that government has a valid case for stepping in with a little oversight and regulation, but let's not kid ourselves. When it's all said and done, we Americans are on our own in this game of "life, liberty and the pursuit of happiness."

I believe we do ourselves a disservice as Americans by ignoring the founding documents of our nation. I don't think it's at all melodramatic (as some might suggest) to say that the United States Constitution was nothing less than a gift from America's founders, a blueprint for how our democratic form of government can best serve us. Not by paying for our kidney dialysis or chemotherapy when our bodies fail us, as some believe. This sort of government "service" has no place in American society. Indeed, it is nowhere mentioned in the Constitution.

The social contract provided in our Constitution rather has to do with *public goods* such as an impartial judiciary and an armed forces beholden to a civilian commander-in-chief. By and large, American judges who sit on the benches of our nation's courts can't be bought. More than anywhere else in the world today— or at any other time in world history—justice in America is mostly *blind*. The world's brutal military commanders who have throughout history held their power through assassination and death camps have no place in our nation's capital. In Washington, the world's finest military leaders answer to a democratically elected president. When that power is transferred peaceably every four or eight years on the 20th of January, as called for in the Constitution, it truly is a marvel to behold.

I appreciate the naysayers. "Oh, *bullshit*, our courts get bought everyday in this country," comes the rebuttal. Just look at O.J. Simpson's acquittal. Attorney Johnnie Cochran's slick "If it doesn't *fit*, you must *acquit*," path away from a place on California's death row didn't come courtesy of a court appointed defense lawyer. I would respond by making the distinction that it is not a tainted bench, but rather the caliber attorney representing the plaintiff or defendant that (no argument here) all too often tips the scales in the wrong direction. The appeals process is good in America, but only so good. In the end it is, like everything else in life, an imperfect system.

And the amazing peaceful transfer of presidential power that I referred to, it too is rife with pitfalls, no doubt about it. The actions of the president and vice president in the area of nuclear proliferation during the Bush years represent a contempt for not only international norms as spelled out in the Non-Proliferation Treaty, but of the U.S. Constitution itself. The fine tuned system of checks and balances codified in the Constitution was inexcusably circumvented.

But, to reiterate, the problem wasn't with the blueprint. The flaw was in the two men the American people had entrusted to "bear true faith and allegiance" to their executive obligations. Our guidelines for a "more perfect union" had simply been ignored by the powers lurking in the Bush-Cheney White House, powers that were never intended by the likes of Benjamin Franklin and George Mason back in 1787.

* * *

Our country's intelligence capability is not some spigot that can be turned on and off at will to suit whatever policies the executive branch chooses to adopt. The men and women who work in the U.S. intelligence community should never be unwitting pawns in a game that only a select few at the White House are party to. If that has become acceptable, then it's certainly time again to examine how the White House and National Security Council function together in the interest of America's national security.

This sort of review of the country's national security apparatus was conducted by the Tower Commission during Ronald Reagan's administration in 1987 in connection with the Iran Contra Affair. It may well be necessary to reconvene such an effort to get to the bottom of what was known—by whom and when—as the Bush administration's hubris and shortsighted planning allowed the spread of terrible weapons of mass destruction, a global problem that this same group of "Neo-conservatives" so hypocritically adopted as their own cause in their toppling of Saddam Hussein.

Equally egregious was Bush-Cheney's flagrant violation of the U.S. Constitution itself. My understanding of the founding document of our country has it that Article II, Section 2 provides that the president "shall have the power, by and with the advice and consent of the Senate, to make treaties..." It would seem to me then that the making and breaking of treaties goes hand in hand. Saudi Arabia, China and the United States are all party to the Non-Proliferation Treaty of the late 1960s. It is significant for the boldness of its aims, but also infamous for the failure of its members to consistently adhere to its key tenets.

At what point will the governments of the world finally be held responsible for the contracts they enter into with one another, particularly on a matter as vital to the well being of the human race as countering the proliferation of weapons of mass destruction?

* * *

In the final analysis, I believe that (more than the Bushes all-too-cozy relationship with Prince Bandar) it was Cheney's influence that had tilted the scales in favor of this unilateral decision to accede to the Saudis' corrupt deal with Beijing. The thinking was that Riyadh already had Bush by the balls, as it were, with America's need for political and intelligence support in an expanding War on Terror. Never mind that many in Congress would have insisted that a line be drawn, that some sort of limit be imposed on how far American principles would be corrupted.

But it wasn't their decision to make, Cheney likely thought to himself of Congress. As Northwestern University professor Gary Wills argues in his book *Bomb Power*, Robert Oppenheimer's invention of the nuclear bomb had ushered in a new way of thinking about America's constitutional form of government. The executive (which Cheney had arrogantly made himself an all-too-potent part of) perhaps really had become the more dominant of the three branches, thus validating the fears of not a few delegates to the convention in Philadelphia.

But beyond Wills' theory, and much more relevant I believe to the Cheney Vice-Presidency, 9/11 had fundamentally changed America's relationship with the world, and in the process had at least temporarily excused an overly streamlined deliberative process on matters of national security. These were strange days in the wake of 9/11, after all. If White House lawyers had successfully cobbled together justification to torture the Islamic Fascists of the world, was it really out of the question for oil-rich Saudi Arabia to be going nuclear without so much as a slap on the wrist?

They just wouldn't understand on the Hill, the vice president decided. Wyoming's svengali would handle this one all on his own.

34 / MELTED PEOPLE

In the fall of 1997, back when I was still in Naval Officer Candidate School, Master Chief Frangione said something off the cuff that I will always remember.

I forget exactly what he had the class doing that Saturday morning except that it was mindless busy work and we were doing it at our desks in a classroom there on Pensacola's Naval Air Station. I was keeping busy not but five feet from the Master Chief when, responding to a fellow classmate's question about his career in the Navy, he uncharacteristically answered.

He commented on the long hours he would spend on watch, manning the nuclear submarines he had been assigned to. How his boats would sit underwater off the coast of some far off country and just wait. "We'd sit there waiting to nuke 'em," he said matter-of-factly.

Nuke 'em. We went back to what we were doing.

But Master Chief wasn't done. "Because that's what we did," he continued to himself a few beats later, his mind clearly somewhere else entirely. "We nuked people. We melted them. That's what we do."

Certainly nothing joyous in that, Mr. Mephistopheles.

* * *

Time for some fourth quarter devil's advocacy:

Q: Regarding the satellite imagery of subsequent arrivals of the Le He and other Chinese vessels (following Charlie Allen's intervention in 2003)—along with all of the related satellite coverage of preparations and post-arrival activity at the various SRF missile bases—why weren't the imagery records and NGA's corresponding analysis of these events similarly covered up? If the administration was really trying to mask an illicit deal between Beijing and Riyadh, wouldn't this analysis also have served to pull the curtain back at the working level of the intelligence community?

A: The subsequent imagery analysis did in fact continue to indicate, strongly in some instances, that Riyadh was trading up to a nuclear capable system. But as I've said, the imagery alone was not sufficient to make an airtight case. I maintain that Charlie Allen and Director Tenet's intervention bought Vice President Cheney some needed time to decide what his position would be on the matter with President Bush.

The inane "distance observation" permitted by Riyadh in response to the White House's futile demand that the containers be returned to China (necessarily an illicit shipment to have justified the administration's request in the first place) was itself confirmation that U.S.-Saudi security relations had completely jumped the track.

Q: How am I so sure, in the absence of a "smoking gun," that the new missiles that the Saudis acquired from China included nuclear warheads?

A: First of all, short of actually laying my hands on one of them—something that the kingdom's defense minister Crown Prince Sultan has likely done himself—I'm as close to certain as I'll ever be that the Saudis acquired an upgraded ballistic missile system from China during the timeframe I've specified. As indicated consistently in satellite imagery, the apparent make and model of these new missiles alone warranted strong intervention by the United States government.

That said, the geo-political situation following 9/11 was markedly different from the late 1980s when Saudi Arabia acquired its initial conventional capability (China's CSS-2), a time when Riyadh still enjoyed a dependable conventional security partnership with the U.S. By 2003, this had all changed dramatically as Iran was now much closer to a nuclear capability of its own and, while the Saddam threat in Iraq would be eliminated by U.S. forces that same year, regional stability from Riyadh's perspective was being viewed with an increasingly jaundiced eye.

Additionally, as mentioned before, the warheads themselves could have been byproducts of the Pakistani nuclear program (rather than shipping directly from China), but I just don't think this was the case. Not only did I never hear or see even a hint of such activity (beyond the rumor mill that analysts in the DI did much themselves to maintain), I very much doubt that the nuclear puppet masters back in mainland China would have risked mixing Pakistani nuclear technology with their own Chinese made ballistic missiles. Likewise, if you're the king in Riyadh, having just recently kissed off your privileged relationship with the U.S. military, not only were you now seeking a new set of *big guns*, those guns would have to be a sure thing, not some patchwork capability drawing from China's surrogate nuclear program in Pakistan. Fortunately for the king, Beijing was more than willing given Saudi's vast oil reserves to provide just such a thing—lock, stock and barrel.

Finally, and returning to my initial point, the installment of a new mobile ballistic missile system in the kingdom (China's CSS-5, based on the imagery) was obvious to any objective observer in Washington with access to NGA's analysis. And yet there was no interest on the part of Cheney's office or anyone else in the administration to determine the type of weapons payload these new missiles were meant to carry. There was no urgency, no regular trips to CIA as there had been when the war drums were beating loudly on the path to Baghdad. This was not due to a lack of interest in an answer. As President and Vice President of the United States, you absolutely must know such things.

The lack of engagement of the same CIA offices that Cheney had milked for a bogus justification for war in Iraq was simply due to the fact that Cheney himself already knew the answer. You don't ask questions you already know the answer to in Washington—especially if you don't want to draw attention to a sensitive subject. And having only recently lost all credibility with the debunking of his Iraq WMD claim, Chinese nukes in Saudi would clearly be a sensitive subject.

Such a revelation would have shaken Washington to its very core. If there had been any evidence of an attempt by Dick Cheney to cover this up—as I have described herein—calls for his and President Bush's resignation would have been swift and merciless. Hence the administration's otherwise inconceivable hands-off approach.

In hindsight, the 2003 imagery black-out was already well beyond what one could deem prudent.

* * *

In a nutshell, there was the initial cover-up, facilitated by Charlie Allen and others at CIA. This suppression of imagery intelligence was a huge red flag that something was rotten in Washington.

Secondly, there was the working level imbalance of priorities that I witnessed personally from inside CIA. Where there was an entire cadre of dozens of CIA officers and contractors working the Iran nuclear issue within its own dedicated branch of CPD, there was just myself and two others working the Saudi puzzle in the Near East Branch.

And finally, there was the policy level hypocrisy evidenced by Dick Cheney's schizophrenic attitude towards WMD proliferation, first with Iraq in the form of the administration's false justification for ending Saddam's reign, followed by the deafening silence from the administration as Saudi Arabia proceeded in its acquisition of a new generation of nuclear capable missiles from China.

Sadly, my claims will be met with fierce denials in Beijing and Riyadh. I can only hope that President Obama will rethink his decision to prolong this madness. Clearly, the legacy of Dick Cheney's decision making was not of Barack Obama's making when he succeeded George W. Bush in January 2009.

* * *

Fixing the dual problems of the executive branch that manifested themselves during the Bush administration—both internal to the White House national security apparatus and the dysfunctional relationship between the White House and Congress—will only be part of a much larger effort to slay the two headed beast that was at the heart of this scandal; the proliferation of nuclear weapons and America's addiction to foreign oil.

The latter I believe is an easy fix. If the United States government was able to put a man on the moon, the powers that be in Washington can certainly convene a panel of top experts and determine how best to wean ourselves from foreign oil dependence over, say, a five to ten year span. Phase one could be a mix of a much smaller percentage of oil from abroad, our own reserves and (most importantly) an accelerated shift to renewable fuels such as solar power and natural gas. This is no longer "rocket science." Let's vote people into Congress who actually want to see progress on this issue and get on with it.

Unfortunately, the other half of this security arrangement between Riyadh and Beijing—the proliferation of nuclear weapons—is inextricably linked to a tragic flaw in the human condition as old as the species itself. I of course refer to the time-honored belief that we can somehow better our own lives over the long run (as a tribal nation, as it were), by arming ourselves and allies to the teeth and, when necessary, ending the lives of others—by *melting* them even. Regardless of the means, this dark side of humanity goes back to the very beginning, long before the formation of the world's great religions and well before the invention of the combustible engine and atomic bomb.

"But what else are we to do," cries the elder statesman, "when they hijack our planes and crash into our buildings?!" Fair enough. But let's not allow these weapons that offer even greater potential for total self-annihilation to become ever more prevalent in the world as we—as Americans first, but also as members of a global community—work towards an ultimate solution.

Obviously, there's much work to be done on both fronts and I'm certainly not going to solve it all here. But underlying this pair of challenges I believe is a more immediate crisis that must also be addressed if the United States is to ever return to its prominence in the world as the shining *city upon a hill* it once was.

35 / FRANKLIN VS. MAO

In the February 6, 2010 "Facing Up to China" issue of the periodical *The Economist*, a series of articles discussed some of the front-burner issues affecting Sino-U.S. relations in the modern era. There was the ever present question of China's Taiwan policy. There was discussion of how in 2010 Beijing is being consistently more assertive vis-à-vis the West to discourage any meddling from abroad in Chinese "internal affairs." Beijing's decision only a month after the issue hit newsstands to completely ban all Google-based Internet searching would serve as a prime example.

The third trend cited disappointed me, but was not a surprise. The article noted how the recent "slump in the West" (beginning in late 2008 and continuing well into 2010) had given way to a "Beijing consensus," one all about "extolling the virtues of decisive authoritarianism over shilly-shallying democratic debate." "In the margins of international conferences," the editors continued, "even American officials mutter despairingly about their own 'dysfunctional' political system."

And why not this despair? Why shouldn't Americans be disappointed in their own political process when even in the worst economic times since the Great Depression of the 1930s, our elected leaders in Washington do nothing to address the roots of the problem? Instead, in the first year of the Barack Obama administration, we saw yet another long drawn out debate over universal health care—a debate this country had already settled several times before, most recently during the Clinton administration in the early 1990s.

In his determined and ultimately quasi-successful attempt to have Congress pass his (and House Speaker Nancy Pelosi's) vision for health care reform, President Obama was all too comfortable employing the "nuclear option" to get the associated bill through the U.S. Senate, a particular parliamentary procedure also known euphemistically as "reconciliation."

The Constitution does actually provide for such reconciliation, whereby a mere 51 vote majority (rather than the generally prescribed 60 votes) can move a bill out of the Senate to the House of Representatives. This math had become critical in January of 2010 when the state of Massachusetts elected a Republican to the upper chamber of Congress to fill a seat that was left vacant—ironically enough—with the passing of longtime universal healthcare proponent Senator Ted Kennedy.

But the Constitution also specifies that this procedure be used sparingly, only on legislative matters pertaining specifically to *taxation, appropriations* or the *federal debt*. Even many of Obama's most ardent supporters in Congress agreed that employing the "nuclear option" to reshape America's uneven healthcare system would be a terrible perversion of the Constitution—if not circumventing it entirely. And yet this was precisely how the bill made its way over to the House for passage.

On the eve of the second critical vote on his vision for universal healthcare in America (which, incidentally, oddly came late on a Sunday night in Washington—and from a practical standpoint was not even considered a true Congressional "vote" on the matter), President Obama was equally indifferent about yet *another* rare parliamentary tactic (related to the first) that had become necessary to ensure passage of the bill, this time through the U.S. House of Representatives. Obama remarked in a televised interview on March 17, 2010 just days prior to the vote:

> "By the time the [House] vote has taken place, not only will I know what's in it, you'll know what's in it because it's going to be posted and everybody's going to be able to evaluate it on the merits."

The president's comment is interesting from a political standpoint in the way it captures Obama's thoughts on the strange circuitous route his healthcare package was taking through Congress at the time. But, to my purposes here, the country's chief executive was also acknowledging just how backwards the whole process had become as he extolled his and Ms. Pelosi's ends—certainly not those of the majority of the American people if the day's polling was any indication—to justify the questionable means. Only *after* the House passed the bill, the president explained, would the merits of the controversial healthcare legislation be weighed.

This blatant abuse of power was evidenced in previous comments made by the Speaker of the House Nancy Pelosi, who herself somehow proudly presided over this short-circuiting of America's Constitution. Only weeks before the House "vote," Speaker Pelosi said the following in reference to her plans for seeing healthcare legislation enacted:

> "We will go through the gate. If the gate is closed, we will go over the fence. If the fence is too high, we will pole vault in. If that doesn't work, we will parachute in. But we are going to get healthcare reform passed."

If the reader is confused by the speaker's mention of "pole vaulting" and "parachuting" as a means of passing healthcare reform, my apologies. I also see no mention of these activities anywhere in the U.S. Constitution.

Perhaps Congressman Alcee Hastings' comments are more illuminating in regards to the chaotic atmosphere that surrounded this debate over government sponsored healthcare and, increasingly, the legislative process itself:

> "There ain't no rules here, we're trying to accomplish something...All this talk about rules....When the deal goes down...we make 'em up as we go along."

Mr. Hastings' preference for blunt language over Pelosi's more nuanced analogies might have something to do with his professional background. Mr. Hastings was once impeached on charges of perjury and corruption and was subsequently removed from the bench as a federal judge *before* being elected to the U.S. House of Representatives by his constituents in Florida's 23rd congressional district.

The corrupt parliamentary tactics used in both chambers of Congress to force Obama's healthcare plans through the legislative process had provided yet more evidence of just how broken things have become in Washington. And not just in the cliché political sense, a reality that will forever characterize the affairs of state in our nation's capital. No, this assault on the principles that serve as the foundation of American democracy would have a much more sobering effect on Americans who grasped the true nature of what had transpired there in the early spring of 2010. The path taken by Obama's healthcare proposal had run quite counter to the guidelines contained in the U.S. Constitution itself.

Regardless of what one thinks of the idea of universal healthcare in America, the rules contained in our nation's founding document had been crudely violated.

* * *

At the ceremonial bill signing held in the East Room of the White House almost immediately after the healthcare package left the House, Vice President Biden made some brief celebratory remarks before introducing President Obama.

As he turned the podium over, Biden remarked to the president, loudly enough for the many reporters' microphones and cameras to hear, "This is a big fucking deal."

Yes, Mr. Vice President, it is most certainly that.

* * *

All of this (stating the obvious) points to an acute crisis of responsible leadership in our nation's capital.

The Bush administration's abrogation of its responsibilities under the Non-Proliferation Treaty; President Obama's decision (thus far) not to reverse the position adopted by Vice President Cheney with regards to the criminal China-Saudi nuclear pact; and finally the Obama administration's inclination to whistle past the fiscal graveyard with its costly prescriptions for the country—these are all indeed symptoms of a dysfunctional democratic system. But (I can't say it enough) the problem doesn't lie with the federal government itself—the thoughtful system of checks and balances provided for in our

Constitution. A root cause of the problem lies with the men and women we've been sending to Washington over too many years to populate the halls of Congress.

As potent as the executive branch can be in tackling some of the nation's challenges, it is the legislative branch that must step up and again assert itself in America's national and international discourse.

With regards to the problem of excessive government spending in Washington, the panacea, I believe, unfortunately does not include (at the moment at least) a series of broad new tax cuts—as many conservatives stubbornly insist, citing Ronald Reagan's bold fiscal strategy of the early 1980s. Successful as it was, the times are far too different for a repeat of this approach. More likely, given the current state of the federal government's balance sheet, the White House and Congress will have to find ways to attack the deficit (and ultimately the national debt) without—and this is critical—further damaging America's business environment for U.S. and foreign owned corporations. Today in 2010, the federal debt and the looming threat of inflation of historic proportions will best be addressed by a comprehensive freeze on federal spending, followed quickly by thoughtful cuts to areas of the federal government that have simply outlived their purpose.

As just one example, I agree with those deficit hawks in Washington who suggest that the U.S. Department of Education should be abolished entirely. Sound radical? It really isn't when you consider that the core functions of kindergarten through twelfth-grade education planning and oversight in America are already well handled at the state and local levels—as it should be I would argue. Far too many federal tax dollars are pumped into this redundant bureaucracy located on Independence Avenue near the National Mall in Washington.

The Department of Education's office building actually sits just behind several wonderful Smithsonian Museums, real national treasures that could definitely use some of the funding that gets siphoned off by its costly bureaucratic neighbors. But such cuts (and they must be comprehensive and, in some cases, *drastic* if they are to achieve the desired results) must be paired with a long term national strategy that is nowhere to be found in Washington these days—at least not in public.

The following are my thoughts on the matter, to be taken with a grain of salt or to heart, as stated in my introduction. Above all, they are intended to spur the reader to herself consider all that is possible for American leadership—both foreign and domestic:

- What is America's new energy policy going to be, particularly in the wake of the bloody course that Dick Cheney and the country's oil executives navigated (at the expense of too many lives) in Iraq?
- How can elements of the country's law enforcement agencies and intelligence community be refocused to better tackle the vile human trafficking networks in Asia, Eastern Europe and along America's own borders?
- How can a private option be implemented to enhance the long-term viability of the federally mandated retirement program Social Security?
- What tax incentives can Congress adopt—while still mindful of the need to balance the federal budget—to once again make the United States a worthwhile place to do business for U.S. and foreign companies?
- How can America build upon the great progress it made throughout the twentieth century in the fields of science and technology?

These questions and many others must not be answered with endless commissions and Congressional hearings. The bureaucracies that already exist in Washington must be given new marching orders in the form of presidential leadership and the fiscal powers of Congress. Time is wasting.

* * *

This pendulum swing in policy-making power between Congress and the White House has defined the political dynamics of Washington throughout our nation's history. Indeed, the sharing of powers amongst the three branches of national government was the subject of much debate at the Constitutional Convention in Philadelphia in 1787.

In the wake of the radical swing in favor of the executive branch during the Bush administration, I'd like to take the opportunity to throw my support behind those calling today for a recalibration (so to speak) of the halls of Congress—to bring it more in line with what the writers of the Constitution originally had in mind for the nation's legislative branch. After all, Congress was meant to be a potent check against executive overreach, a major reason the British were given the boot in the first place.

The usurpation of the Constitution by Vice President Cheney and, ultimately, President Bush—by their obtuse unilateral approach to the Saudi nuclear issue—would have been stopped in its tracks by an open, more democratic flow of information. Unfortunately for President Bush, he had only his biased (almost familial) relationship with Prince Bandar and the equally tainted filter of Dick Cheney to rely upon in deciding which course to take on the matter. The result was hardly democracy at work. It was the stuff of quasi-monarchy and crude oil dynasty—both at home and abroad.

I believe the legislative branch can be made strong again by an American electorate that begins to look beyond only matters of party affiliation. This tendency to vote "straight Republican" or "straight Democrat" must give way to new ways of thinking. Our world is too complex today for such a simplistic approach to self governance. Critical questions pertaining to bioethics and America's path in foreign affairs can't be left only to the judiciary and executive branches.

In the interest of this needed fresh approach in Washington, why not a full sweep of Congress? Both houses. A congressional election in the not-too-distant future could take on renewed significance. Any and all incumbents who have already served four full terms in the House (eight years), or two full terms in the Senate (twelve years)—they simply get voted out during their states' next election cycle. Republican, democrat, or otherwise—it doesn't matter. The result would be a House of Representatives and Senate with nearly all new representation coupled with a much smaller group of "business as usual" incumbents.

To be clear, I'm not advocating term limits, per se. Over the long run, I think such limits do a disservice to the country by excluding individuals who actually should be in office for *longer* periods of time. Not all politicians are bad, after all. I'm simply proposing a one-time effort to, in a sense, "reboot" the system.

In this way the legislative branch of our nation's government (as provided for in the Constitution) would have a fresh set of minds to decide what works and what doesn't for modern America. This new Congress could, if only briefly, be free of much of the partisanship and backroom deal-making that has weighed the body down for too long.

Maybe the argument against this is that Congress would grind to a halt. Perhaps all these freshmen legislators running around would result in such a leadership vacuum on Capitol Hill that another Cheney might come along— perhaps as the *real* commander-in-chief this time—and proceed to have his way with a less experienced legislative branch. But such hesitancy would be based on a misunderstanding of the way things actually work on Capitol Hill.

In both the House and Senate, there are interns (who know nothing), junior staffers (who know enough), but then "professional" staffers who enjoy almost a tenure-like status. The professional staffers are the key players on the Hill; they make the all important Congressional committees function as they do—albeit not so well at times. Capitol Hill's professional staffers would still be in town following this proposed special election.

As job market forces provide, they would find work supporting the new Congress. Only now, the offices and committees they work for would be under very new management. Not a bad thing for a democracy, I don't think, particularly given the current state of affairs in Washington.

* * *

"Oh, but our debt!" the skeptics might continue to lament. Yes, it will be right there staring us in the face for quite some time. It took years of reckless government spending to get into this mess and it will take years to get out of it. But at least we'll be headed in the right direction.

And if the history of the United States is any indication, things can often get turned around quickly in favor of the American Dream. Whether it's American "exceptionalism" or just a solid foundation in the U.S. Constitution, our future as Americans remains bright.

36 / THE GOLDEN STATE

The two bedroom apartment my family and I are now living in as I write this from South Pasadena, California is a world away from the near waterfront home we enjoyed in St. Michaels only a few short years ago.

Our apartment building sits in a neighborhood called Raymond Hill, which borders on the much larger city of Pasadena where the famous Rose Bowl parade is held every January 1st. We didn't go this year. We decided that the girls wouldn't make it in the cold for any length of time and, truth be told, the cheapest tickets I saw online were $45 a piece. That kind of cash is in short supply for us these days.

The latest community circular from South Pasadena's chamber of commerce had an article about how Theodore Roosevelt visited the town back in 1903 as president. As the article recounts the event, prior to leaving town by train TR paused at the base of Raymond Hill and declared, "I am sure I need not say how much I enjoyed my visit here. It has been delightful, delightful."

I like it just fine here myself. I'm quite confident that California is where my family and I are meant to be at this point in life, my time working in Washington forever behind me now.

* * *

My mother eventually moved back east from Roseville after my father's passing in 2003 in northern California. While much of her family lives in Massachusetts where she grew up as a child (her mother, brother Steve and his family continue to live in the town of Blackstone), she decided on a retirement community outside Raleigh, North Carolina, not far from her sister, my Auntie Lorri.

Fortunately, I have family from my dad's side nearby here in southern California. One of his uncles, Charlie, lives with his wife in the town of Falbrook. Two of my dad's cousins live south of Los Angeles in the San Diego neighborhood; one in La Mesa, the other out on Point Loma overlooking the same bay I once helped steer the cruiser USS Princeton on her way out to the Pacific.

The U.S. Navy might not be as big numbers-wise as it once was in the days of Teddy Roosevelt's Great White Fleet, but it fortunately remains a most potent force for democracy on the seas and oceans of the world. Following the fleet's circumnavigation of the globe from December 16, 1907 to February 22, 1909, Roosevelt spoke in the twilight of his presidency in Hampton Roads, Virginia to mark its historic return.

"Other nations may do what you have done," President Roosevelt predicted, "but they'll have to follow you."

* * *

My father is buried up north in Rocklin, California, where the Sierra foothills begin just east of Sacramento. His grave is actually not far from those of his Aunt Sta and her husband Corey. My dad always spoke fondly of his Uncle Corey, very much as the father he never had.

It's been years since I visited his grave and it will likely be a few more before I do. I'm going to get things rolling again before I pay him a visit.

One of the last things he said to me with his signature melancholy was, "I wish things could have been better for you." I was only 27 at the time, for Christ sake! My life was just getting started.

But I will visit. In time.

* * *

My grandfather, Paul Edward Scherck, Senior is supposedly buried here in the Los Angeles area. He apparently died from lung cancer in the late 1960s, which would have made him about as old as my father was when he passed in January 2003.

During my father's last month on this earth, he told my brothers and me the story of how our grandfather had never returned to Fayetteville, North Carolina after he was born at the end of World War II. My dad used to say how his mother could hear the church bells ringing to signal the end of the war in Europe as she and my father were driven home from the hospital, his own father far away somewhere overseas at the time.

My grandfather, my dad continued, had run off with a nurse he met while serving in the Army. He later divorced my grandmother once he returned to the States. My dad never met his father, he said with tired regret, handing my brothers and me a small black and white wallet-sized picture of his father. He pulled them from the breast pocket of his button-down shirt as he spoke. He had them made up especially for this planned confessional to me and my brothers.

My mother had shown me a very different picture of our grandfather years earlier while we were still living in Virginia. She had also briefly mentioned once what happened between my grandmother and grandfather, but not in any great detail. The picture my mom showed was of a Paul Senior beaming directly into the camera. That picture was in color. My grandfather was wearing his WWII era military khakis as he posed with one foot propped up on a golden bale of hay. He was a good looking man, my mom commented as she put the picture away.

While finishing this book, I reached out to my mother back in North Carolina, not far from where my father was born actually. I wanted to know whether (today in 2010) she had any more details on my grandfather. The single sheet of paper my mom sent in response was a photocopy of notes that my grandmother had clearly typed up herself.

I knew these notes came from my grandmother because I could recognize the particular font from her typewriter, the one she used later in life when she was a grandmother to her only son's three boys. I especially remember the quote from Albert Einstein that she had typed up on a small index card and posted with a magnet to the refrigerator door in her kitchen. I would read the Einstein quote most every time my family and I went to visit her in Blackstone, a long ten hour drive in the family Dodge Caravan from our home in Montclair, Virginia, back when I was a boy.

"I live in that solitude which is painful in youth, but delicious in the years of maturity," the card read.

* * *

Like me, my grandfather was born in New England—April 22, 1909, in the town of Lynn, Massachusetts. Lynn is less than a twenty minute drive from where I was born in Woburn. He had a brother by the name of Louis who lived in Houston. Their father, my great-grandfather, was Leon Henry Scherck, born in New Orleans.

My grandfather was a student at Harvard University, but for only two years. While there he studied economics and history. "Speaks, translates & reads: French & Spanish," my grandmother's notes read.

After leaving Harvard, it appears that Paul Sr. worked in real estate for a number of years. Finally on January 17, 1941, he was drafted—"inducted" my grandmother typed—by Uncle Sam for the war. Living in Houston, Texas at the time, my grandfather weighed 178 pounds and stood at just 5'10". Who knows why my grandmother recorded such details, but there they were. He was shorter and a little thicker in his early thirties than I am today at the age of thirty-five. Height-wise, I'm the runt of my parents' three sons; Mike is somewhat taller than me and Jeff towers over us both at 6'4".

From that January of 1941 to February of the following year, our grandfather was in training as a member of the Texas Air National Guard's 111th Observation Squadron-Photographic in Brownwood, Texas. Some research revealed that the 111th specialized in aerial reconnaissance. My grandfather was being trained to be an overhead *imagery specialist*. I almost couldn't believe what I was reading given how consequential satellite imagery had been during my time as a CMO on the Saudi account at CIA. It would be almost another twenty years before the first satellite images of earth were generated by an American satellite in 1959, and yet there my grandfather was getting trained to fly with a camera in a Texas Air National Guard airplane to capture the next best thing.

From Texas, my grandfather was transferred to Pope Field, an Army Air Corps Base at the time (now Pope Air Force Base) immediately adjacent to the U.S. Army's beloved Fort Bragg in North Carolina. U.S. military personnel managers had decided to pluck him from Texas' 111th and make him a private in the Army Air Corps' 23rd Observation Squadron.

After attaining the rank of sergeant at Pope, he was sent back to Harvard in January 1943 to attend Officer Candidate School—all straight from my grandmother's notes. Uncle Sam wanted to turn my grandfather into an Army officer. But, as my grandmother noted simply, "Did not make it—so returned to Ft. Bragg, N.C."

The last paragraph of my grandmother's notes on Paul Sr. reads verbatim as follows:

"Later sent to various A.F. Bases—Lowry I think (Colorado) & Salt Lake City ?? returning home from trips. Then to Charleston, S.C. for shipment late in September 1943 to Pacific Theater. Based in Karachi, then in India. Now Karachi is Pakistan. Returned to States in November 1945."

Based on these notes—and they're all I have—my grandfather was somewhere in India in June of 1944 when my father was born. He was serving as an airman on a lesser known front of World War II, referred to as the China-Burma-India (CBI) theater. Under the command of American General Joseph "Vinegar Joe" Stilwell (known for his acerbic nature according to the history books) CBI was largely an air transport supply mission supporting Allied and Chinese military forces operating in the rugged terrain of North Burma against an entrenched Japanese occupation.

The Japanese had taken over the strategically significant Burma in early 1942, and with it China's only remaining overland connection to the outside world, the critical 700 mile Burma Road. Forcing the Imperial army back off the mainland had become key to the Allies' overarching strategy for victory in the Pacific theater. It was a long fought struggle, but by early 1945 General Stilwell had commanded his American, British and Chinese forces to victory over the Japanese.

When my grandfather returned to the States in November of that same year, it wasn't to be with my grandmother and father, by that time both living back in Massachusetts. Not in my grandmother's notes was that my grandfather went on to have at least one more wife and some unknown number of children in Texas and California.

* * *

The black and white photo of my grandfather that my father had chosen to give us as death approached in December 2002 was very different from the photo my mother had shared years earlier. You couldn't see my grandfather's eyes in the one my father gave me. Paul Sr. was looking away from the camera in this shot, almost as though someone had taken the picture without him knowing.

My dad got only an occasional letter in the mail from him while growing up as a young boy in Blackstone. My grandmother, as my dad told the story, never allowed my grandfather to meet his son face-to-face after returning from overseas. My grandfather's infidelity must have been just too painful for her. The letters eventually stopped.

And there my brothers and I were in Roseville, California, not quite sixty years later, listening to our father describe the pain he had tucked away as a young boy. It was this pain from not knowing his father and the resulting resentment of his mother that he would hold onto his entire life. This had been at the heart of the "look at the seagulls" ridicule I witnessed as a child.

This had been the answer my father was looking for one day when he asked me late in his life, completely out of the blue, "Why can't I be happy?"

I just didn't know what to say.

* * *

In the summer of 2000, several years before my father was stricken with cancer, he and I were strolling once more along the beaches of the Outer Banks in North Carolina, right where we had played "Imperial Japanese Navy" (a product of my dad's playful imagination) with my brothers when we were younger. I was still in the Navy at that point in 2000 and had just transferred to Norfolk from San Diego. Christa and I had yet to meet. The resulting wedge between father and son—a wedge that never needed to be—had yet to form.

Even then in 2000—before getting out of the Navy, before that detour to U.C. Berkeley, before 9/11 even—I had been thinking of applying to the CIA. My older brother Mike was making good progress at the time with his own application to the FBI. Walking along the beach with my dad, I predicted a promising career in the federal government for two of his three sons—even though both had yet to begin. I was trying to cheer up the old grump.

"You'll have one son in the FBI and another in the CIA," I estimated. "How about that?" Will *that* make you happy, I thought to myself as we ambled along the edge of the surf.

He just stared off into the Atlantic, those damn seagulls almost certainly still in view.

* * *

Our careers have gone their separate ways, as brothers tend to do in life. Mike (four years my senior) eventually did his time at the FBI Academy in Quantico, Virginia and is now doing valuable work for the country in the ongoing War on Terrorism. He and his wife live in northern Virginia and are blessed with three beautiful daughters.

Younger brother Jeff broke from tradition and opted to pursue a career other than working for Uncle Sam. After establishing himself as an account-ant in Vegas, he continues to live the bachelor life in the Boston area now, tak-ing in the occasional Celtics and Red Sox game.

I think Mike and I would probably agree that Jeff was (in some ways) wis-est of the three boys in his choice of career paths.

* * *

I'm rather certain that if he were still alive today that my father would be proud of me for having finally done what needed to be done to shed some light on the shortsighted policies of the Bush-Cheney administration. I like to think that, whereas he had dedicated twenty-six years of his life to service in the U.S. military, he would also see that I had found my own path to being not only true to myself, but also (in my own way) a patriot.

But more than this connection to some higher cause known as the U.S.A. which, in the end, we can only imagine, I wish that my dad could have learned to enjoy the more immediate and lasting side of life—that of family.

* * *

Don't get me wrong, career is important. Finding what you love to do for a living and pursuing it *to the death!!* is a big part of what this is all about.

But my wife and I are just unbelievably blessed to be parents to two such wonderful little girls. They bring such joy to me and Christa each and every day. (Well, ok, *almost* each and every day.)

We were at the Swedish furniture store IKEA in Burbank recently getting some things for our new apartment. When we returned home, Chloe and Sidney proceeded to dub the stepstool we bought for the kitchen the new "apple picking stool."

"The what?" I asked, not understanding. There's not an apple tree anywhere near our apartment. But guess what? We now have the only "apple picking stool" in the greater Los Angeles are—right here in our very own kitchen.

Sidney just got potty trained recently, something she's very proud to announce even to perfect strangers on the playground in South Pasadena's nearby Garfield Park. But at home, she's prone to forgetting to put her underwear back on after doing her business. She'll run straight out from the bathroom at Chloe shouting, "Hey, Clo! Hey, Clo! Guess what kinda undies I have on?!" She spins around lifting up her dress to show her naked backside. "*These* kinda undies!!" she shouts uncontrollably. How great is that!

And you know those credits at the end of the movie when the song begins to play? Christa and I used to be quick to just shut off the DVD and head to bed. But not anymore. Now the volume on the television goes up as Chloe turns to me and asks, "Do you want to dance, daddy?"

37 / OF LAWS, NOT MEN

However this account of my time working at CIA ultimately plays out, I'm comfortable knowing that I did it motivated not by any sort of personal vendetta against the Bush administration or the intelligence officers I tried my best to support in the Counter-Proliferation Division of CIA. Above all, I wrote this for my two daughters so that they someday understand what their father was going through during their first years of life.

As an American I truly did feel honored to shake the hand of President Bush as my time working for the federal government drew to a close there at NCTC. And the Agency professionals above me years earlier in CPD and the "seventh floor" (although I never had the pleasure with the latter) were, at the end of the workday, just doing their jobs best they knew how. Unfortunately, they just didn't know when to say "no" to management downtown. They just didn't recognize how their actions were actually undermining what needs to be America's long term goals in the world.

As for Mr. Cheney, the man was President Ford's chief of staff when he was my age. Regardless of how shortsighted some of his decision-making was as vice president, it should not altogether cancel out the good things he has done for this country over the course of his long career in politics. I have my doubts that this professionalization of American politics is good for the country, but that's another conversation entirely.

Say what you want about the CIA's water boarding of high value terrorists (a program essentially underwritten by Cheney's own lawyers), the country did not suffer a single more terrorist attack during the remaining seven years of the Bush administration. As terrible as it is to think that human beings were tortured in the name of American national security, if the lives of my two

young daughters or anyone else's children were saved by Cheney's and Addington's blurring of that thin line between self defense and atrocity, I must admit
I'm glad it was done.

And, Nancy Pelosi's outrageous equivocation on the subject in early 2009
aside, the CIA's questionable torture tactics during the height of the Bush administration's war on Islamic Fascism do not present the same Constitutional
balance of power dilemmas as the Saudi nuclear debacle. Unlike the Bush administration's secretive complicity in the transfer of a nuclear capability from
China to Saudi Arabia, Congress was duly informed (Ms. Pelosi included)
of the extraordinary measures being taken with a small number of America's
worst enemies. Congress had a chance to voice its disapproval when it mattered
most. Its leadership on both sides of the political aisle chose not to do so.

*　*　*

And what about Israel? Clearly, as the content of this book hits Tel Aviv—
once Bibi Netanyahu reads about how things went down during the Bush administration—won't there be some reaction? Might there be a knee-jerk air-
strike against some of the Saudi bases already on the Israeli Air Force's radar?
Perhaps something *worse?*

I don't believe so. I tend to think the Israelis have been reading the tea
leaves on their own all along. They quite possibly gathered themselves at the
time that something was going on between China and the Saudis and, perhaps,
that Washington was looking the other way, choosing not to make a big deal
of it as Bush focused more on pushing democracy on that part of the world.
In addition to the situation in Iraq, the Israelis were seeing up close how the
Chinese were sinking their claws more and more deeply into Saudi oil fields
and even certain parts of Africa, to include the Sudan.

But what if this is wrong? What if this claim I'm making hits the front
pages of the world's newspapers—from the *Albuquerque Journal* to the *Zimbabwe
Herald*—and all hell breaks loose. What if my particular optic on this issue prevented me from seeing the complete picture (assuming there is such
a thing in this). It might be that there are U.S. military personnel secretly
on the ground in Saudi at the request of the king, as someone once obliquely

suggested, whose sole purpose is to safeguard the dozen or so nukes against the possibility of an Al Qaeda-led coup against Riyadh. Thus, perhaps yet another complicating twist to the overall mess. What then?

Again, I wouldn't have written this if I thought that some catastrophe would result in its publication. But if "it" does happen, I hate to use the cliché, but it's a cliché for good reason: don't shoot the messenger. In no way could the higher-ups of the Bush administration (Bush, Cheney, Hadley, Rumsfeld, Rice—and of course others now, given the change in administrations) have thought that such a policy decision could remain under wraps forever. If they did, they were stupid. And if they did, they were obviously wrong.

In the end, any unintended consequence of my attempt to expose this grossly flawed approach to national security policy making rests solely on the shoulders of those who committed *We the People* to it.

* * *

That said, I've also done this to preserve something that I learned as a young man is no less than the foundation for the success of this country.

The American Legion website states that the organization's now seventy-year-old Oratorical Competition "exists to develop deeper knowledge and appreciation for the U.S. Constitution among high school students." The title of the ten-minute speech I prepared for this same competition when I was a high school student was "The Secret of the Constitution's Success." I chose to focus on Article V which lays out the process by which the Constitution can be amended.

I spoke of this aspect of the framework for our nation's government as a powerful mechanism that makes the Constitution a "living and breathing document." It is Article V that allowed for the first ten amendments to the Constitution, known near and far as the United States Bill of Rights—the freedom of speech, religion and the right to a free press. But while I still consider this part of the Constitution to be one of its principle strengths, I realize years later that there are other elements that make the Constitution the cornerstone of our great democracy.

John Adams, one of our country's founders (and George Washington's successor as the nation's second president) was responsible for drafting the

Massachusetts Constitution and Bill of Rights—later serving as the basis for the United States Constitution. In article 30 of the Declaration of Rights, ratified in 1780, Adams addressed the essential need for proper separation of powers amongst the three branches of government.

"To the end," Adams' bill of rights reads, "it may be a government of laws and not of men."

* * *

As the man with the president's ear on all matters related to national security and foreign affairs, Vice President Cheney's carefully shrouded decision to forego any forceful intervention in the illicit deal between Riyadh and Beijing represents an abdication of fundamental executive branch responsibilities outlined in the Constitution. Responsibilities envisioned by men like John Adams.

My view of the Bush administration's inaction—of Vice President Cheney's in particular—is no more naïve or unrealistic than it is reasonable and responsible to claim that turning a blind eye had been the optimal course of action due to America's involvement at the time in the ongoing War on Terror and the still precarious and increasingly bloody situation in Iraq. The failure to take steps to prevent the nuclearization of a regime as unstable and fickle as that in Riyadh—be it with the help of an advancing China or any other nation—has potential consequences that far exceed any such near-term objectives.

In a perfect world, as global leaders come to grips with the startling reality I have described here, there will hopefully be a burst of momentum in the effort to reign in the proliferation of nuclear weapons, a goal that Barack Obama rightly promoted early on in his presidency. Ideally (says the man dreaming) political pressure might come to bear on both Riyadh and Beijing to undo this terribly dangerous situation. Perhaps Riyadh might actually show some leadership for once by simply returning the dangerous arsenal to China.

Yes, that simple. Such a selfless act of peace would be a welcome surprise from a country whose prominent status on the world stage was literally handed to them in March of 1938 when the American firm California-Arabian Standard Oil first discovered oil north of Dhahran. By returning the weapons, I believe it's possible—though far from certain—that Riyadh might actually create a new dynamic of security for itself and much of the Middle East. If Riyadh, Beijing and Washington could together own up to their carelessness in this whole affair, I suggest that such cooperation might serve as a strong deterrent to any further saber rattling out of Tehran. One of the main reasons behind Riyadh's interest in acquiring a nuclear capability in the first place might simply dissolve as China rethinks its support of Iran's nuclear program. Pandora's box may have a lid after all.

One can always hope.

* * *

Washington's stance on WMD proliferation throughout the world—nuclear, chemical and biological alike—must not be contingent upon extenuating circumstances that have and will continue to arise over the course of our nation's history. The proliferation of weapons of mass destruction is either acceptable—from the standpoint of what is right and just for the future of the human race—or it is not.

Although I very much doubt it (given the close relationship between the House of Bush and House of Saud), even assuming attempts were made by the Bush White House to try to reverse this spread of nuclear weapons from China, any such efforts came up short in the end. The devil had gotten his way in Riyadh and—more ominously given China's reinvigorated presence on the world stage—Beijing. And Washington said nothing.

Look, the world's leaders made a collective commitment to oppose the proliferation of nuclear weapons back in the late 1960s. President Obama's Nuclear Security Conference held in Washington in April 2010, focusing on the need to keep nuclear material worldwide out of the hands of international terrorists, was without question a step in the right direction. But such tactical level efforts will only go so far in reigning in the spread of nuclear weapons throughout the world.

The defining Nuclear Non-Proliferation Treaty (NPT), first signed at Washington, London and Moscow on July 1, 1968, contains three fundamental "pillars": Non-Proliferation, Disarmament and—increasingly important in the modern era—the Right to peaceful use of nuclear technology. A much needed month-long international conference was held in New York only weeks following the 2010 Nuclear Security Conference in an effort to revive the essential mandate of NPT. The goal of Non-Proliferation is stated in the Treaty in stark, unmistakable terms:

"Considering the devastation that would be visited upon all mankind by a nuclear war and the consequent need to make every effort to avert the danger of such a war and to take measures to safeguard the security of peoples... [parties to the Treaty have] agreed as follows:

Article I: Each nuclear-weapon State Party to the Treaty undertakes not to transfer to any recipient whatsoever nuclear weapons or other nuclear explosive devices or control over such weapons or explosive devices directly, or indirectly; and not in any way to assist, encourage, or induce any non-nuclear weapon State to manufacture or otherwise acquire nuclear weapons or other nuclear explosive devices, or control over such weapons or explosive devices."

China's violation of this paramount goal of NPT in its relationships with North Korea, Pakistan and now Saudi Arabia, while worthy of censure, is of course consistent with China's own nuclear doctrine. Beijing's policy on nuclear weapons is guided by the principle that a nation simply doesn't need thousands of warheads (as the U.S. and former Soviet Union clearly believed) to secure a nuclear deterrent—China's stated goal for building and maintaining a nuclear arsenal. And, on paper at least, Beijing subscribes to a "no first use" policy.

NPT obligations notwithstanding, Beijing's nuclear doctrine was thus consistent with how China's decision-makers likely perceived (and no doubt still do) the nuclear power status afforded by them to Riyadh's ruling elite. In exchange for an ever greater share of the kingdom's oil, Saudi royals would—after decades of disavowed interest—finally be in control of their own discreet stash of nuclear missiles, just enough to provide the requisite deterrent against Israel and a rising nuclear power in Iran.

The exact size of the arsenal is anyone's guess in the West, as perhaps even the King himself is unaware precisely. But they know in Beijing: just enough to keep the oil flowing. No more, and no less.

* * *

And so the rationalizing is as easy on this side of the Pacific as it is on China's end. But at the end of the day, it is only that.

And while Beijing's communist leaders have obviously granted themselves the luxury of deciding when and when *not* to abide by the NPT, America's leaders in Washington are ultimately beholden to a higher standard—the U.S. Constitution. It had been the United States Senate, after all—in accordance with the "advice and consent" power enumerated in Article II of the Constitution—that first ratified the Non-Proliferation Treaty on behalf of the American people on March 13, 1969. And, by law, it was only the Senate's prerogative to undo that commitment. Consequently, the Bush administration was flat wrong to have folded as it did.

This debate (assuming there even was one between the office of the vice president and the Oval Office) should have been carried out openly between the Bush administration and Congress. Hearings should have been held both on television and behind closed doors—but not too many closed doors. Cabinet secretaries, military flag officers and intelligence agency directors should have been called as witnesses. It should have been a public national debate not unlike what we see today in 2010 over what should be done in response to Iran's potentially belligerent nuclear aspirations. What should America's response be to China's flagrant disregard for the fundamental goal of the Non-Proliferation Treaty?

It's not American "exceptionalism" so much as it is a cold, hard reality: If not the United States of America to stand up against the proliferation of weapons of mass destruction—then who?

* * *

In seventeenth century England, the British political philosopher Thomas Hobbes observed in his book *Leviathan* that, without a strong centralized government, life in human society tends to be "solitary, poor, nasty, brutish, and short." And, given that Hobbes had little use for the doctrine of separation of powers in government, it's likely he would have approved of Dick Cheney's national security shell game which—while resulting in the proliferation of WMD—did serve to preserve (at least for a time) America's easy access to the world's largest natural repository of petroleum.

When I first learned of Hobbes' thinking back in college, I will admit that I was rather inclined to agree with his staunch support of an all-powerful sovereign. Things are just easier when only a single decision-maker is involved. No needless debate, no labyrinth of bureaucracy to contend with. But I, for one, am convinced that the abuse of power perpetrated by Vice President Cheney in his oversight of American intelligence fails to qualify as what Hobbes would have perhaps suggested is the "price of peace."

It's worth noting that Hobbes did not rule out the necessity for rebellion in cases of undue abuse of power. And while I'm not about to pick up the pitchfork against Washington (a vastly more benevolent power by Hobbesian standards), I was not about to let this grave misstep in America's foreign policy go unnoticed.

38 / CALLING ALL COOLER HEADS

The details of George W. Bush's and Dick Cheney's working relationship in relation to the Saudi question are, in the end, something only these two men alone know for certain. Likewise, only China's leaders in Beijing know the intimate details of the calculus that resulted in the transfer of doomsday weapons to a regime as capricious as that in Saudi Arabia.

That said, while visits by the Dalai Lama to the White House over the years have caused considerable consternation in Beijing, this wake-up call to America's leaders in Washington absolutely must help bring an end to the overly politic kabuki dance in post-Cold War Sino-U.S. relations.

I will leave it at that, however. As has been the case throughout world history in the relationship between rulers and those they rule, the needed critique of China's political leaders will best come from the Chinese people themselves.

* * *

The Cuban missile crisis of October 1962 began at the highest levels of our government, ironically enough, with satellite imagery that informed a young President John F. Kennedy of the Soviet Union's attempt to arm Cuba with nuclear tipped missiles, only ninety miles off the coast of Key West, Florida.

The news media was involved from the outset, broadcasting statements on the status of events directly from President Kennedy himself. Where was this same interplay between the Bush administration and the nation's news media in covering the *many* illicit shipments between China and Saudi Arabia?

With this in mind, a complete and honest assessment of ourselves as Americans in this whole ordeal must include a hard look at what has become of

America's journalistic community. As far as mainstream American journalism has drifted in recent decades from the strong foundation built by journalists like Edward R. Murrow and Walter Cronkite, the Cuban missile crisis serves as a valuable reminder of the powerful role the news media can play in bringing needed transparency to global crises as they unfold. In this sense, it is tempting to consider how the deal between China and Saudi Arabia may have been peaceably resolved had there been some participation by an informed and objective American news media.

As determined as the Bush administration was in keeping the White House press corps at bay—out of reach from the realities of a wide range of questionable wartime (and energy) policy decisions—the American media establishment was guilty of gross bias in its coverage of, for example, Hurricane Katrina and its catastrophic aftermath in 2005. By the time this powerful act of God had pummeled the city of New Orleans in late August of that year, who could possibly argue that the damage hadn't already been done? Well, certain elements of America's media establishment could. Most of the Washington and New York-based media continue even to the present day to blame George W. Bush by name for the federal government's failed "handling of Hurricane Katrina."

How is this rational? Neither man nor government agency can effectively "handle" acts of God, although, when he arrogantly tries, the results are almost invariably sad and even grotesque, as some things we do on this earth just aren't what nature intended. It's true that the Federal Emergency Management Agency (FEMA) stumbled in its response to the aftermath of this terribly destructive storm, but President Bush was quick to recognize this and accepted the resignation of FEMA's director Michael D. Brown only weeks after Katrina had blown through a devastated New Orleans.

The real error in judgment with Katrina, in my view, was made at the state and local levels in the days *prior* to the storm ever making landfall. To be fair, part of the problem was the erratic and unpredictable nature of Katrina itself. But that factor aside, damage control preparations and timely population evacuations in some of the hardest hit areas along the Gulf coast simply weren't coordinated effectively enough by too many city managers and parish leaders. And yet these same elected local officials (particularly those of Louisiana) who were actually in a position to make a difference during those critical days and hours before the storm hit have been strangely immune to anything even approaching the censure Bush has been subjected to on the national stage.

A free and robust press is vitally important to a healthy democracy, but political bias must not dominate as it does today when it comes to the contributions made by trusted members of the journalistic community—on everything from our government's response to natural disaster to matters of national security.

* * *

Another example of this damaging bias comes from journalist-columnist (any meaningful distinction between the two in the field went out the window long ago) Frank Rich who wrote the March 27, 2010 *New York Times* column titled "The Rage Is Not About Health Care."

The rough outline of the piece is the following: a rehash of the previous weekend's Sunday morning political talk-show one-liners, followed by a carefully edited account by Rich of the many public demonstrations that had been taking place around the country at the time in opposition to the Obama-Pelosi healthcare legislation. But then, rather than addressing some of the legitimate criticisms that these demonstrators had (and still have) of the legislation, Rich chose to fixate on the more sensational tactics that demonstrators (both liberal and conservative alike, of course) tend to use to draw attention to their respective causes.

In this way, writing just a few pithy paragraphs for the sizable nationwide readership of the *New York Times*, Rich had managed to grossly mischaracterize the considerable opposition in America to the Obama-Pelosi legislation. He referred to it derisively as a "tsunami of anger," a swell of political opposition that he curiously made sure to point out was "virtually all white" in composition. Not surprisingly, this angry *white* mob was dismissed as nothing more than "illogical" with a vacuous snort from Rich's pen.

Now, unless of course one supports the creation of yet another federal program *on top* of Social Security and Medicare (programs the federal government already can't afford) in what way is it "illogical" to be opposed to legislation that does just that by creating a new government-backed healthcare entitlement? Methinks opposition in this case is an excellent example of the exercise of *logic*, no?

On the other hand, had I been of the mind that government should in fact pay for my blood pressure medication if I can't afford it, would it still have been "illogical" to take issue with the way the bill was clumsily jammed through the lower chamber of Congress late on a Sunday night? Pray tell, Mr. Rich.

The reader of this malignant missive is sadly left wanting for an answer. Instead, this journalist-columnist's chronicling of developments surrounding the healthcare debate goes from a distorted treatment of the thoughtful arguments made against the Obama-Pelosi legislation to a sickening defense of the president's "reform" of America's healthcare system. Without addressing any of the supposed merits of the legislation, Mr. Rich dressed up his own unexplained support of it with several outright lies, one of which in particular warrants fierce rebuke.

Striking entirely below the belt with a most insidious lie (and demonstrating a grossly flawed understanding of U.S. history, no less), Mr. Rich observed that opposition to the Obama-Pelosi healthcare bill was akin to being an opponent of the American Civil Rights Act of 1964. Referring to several supporters of the healthcare bill who, by virtue of the color of their skin or sexual orientation should—according to Rich at least—be regarded as "minority" members of the House of Representatives, Rich wrote:

> "It's not happenstance that [these "minority" representatives] received a major share of last weekend's abuse. When you hear [Obama-Pelosi healthcare legislation opponents] chant the slogan 'Take our country back!,' these are the people they want to take the country back from."

With these words, by recklessly juxtaposing legitimate political opposition with the demons of racism (a particularly vile ploy in modern America) this journalist-columnist had branded millions of Americans as bigots for their opposition to President Obama's healthcare legislation. If you aren't a supporter of the Obama-Pelosi bill, Mr. Rich was insisting, you are very likely a racist and even a homophobe.

As one of millions of Americans falsely vilified by this *New York Times* sanctioned op-ed column, I'd like to make one thing clear as I close, and I believe Abraham Lincoln himself would back me on this: I don't want my country "taken back" from a black man, a gay man, a former oil executive or any other man or woman for that matter. Despite pervasive rumors to the contrary, my country is still mine. And I say this not so much as a white heterosexual male who used to hunt pheasant with his dog and twelve gauge shotgun in northern California. I say this as an American.

What I would much rather see is simply respect once more for this country's Constitution coupled with an American news media that again strives to do nothing more than inform me and, years from now, my own daughters on what's new in the world.

* * *

On the foreign policy side of this same coin was the failure of our own democratically elected leaders in the White House to intervene with some more rational solution to the Faustian pact consummated between Riyadh and Beijing. As Faruk Tabak used to say, "Cooler heads must prevail." They did not.

The wisdom of America's founders bears repeating during these challenging times. We remain a country of laws, not men. But we as a people must be ever vigilant in our efforts to remain so, for America's special place in history as having a government *of the people, by the people and for the people* is most assuredly at risk.

NOTE FROM THE AUTHOR

In accordance with my obligations as a former employee of the Central Intelligence Agency, *Patriot Lost* was submitted to the CIA's Publication Review Board on April 12, 2010. Typically, the Board aims to complete its review of manuscripts within 30 days of submission.

Following repeated unanswered requests for an estimated completion date from the Board, I published *Patriot Lost* over the Internet on June 5, 2010. I began publicizing it as an "eBook" on the morning of the 7th.

On Wednesday that same week, I received a package in the mail here in California containing a letter from the Board. It was dated June 7, 2010. The Board also provided me with a copy of the "edited" (blacked out) pages to assist in my understanding of what they deemed "inappropriate for disclosure in the public domain."

The reader should know that had I revised the print version of *Patriot Lost* to comply with the Board's requested redactions, this book would have contained no mention whatsoever of any missile deal between Saudi Arabia and the People's Republic of China.

From Los Angeles – JS
June 2010

16330573R00150

Made in the USA
Lexington, KY
17 July 2012